GW01454488

History Workshop Series

General Editor

Raphael Samuel, *Ruskin College, Oxford*

Routledge & Kegan Paul
London and Boston

edited by

Raphael Samuel

Tutor in Social History and Sociology
Ruskin College, Oxford

Village Life and Labour

First published in 1975
by Routledge & Kegan Paul Ltd
Broadway House, 68–74 Carter Lane,
London EC4V 5EL and
9 Park Street,
Boston, Mass. 02108, USA
Set in Monotype Modern Extended
and printed in Great Britain by
The Camelot Press Ltd, Southampton

ISBN 0 7100 7499 9 (c)
0 7100 7500 6 (p)

Contents

Illustrations

Plates

between pages 202 and 203

The place of harvesters in nineteenth-century village life

1 Westmorland farm labourer with scythe, *circa* 1890 (Radio Times Hulton Picture Library)
2 Women harvesters in Norfolk (Colman and Rye Libraries of Local History, Norfolk)
3 Fagging wheat in Herefordshire (Hereford and Worcester County Libraries, Hereford and the Museum of English Rural Life, University of Reading)
4 Two men and a woman (Museum of English Rural Life, University of Reading)
5 The harvest field just before stooking (Museum of English Rural Life, University of Reading)
6 Fagging wheat, *circa* 1900

Country work girls in nineteenth-century England

7 Washing day (Radio Times Hulton Picture Library)
8 Out-door kitchen, *circa* 1860 (Radio Times Hulton Picture Library)
9 Water carrier (Radio Times Hulton Picture Library)
10 Gleaners, 1857 (Radio Times Hulton Picture Library)
11 Women hop-picking, Hurstmonceaux (Mansell Collection)

Figures

Notes on contributors

David Morgan started work on the land in 1940 and was a cowman for over twenty years. He was a student at Ruskin College from 1967 to 1969. His chapter on Harvesters was first given at a History Workshop on the English countryside in the nineteenth century (in 1967), and later extended into a thesis at the University of Warwick.

Jennie Kitteringham comes from a farm workers' family and spent her childhood on farms in Dorset and later Warwickshire. She was a student at Ruskin College from 1969 to 1971 and is now at Hull University. Her chapter stems from work begun for the History Workshop on childhood (1970), and a version of it appeared as a History Workshop pamphlet.

Raphael Samuel has been tutor in social history and sociology at Ruskin College since 1963. An early version of the chapter on Headington Quarry was given at the History Workshop on proletarian Oxfordshire, in 1968.

A worker's questions while reading

Who built Thebes of the Seven Gates?
In the books stand the names of Kings.
Did they then drag up the rock-slabs?
And Babylon, so often destroyed,
Who kept rebuilding it?
In which houses did the builders live
In gold-glittering Lima?
Where did the bricklayers go
The evening the Great Wall of China was finished?
Great Rome is full of triumphal arches.
Over whom did the Caesars triumph?
Were there only palaces for the inhabitants of much-sung
                              Byzantium?

Even in legendary Atlantis
Didn't the drowning shout for their slaves
As the ocean engulfed it?
The young Alexander conquered India.
He alone?
Caesar beat the Gauls.
Without even a cook?
Philip of Spain wept when his fleet went down.
Did no one else weep besides?
Frederick the Great won the Seven Years' War.
Who won it with him?

A victory on every page
Who cooked the victory feast?
A great man every ten years.
Who paid the costs?

So many reports
So many questions.

Bertolt Brecht

General editor's introduction: people's history

It is remarkable how much history has been written from the vantage point of those who have had the charge of running – or attempting to run – other people's lives, and how little from the real-life experience of people themselves. The history of education is a prime example. It is either a history of great headmasters and reformers, or else about organizational change. The student is expected to memorize (for examination purposes) the more controversial clauses of the different Education Acts, to summarize the findings and recommendations of various Royal Commissions, and to set education in 'a wider context' of denominational rivalries and party politics. He does not need to know much about the children – where they sat, what they learnt, how they were disciplined (or bribed) into obedience; nor will he be invited to inquire into the wider context which the child itself experienced – the interplay of family, work and home, or the way in which schooling helped to teach behaviour and inculcate sex and class roles.

Trade-union history, though ostensibly devoted to the workers, is often quite as bureaucratic. This is partly because of the nature of the documents available (chiefly executive minute books), partly because of the teleological way in which the subject is defined (the origin and growth of national organization), and partly, perhaps, because of an inherited bias from the Webbs, who first gave the subject shape. Everything is seen from Head Office. The General Secretary walks in and out, a familiar figure; the rank and file, on the other hand, remain anonymous, a dark outside, and appear in the records only as troublemakers, or seceders, or members in arrears. Housing conditions, to take another nineteenth-century example, are still seen through the eyes of the sanitary reformer rather than those of the people who actually lived in them as tenants or lodgers. The problem is defined as hygienic. We are told about overcrowding but not about its consequences for family and street life; about mortality rates and epidemics, but not about the ways in which illness was treated, pregnancies coped with, or families reorganized at death. The student will be more familiar with the medical officer of health than the 'threepenny' back street doctor. (See, however, *The Threepenny Doctor*, a pamphlet produced by Hackney WEA containing local people's reminiscences of such a doctor.) Labour conditions, in the same way, are apt to be seen through the eyes of the Factory Inspectors rather than of the working man, woman or child. The inner life of the workplace – the subject of five of the volumes in this series – remains unknown terrain. Finally crime. The student will learn more about prison reformers than about the prisoners themselves, about Game Laws than poachers, thief-takers than theft.

Some of these biases may be accounted for by the materials on which the historian works. In a county record office, for example, the democratic classes (through no fault of the archivist) are almost entirely unrepresented by documents of their own, but have to be seen through the eyes of intermediaries. The chief medieval documents to survive are the manorial court rolls, while in more modern times there are estate papers, solicitors' accumulations, business records and a huge number of conveyances, wills and deeds, which take up page after page in the catalogues. In the quarter sessions records, which form the original nucleus of many county record office collections, it is the more bureaucratic type of document which tends to be preserved (indictments, for instance, which give a formal statement of an offence, but no details), while the 'human' ones – the depositions which give a transcript of evidence in individual cases – have either vanished, or else have been heavily thinned. In the British Rail archives, too, the more plebeian class of document seems to have been systematically weeded out. The visitor will find ample documentation for proceedings in the board rooms – big, fat volumes minuting the meetings of each set of company directors – but very few working papers, and little to encourage inquiry about railwaymen themselves: the diary of driver Baron, which Frank McKenna makes the centrepiece of his account of Victorian railwaymen, is, so far as I know, the only one there of its kind. Workhouse records are also administrative in bias. Well over two hundred different classes of nineteenth-century Poor Law documents are said to exist, but the hopeful researcher who makes his way into the muniment room of the town hall or library is likely to find that only the minute books of higher committees survive, and bound volumes of accounts. Even with these it is occasionally possible (though only after long winnowing) to find brief entries which give a glimpse of, for instance, workhouse inmates, like this woman in Newcastle:

16:8:1860
It appearing by the Pauper Offence Book that Sarah Conolly aged 32 an Inmate of the Workhouse had misappropriated Worsted for making stockings Ordered that she be not allowed to go out for two months.
30:8:1861
It also appearing that Sarah Conolly aged 33 had been guilty of introducing Rum into the Workhouse contrary to the Rules Ordered that she be not allowed to go out for six months.
21:3:1862
And it appearing that Sarah Connelly [sic] aged 34 had been absent without leave Ordered that she be not allowed to go out for three months.
(Newcastle City Archives, Board of Guardians Minute Book)

The question of sources is important because they can, of themselves, push work in a certain direction, and give it an unarticulated bias which has to be recognized if it is to be successfully resisted. The magistrate's clerk – or the police officer – guides the researcher on his journey into crime, the senior partner takes him by the arm when he looks at business, the temperance advocate leads him in and out of the pubs. Unless he is careful the historian may end up as their mouthpiece. Organizations can swallow the historian up if he approaches their records unwarily, because they offer a ready-made subject for research, with all the materials perhaps to hand, an office space and (if he is fortunate) a generous supply of tea. The researcher may begin by wanting to find out about a group of workers and end up – like historians of the miners – writing about their union executives instead; or embark on an inquiry into, say, mid-Victorian prostitution, and finish up by writing not about women (or even their clients) but about one of the agencies set up to deal with them, a rescue society or

Josephine Butler's League. Administrative records have similar pitfalls since they are more informative by far about the administrators than about those whom they investigated or oppressed. It is much easier for the historian to write about nineteenth-century Poor Law administration than about the inner life of workhouses or – to take an example from earlier times – about the Elizabethan statutes on vagrancy than about the 'sturdy beggars' they were intended to attack. There are shelf-fuls of books about factory legislation; not one about factory girls.

Parliamentary Blue Books, a major source for nineteenth-century history, are nevertheless insidious, because they encourage the historian to rely on second- and third-hand opinion – heavily class biased – whose worth he cannot begin to assess unless he has primary material to use as a yardstick. Poverty inquiries (there are hundreds of thousand-page volumes of them) are in many ways the most treacherous to use: their question and answer form and the fact that the witnesses were outsiders – sanitary reformers, temperance advocates, chief constables, chairmen of boards of guardians, philanthropists, clergymen, 'lady' visitors – make it questionable whether they should be treated as primary sources at all (except for the appendices). There is an enormous amount of value to be gleaned from the Blue Books, but only if the historian works against the grain of the material, refusing to accept the witnesses' categories as his own, ruthlessly winnowing out opinion and harvesting the residue of fact however small.

The historian's own sense of personal identity places further limitations on his work, though at the same time giving it thrust and direction. Once he might have been a scholar and a gentleman, ready and indeed eager to hob-nob (metaphorically speaking) with the great. Today his social sympathies may not reach so high. As a professional man (history is very much a profession, and very much a man's profession at that: there is only one woman lecturer in a faculty of thirty at Cambridge) he shares a similar class position to the nineteenth-century administrator, in the middle or lower echelons of the bourgeoisie; his orderly ways and college duties may have given him other affinities besides. His vocation, as an historian, places him far above the madding crowd; he surveys them, retrospectively, from a height, as objects of reform rather than as the active agents – or subjects – of change. He may feel sympathy for the mass, but hardly solidarity. Labour historians have done much to correct this bias, but they have tended to reproduce in it another field, though their identifications, of course, are by no means the same as those of their bourgeois colleagues (except in one respect: they are as likely to be male). Their interest has on the whole been confined to the 'organized' working class (a small minority in nineteenth-century England), and their identification has been with the cadres. They will take sides with Potter or the Junta (rivals for the soul of trade unionism in the 1860s), and debate with passion the respective claims of 'physical' and 'moral' force (the issue dividing Lovett and O'Connor in Chartist days), but when it comes to the street girl on the Haymarket or to Mayhew's 'wandering tribes' they are not so sure.

Women have been virtually excluded from working-class history in much the same way as the *lumpenproletariat*, and for very much the same reason: they were not 'organized'. Women make their appearance as the objects of factory legislation, in the 1830s and 1840s, and later on as the subject of Royal Commissions into 'sweating', but they are allowed no collective existence of their own. This is not because there were no women workers. In cotton textiles they made up more than half the hands in many mills, though employed on the lower classes of labour (three-fifths of the Blackburn weavers in 1901 were women). They made up one-third of the labour force in the worsted textile mills in 1871, and a rather larger proportion in woollens; in linen, jute and flax they outnumbered men by 60,166 to 49,676 (Dundee was a 'woman's town' when Bob Stewart began working there in 1887). They had a preponderant role in some of the Black Country and Birmingham trades; in the silk industry; in waterfront industries such as rope making and fish curing; and in certain branches of agricultural labour (market gardening, fruit picking, weeding). Beyond this there were all kinds of women's work which do not figure in the censuses at all, but which might play a greater part in keeping the family together than the man's wages. (Sometimes, of course, there would not be a man at all, because he was away on tramp, or because he had gone off with someone else, or because he was dead; or again he might be ill or unemployed.) In many households the woman produced a good part of her own and the family subsistence – by taking in washing, by long hours at the needle to keep the family in clothes, by taking the children out to gather winter fuel ('wooding' in country districts, like coal-picking in mining ones, figures largely in court cases against women), by pickling and by salting (as in the cottage economy described in this volume by Jennie Kitteringham), by gleaning, and in both countryside and the back streets of the town by the multiplicity of little contrivances by which the woman of the poor manipulated rent arrears and debt. In the volumes on work we try to redress this balance, not only in the book specifically devoted to women's trades, but also in the others – domestic service as one of the components of the 'uniformed' working class, women bookbinders and tailoresses in the volume on the workshop trades, country work girls in the volume to hand, while in the volume on family and marriage attention is focused on the history of housework.

The fact that some subjects get more attention from historians than others – and some, like childhood, almost none – is no testimony, by itself, to their comparative importance, but may have more to do with the state of the documents, or the way in which research is organized and shaped. Too often research is simply a stage in the historian's career and its context the enclosed world in which the 'new' interpretation may count for more than the substantive importance of the subject or the way in which it contributes to a wider understanding of society. The historical 'discipline' – like others – encourages inbreeding, introspection, sectarianism. The problematic is likely to come from within. Often it is suggested by 'gaps' which the young researcher is advised by his supervisor to fill; or else by an established view which he is encouraged to challenge. Fashion may direct the historian's gaze; a new methodology may excite him; or he may stumble on an untapped source. But whatever the particular focus, he will be working within an existing frame of inquiry, respecting its limits (however chafing) and eschewing any suggestion of social or political bias. Historiography provides the measure of significance, not life.

These volumes have taken shape in a rather different way. Instead of taking our cue from the state of the archives – or the more or less chance configurations of controversy and research – we have been guided, in the first place, by the intrinsic interest and importance of our subjects, as fundamental elements in social life – work and class relations, sex roles and family life, popular culture and education. They are an attempt to bring history closer to the central concerns of people's lives, both through the framework of inquiry (the questions asked and the way in which evidence is evaluated), and through the use of personal experience and oral testimony to reinterpret the records of the past.

The purpose of these volumes is not so much to 'fill in gaps', a task which is anyway beyond us and will demand years of collaborative and individual research; but rather to offer some examples of what 'people's history' is or might be about, and to suggest some ways in which the boundaries of history might be brought closer to those of people's lives. The writing of such history need not involve evacuating (as E. P. Thompson fears) 'whole territories of established economic and political history'; rather would it be a matter of travelling over them in a different way – on foot instead of in armoured car or tractor. There is no necessary disjunction between the particular and the general: on the contrary there is – or ought to be – a dialectical interplay between them. We need to know about the inner life of the household – the competition for authority and love, the allocation of domestic roles – if we are to give a convincing account of the way it is shaped by external forces, or (as in the case of gypsies) proved recalcitrant to them. We need to know how class relationships were mediated in the workplace if we are to understand why they held – as binary oppositions – in the society as a whole. The same is true of moral discipline and social control: they are generated from within as well as imposed from without.

No subject in history is intrinsically 'micro' or 'macro', mainstream or marginal, big or small. Everything depends on the way it is studied. The local study may be myopic, but then it is possible to hold eternity in a grain of sand.

The socialist historian has the privilege of keeping the record of resistance to oppression, but also the duty of analysing the enemy's campaign, and showing how men and women become accomplices in their own subjection. Of every event one should be able to ask, what meaning did this have in people's lives; of every institution, how did it affect them; of every movement, who were the rank and file.

These volumes are based on History Workshops held at Ruskin College over the past eight years. Originally there was to have been one volume – a general collection showing the kind of work the Workshop was trying to do. Now there are twelve, loosely organized around the theme of 'Family, Work and Home'. All are in a more or less finished state. Five of the volumes are on Work – Village life and labour; Miners, quarrymen and saltworkers; the Workshop trades; Women's trades; and the Uniformed working class; two are on Childhood; two on Education (both adult and school); two on Popular culture; one (or possibly two) on Family and marriage.

The Workshop began as an attack on the examination system, and the humiliations which it imposed on adult students. It was an attempt to encourage working men and women to write their own history instead of allowing it to be lost, or learning it at second and third hand; to become producers rather than consumers; and to bring their own experience and understanding to bear upon the record of the past. For some it was in the nature of an exercise – the return to primary sources – but for a few it developed into a passion, even the start of a lifetime's work. No grants from the SSRC facilitated them in their work (though the National Assistance was sometimes a help): one student financed his research by cleaning the rafters in the British Leyland Motor Works at Cowley; another by selling his car; a third by living on baked beans; most by going short. In the early years, when such research activity was wholly unofficial, even – from the point of view of the curriculum – clandestine, there was not even recognition or support from their own college. All that sustained them was the seriousness of their commitment, and the awakening pride that comes from mastering a craft for oneself.

The Workshop has profited from the participation of historians who have responded to the informality of its proceedings, and who shared its preoccupations and concerns. It has been associated, from the start, with the work of the Oral History Society, and it has enjoyed a fraternal relationship with the Society for the Study of Labour History, even though its biases, and focus of attention, are not always the same. It has also profited by (and hopefully made some contribution towards) the growing support for social history, and the change which has taken place in the climate of historical opinion under the impact of *The Making of the English Working Class*. Another association has been with the women's movement. The first women's national conference was held at Ruskin in 1969, and it was convened by a group of women who had met together, as a faction, during the History Workshop of 1968, to express their discontent at the male-dominated character of the proceedings. The movement turned up in force at an explosive Workshop on 'Women in history' in May 1973, and the travails of that occasion – and the self-criticism it provoked – have helped to produce two of the volumes in this series, as well as to change the others.

Much of the editorial work on these volumes has been done by Anna Davin, taking time off from her own work to help the individual chapters and projects forward. The whole shape and character of the series has been profoundly influenced by her own work, and the comradeship she has given the editor and many of the contributors. Without it these volumes would have remained – at best – in a half-finished state; they would have been impoverished of some of their best materials (including her own chapters which appear in five of the later volumes), and they would certainly not have taken the direction they have.

We have lived with these volumes together; they represent a joint historical concern. The manuscripts line the passageways, crawl up the stairs to sleep at night, and invade the children's bedroom. For us, as for many of the contributors, they are the troubled product and labour of love.

Acknowledgments

So many people have helped with the making of these volumes that it is impossible to thank them individually. Librarians and archivists, fellow students and historians, History Workshop stalwarts who at the various stages have heard and discussed each piece of work, and helped to check and prepare the final texts, have all by their encouragement and interest and time made invaluable contributions for which we are most grateful.

We are also grateful to the Master and Fellows of Trinity College, Cambridge, for permission to quote from the manuscript diaries of A. J. Munby; and to Eyre Methuen Ltd and Suhrkamp Verlag for permission to use Bertolt Brecht's 'Questions of a Studious Working Man' from *Tales from the Calendar*, in a translation by Nicholas Jacobs. Original poem copyright 1939 by Malik-Verlag, London; translation copyright © 1975 by Stefan S. Brecht.

Part 1

Village labour

Raphael Samuel

The village labourer of the nineteenth century remains a curiously anonymous figure, in spite of the attention given to agriculture, Speenhamland, and Captain Swing. We know a certain amount about his movements (though the years from 1830 to 1872 remain uncharted territory), but very little about his life. We do not know whether he was man, woman or child, though often it is assumed that he was the first (yet 143,000 women farm servants and agricultural labourers are recorded in the census of 1851); nor where he lived (whether in 'closed' or 'open' villages, by a green or on the waste); nor what he worked at during the different seasons of the year. Drainage is discussed as a factor in agricultural 'improvement' or in relation to the Corn Laws (some £12 million of public money was borrowed for it under Peel's Land Drainage Act of 1846, with the aid of which between two and three million acres of land were drained),[1] but not as a source of work. There is a whole spectrum of occupations which historians (following the census enumerators) have overlooked, either because they were too local to show up prominently in national statistics, like coprolite digging in Cambridgeshire and Bedfordshire,[2] or because they were too short-lived to rank as occupations at all. (Perhaps this is why the well-diggers are statistically invisible; the job was often taken on as an autumn or winter standby, and unless rock was encountered would be over in a matter of weeks.) Industrial occupations in the countryside, such as lime burning, brick-making, or quarrying, are ignored. So too is the whole range of country navvying jobs which kept the out-of-work farm labourer employed – sand getting and gravel drawing, for instance, clay digging, wood-cutting and copse work, and such locally important occupations as river cutting and dyking in the Fens. (At Cholderton, in Wiltshire, the Rev. T. Mozley recalled of the 1830s, there was a 'regular craft' who made pond-making for the local sheep keepers their chief resource.)[3] We know very little about the alternative sources of employment open to the labourer; the census enumerators very largely ignore them. 'Field labour' covers all.

The notion of occupation in the countryside is one that needs to be complicated and refined. Many of those who worked in the harvest fields had other jobs besides. Three-quarters of the

farm labourers of Monmouthshire, according to a report of
1892, engaged in wood-cutting, quarrying and mine-work.
'With respect to many of them, it is difficult to determine
whether they may be styled wood-cutters and quarrymen,
coming to the land for hoeing, harvesting, and sundry piecework, or whether they are in the main agricultural labourers,
going to the woods, quarries and mines in the winter months.'[4]
In Suffolk, George Ewart Evans tells us, there was a whole
class of farm labourers who, when they were turned off after
the harvest, went to spend the winter in the 'maltings' at
Burton upon Trent.[5] Others from the same parts went off to
Lowestoft and Yarmouth, where the herring season lasted from
Michaelmas to December. 'By far the greater part of them are
farm labourers,' wrote a *Morning Chronicle* commissioner in
1850 of the herring crews at Yarmouth. 'Immediately after the
harvest they start off in search of employment at Yarmouth,
and various other small ports on the coast of Norfolk. . . . When
mishaps . . . take place, the children or widow of the lost man
receive the full share of the earnings which would have been
paid . . . had he been alive.'[6] The Norfolk Broadsman pursued
a more local cycle of work:[7]

> When mowing the marsh-hay is over, after the hay is poled
> and stacked, he turns his attention to the gladdon, which
> had already begun to show the yellow leaf. He is now seen
> daily in his huge marsh-boat, with his meak, cutting and
> sheaving the long leaves, which he sells at a good profit. As
> the winter draws on he dries and packs his eel-nets, locks
> his cabin door, and those haunts know him no more until
> the following summer. Now, at even-tide, you will see him
> in his boat with dog and gun, hidden in a clump of reed,
> waiting for the flight of duck and plover; there he will sit
> patiently until the darkness sends him home, generally with
> a bird or two for his supper. When the first ice covers the
> Broad he is up betimes, and with his whole family, in an
> old hulk, you will see him busy breaking and gathering the
> thin ice, which he afterwards sells to the Yarmouth
> smacksmen. A little later he is to be seen, in tall
> marsh-boots, standing in the icy water, and cutting the
> reed with which he makes his fences and thatches his roof.
> In early spring he devotes himself to babbing for eels. If a

very zealous naturalist, he will also be taking eggs for the dealers.

Occupational boundaries in the nineteenth-century country-side were comparatively fluid. They had to be, where so much employment was by the job rather than by the regular working week, and where work was difficult to get. In the country building-trade jobs were chronically short-lived, and there was a great deal of movement from one class of work to another. The country craftsman or mechanic was a man with two or three strings to his bow. The thatcher might turn hay trusser for the summer season,[8] the hurdle maker to repairing carts and wagons,[9] the stonemason, when out of work, to jobbing carpentry.[10] A Wiltshire thatcher whom Alfred Williams writes about at Liddington turned his hand to making sheep-cages when there was no thatching to be done; he also built cottages of wattle and daub, or chalk stone, letting them out to poor labourers at 1s. a week, or selling them off.[11] Joseph Arch, the farm workers' leader in 1872, carved out a modest independence for himself through jobbing.[12]

Finding, two or three years after his marriage, that he could not, as a regular farm labourer, support his wife and family – for by that time he had two children, a boy and a girl – he determined to try his fortune as a jobbing labourer. Taking with him some necessary tools, he therefore left home and sought piece-work in various localities. He began by gravel-digging; from that went to wood-cutting. Then he got some draining work to do, having, it is said, whilst occupied in this work, to stand sometimes for as much as twelve and thirteen hours a day up to his ankles in water. After this he took to hedge-cutting, and became so proficient in this kind of work that he got to be much in request by the farmers in the districts around.

As well as being what he called an 'experienced' agricultural labourer ('master of my work in all its branches'), Arch also took jobs as a country mechanic, being employed by one of his friends as a carpenter 'when he got very busy coffin-making, or putting on roofing, or making church work. . . . Then my skill at hurdle-making and gate-hanging would come in handy . . . Being a good all-round man I was never at a loss for a job.'[13]

Another neglected area for investigation concerns the cottage
economy, and the unofficial sources of income on which a
labouring family (to keep off the parish or the workhouse) had
often to rely. Poaching, for instance may be discussed in
relation to the game laws, or else as a colourful page from the
past, but there is no attempt to relate it to the seasonal cycle
of plenty and want (the rabbiting season began in September
or October), to the local lie of the land (there were more rabbits
in wooded than in open country), or to the range of totting and
foraging activities of which it formed a part. Gleaning, so far as
I know, has yet to be the subject of an article in a learned
journal, though village autobiographies – and police court
reports – are full of the kind of evidence on which a discussion
might be launched. Nor has anyone thought it worth paying
research attention to the cottager's pig, though (as Flora
Thompson shows in *Lark Rise*)[14] there was a whole nexus of
economic and cultural relationships which formed around it.
Land, too, could be a source of secondary incomes. The whole
question of proletarian landholding in the countryside cries out
for investigation (it might lead to quite substantial redrawing of
the map of British farming); so does the equally neglected
question of common rights (heaths and commons did not
disappear from the countryside with the advent of enclosure,
though their size was drastically curtailed: in the open villages
east of Oxford there was a whole class of cow-keepers still
profiting by them in the 1860s).

In the absence of satisfactory statistics historians have often
neglected the question of family earnings (difficult or even
impossible to quantify) and instead have argued from wage
rates – such as those published in the Parliamentary Blue
Books – to judgments about the standard of life. The published
figures, as Wilson Fox pointed out long ago, 'probably relate
to the men in fairly regular work attached to the staff of the
larger farms'.[15] Moreover, they cannot tell us much about net
earnings. Wage rates may be useful as a barometer for secular
trends, but they can tell us little about the kinds of vicissitude
which a labouring family experienced from one week to the next.
Farm labour books, such as those used by David Morgan, make
possible a more realistic account: they deal with net earnings
rather than average rates, and show that even for the regularly
employed farm servant there could be quite sharp variations in

earnings according to the job in hand (a great deal of nineteenth-century farm work was given out on 'piece' or 'task' work, even to the annually hired). They cannot tell us much, however, about what happened between periods of employment, or about the economy of the household group. One crucial variable, especially in the earlier nineteenth century, when wood was still more generally used than coal, concerns accessibility or otherwise to fuel, a major item in the household budget to those who could not get it free. (Cobbett believed the labouring family of the woodland districts comfortable on this count alone, and compared them with the 'poor creatures' he had seen about Bedwin and Cricklade, 'where I saw the girls carrying home bean and wheat stubble for fuel', and with those at Salisbury where firing was so scarce that poor families had to take it in turns to boil kettles for their tea.)[16] Another concerns the availability or otherwise of winter work (the comparative well-being of labouring families in the hop growing district of Kent seems to have been due to the fact that the cycle of employment for both men and women began in the autumn rather than the spring).[17] Then again there is the question of family size and of the existence or otherwise of independent sources of income. These are not questions which this book claims in any way to have resolved, but perhaps it will help to point to their importance.

Woodland villages had an economy all of their own, and experienced a kind of inverted seasonality of employment. Their two native harvests – fern cutting and bark stripping – occurred in the autumn and the spring, and there was a good deal of winter employment in the woods. Bark stripping, which began in March and lasted for about six weeks (it provided 'flaw' for the tanners) was a major harvest, drawing extra hands from afar as well as providing employment for woodlanders themselves. As in corn harvesting the work was undertaken sometimes by men, sometimes by family groups, sometimes by travelling gangs.[18] 'Faggoting the lop' was done by men, while women and children did the 'hatching' (cleaning the bark of moss):[19] 'A good "woman hand" may earn 8d. a day; a child (doing the work badly) perhaps 3d. . . .'[20] In summer wage-paid employment in the woodlands was liable to give out. Farms in such vicinities were characteristically small (they would have originated in squatters' intakes on the wastes) and those who wanted work had to travel – as far away as 'the market gardens near London, and even to a small extent to the fruit districts of Kent' in the case of the very migratory inhabitants of Pamber and Tadley, two adjoining villages on the Hampshire–Berkshire border.[21] The crofters of Ashdown Forest, Sussex, moved within a nearer vicinity, since there were hop gardens nearby and a local demand for harvest labour. They settled back on the forest in October, mowing bracken and selling it to local farmers at a rate of 8s. the waggon load; cutting turf for sale was another of their autumn trades, while the gypsies among them hawked clothes pegs in the neighbouring towns and villages.[22] (Earl De La Warr, lord of the Manor of Duddleswell, carried on a long war against these depredations, but in spite of decisions favourable to him at the local magistrates court – and eventually in the High Court – he does not seem to have been able to put a stop to them, until the trades died away of themselves.)[23]

The forest villager, though a labourer, was often a landholder as well, and sometimes a cottage manufacturer besides. At Nomansland, Wiltshire, a very proletarian village on the northerly edge of the New Forest, most of the cottagers had 'ground', some having thirty to forty poles, others as much as three acres. 'The men who have two or three acres of land cannot take regular work as labourers', the Agricultural Employment Commissioners were told in 1868. 'They grow chiefly vegetables and roots for the cows; they are better off than men who have regular employment.'[24] On the New Forest, pasture rights were even more important than holding land. They enabled the labourer to raise himself by degrees to the status of a peasant proprietor, chiefly by keeping cows or ponies, or fattening pigs. Eyre has left some fine examples in his paper of 1883:[25]

Z. is the son of a stable-helper and labourer who earned 10s. per week, and lived in a lifehold cottage (quit rent 2s. 6d. yearly) on the edge of a common excellent for milch cows, and connected with the Forest. As a boy he worked for a carrier for some years at 3s. and 5s. per week, and, at 20 years of age, while living at home, set up as a carrier, with two ponies and a van purchased with a windfall of 40l. that fell to his parents. The carrier's business not paying was sold at a loss of 10l.; a mare was

reserved and turned out upon the Forest, and 2 cows were
bought for 20*l.* The father died; the widow maintains
herself by a cow and pig kept almost entirely upon the
common. Z. began to rent a cottage and 2½ acres of land at
a very high rent, and married. At 25, he keeps 3 cows
which produce about 40*l.* per annum in butter, maintaining
themselves almost entirely upon the common in summer,
and in winter living on the produce of his plot and land,
supplemented by about a ton of hay (say 4*l.* 10*s.* 0*d.*) and
about 5*l.* worth of food. He sells 2 calves yearly, keeps 2
sows, and sells 18 to 20 piglings (6 weeks old). He
calculates that he clears about 12*s.* to 13*s.* per week, though
burdened by a very heavy rent paid to a small freeholder.
He is prepared to take a 'little place' of 5 to 6 acres.

Y. is a labourer aged 52, earning 12*s.* a week (including
occasionally skilled task-work). His 10 children have all
turned out well and helpful. Rents a cottage, garden, and
plot, about 1¼ acre. On his marriage, he bought a calf for
10*s.* on credit, and paid for her when a milch cow by sale
of her milk, rearing her on the common, and in winter by
the hay grown at home, say 1 ton, supplemented by an
out-of-pocket cost of about 30*s.* The annual stocking of his
garden does not cost 20*s.* Made 4 lbs. of butter a week, and
sold it to a dealer at his gate for an average price of
1*s.* 2*d.* per lb. Sold a calf; bought a sow, and sold upwards
of 15 pigs yearly at 25*l.* Owns a mare and 2 good colts,
and is about to take a little farm of 12½ acres; his son,
aged 26, is able to retain the old home, and inherit his
father's improvements.

X. is a woodman and farm labourer, a first rate workman.
By working early and late, especially at hurdle-making, and
in the barking or 'rinding season', he saved 100*l.* before he
married, though living in a parish 'without chances',
i.e., where there were no commons. With great difficulty,
he was able to keep his savings and the interest intact,
while his family increased and grew up. He then took a
woodman's and underkeeper's place on the edge of the
Forest, but was unable to add to his fund, though his
hard-working wife earned as much by taking in washing
as he earned abroad. At 45, his family being nearly

independent, he hired a 2 acre field and house plot of about
¾ of an acre, and bought a cow and kept pigs. Sold the
first calf for 4*l*. before winter, and being accidentally able
to earn 10*l*. during the 2 years following bought a second
cow for 14*l*., and took a small place of 5½ acres, and
increased his pigs. Has since taken a grass farm of 35 acres
by means of his original capital. In 3 years, he has a
dairy of 10 cows, a horse and foal, 2 sows, and makes
about 16*l*. per annum profit by breeding and selling pigs.

The English countryside in the early and middle years of the
nineteenth-century – in many places down to the 1870s – was
more densely peopled than at any other time before or since.
This was partly due to the rise in population, general from the
1760s, steepest of all in the years from 1780 to 1821, partly to
the extension of agricultural and industrial employment, and
partly to changes in the pattern of settlement. The demographic
explosion of the later eighteenth and early nineteenth
century was almost as marked in the countryside as in the towns.
In Cambridgeshire, for instance – 'a purely agricultural country,
no manufactures being carried on', according to the county
report of 1846[26] – the population rose between 1801 and 1851
at slightly more than the national rate.[27] In Lincolnshire,
where 'large increases' in population became marked from about
1770, the population of many rural townships doubled between
1801 and 1851.[28] In Suffolk in the same period the population
increased by some 86 per cent.[29] The causes of this increase –
whether falling death rates, rising fertility, or changes in the
economy – are a matter for scholarship and dispute, but the
consequences are not in doubt: by the 1830s, when the Poor
Law commissioners set about trying to reduce it, the 'superabundance of labourers'[30] was as much a feature of the English
countryside as shortage of population had been a century before.
   One result of this 'superabundance' of labour was the decline
of living in. In the eighteenth century labour had been a scarce
resource. The typical farm servant – a young, unmarried man
or woman – was boarded and lodged by the farmer until able
to set up in an occupancy or tenancy of their own, whether as
farmer, farmer's wife, or cottager. Living-in survived strongly
into the nineteenth century in pasture districts, where there
was constant work for stockman and dairy maid; and in sparsely

populated counties like Westmorland, something like the old system of informal farming apprenticeships prevailed.[31] But in much of the country radical changes were taking place in the relationship of the farmer to those he employed: 'servants in husbandry' were becoming 'hands'.[32]

On the large arable farms of east and southern England, living-in servants were replaced by outside labourers and hands, and this labour force came to be divided into two, with a nucleus of 'regulars' – ploughmen, stockmen, and shepherds, and labourers hired by the year – and a wider periphery of men, women and children, employed by the day, the week, the month, or the task. This extra labour force was decisive at harvest time, as David Morgan shows, but it was by no means only then that farmers had to call on it. Hoeing and singling, for instance, was very often undertaken by the task. In Norfolk and Lincoln these jobs would be done by the travelling gangs of juveniles whom Jennie Kitteringham writes about in 'Country work girls'. On the leviathan farms of Salisbury Plain, Caird reported in 1851:[33]

> the turnip crop is hoed by men at task-work – strangers
> who migrate into the district every season, and work late
> and early, that they may earn good wages. They are paid
> from 7s. to 8s. an acre, besides beer, and expert hands can
> make 3s. to 4s. a day at this rate, beginning work, of
> their own accord, at three o'clock in the morning, resting
> during the mid-day heat, and after resuming their labour
> in the afternoon, continuing till eight o'clock in the
> evening.

Strangers were also an important element on the grass lands of Middlesex, though for rather different reasons. Here the land, 'celebrated for the quality of its hay',[34] was divided up into numerous farms, rented by dairymen or small tenant farmers. The number of agricultural labourers was comparatively speaking low (three labourers to every farmer at the time of the Census of 1831). At Perivale, when Henry Tremanheere visited it in 1842–3, there were no resident labourers at all, though there were five farms in the parish 'the largest of which comprises 179 acres'.[35] At haymaking time the deficiency of hands was made up for by a large mobilization of itinerants; Cobbett wrote in 1822 that it was the 'first haul' of the Irish

'and other perambulating labourers';[36] and the situation was
very much the same when Clutterbuck made his report on the
agriculture of Middlesex in 1869, though according to him the
Irish element, 'which at one time bore a large proportion to the
whole casual supply' was 'nearly extinguished':[37]

> The mowing is for the most part performed . . . by
> strangers who come in companies from the counties of
> Bucks, Berks and Oxford, and other places. Mowing . . .
> is . . . undertaken by the acre, the price varying very much
> with the state of the weather, the supply of labour,
> the condition of the crop, and such like variable incidents.
> The haymakers, like the hop-pickers of Kent and Surrey,
> are often strangers from various quarters seeking casual,
> and, for a time, well paid employment.

Among the mowers would have been the six or eight men who
went up each year from Filkins in Oxfordshire. '. . . When the
haymaking was done, they worked their way back by doing
hoeing for market gardeners . . . by the time they got to
Wantage, the harvesting was ready.'[38] In the orchards and
market gardens of Middlesex, seasonal disparities in employment were pronounced. 'They afford occupation during the
winter months to three persons per acre', wrote Henry
Tremanheere of the garden grounds at Ealing, 'and in the
summer at least five more; and in some of the gardens during
the fruit season the whole amount of industry called into
activity, including market people, basket women, dealers, and
hawkers cannot be estimated at less than 30 persons per acre.'[39]
　Women played a large part in the new labour force, as day
labourers employed on the roughest, if not the heaviest, classes
of work. Women and girls predominated for instance in the
stone-picking gangs of East Anglia and the fens, 'a form of
organised labour which have chiefly sprung up within the last
twenty-five years' according to an account published in 1864.[40]
They went out stone-picking after the land had been ploughed
and harrowed. Later on, when the crops began to grow, they
were employed as human weed-killers, 'charlocking' or picking
twitch and thistles, and they returned to this work at the end
of the year with the autumn ploughings. Another winter job
done by women, in Norfolk at least, was cleaning turnips and
beet for cattle. 'They would come home up to there knees in

mud and whet, and then they would have the household work
to do, washing cooking mending, and all the other Jobs which
came along wen there is a big famley to do for.'[41] The cycle of
women's work at Bramley, in Hampshire, was recalled by
William Clift, writing in 1897 about his childhood fifty or sixty
years before.[42] It began on 14 February with bean setting.
'The price paid was 3d. or 4d. per gallon; so that supposing a
woman had two children to help her she might add 12s., or 13s.
to her husband's earnings in a week. Good and quick setters
could earn more.' The next job women were called on to perform
was the hoeing of wheat – 'this was begun about the middle of
April, and carried on until haymaking'. At haymaking they
were employed at tedding and raking out ('each woman had
to find a rake and prong of her own'); finally came 'a full month's
work' at harvest. The women at Bramley were the wives of
regularly employed farm labourers, but they also did jobs for
outsiders.

> Some families used to ask their employers to let them go
> out to where corn ripened sooner than here (say at
> Chichester, or some such forward place); there they would
> get a fortnight's harvest work before our corn was ready.
> And after harvesting our corn, they would also ask for
> another fortnight to go into more backward counties
> (say, Wiltshire or elsewhere) and get another two or three
> weeks' work.

The proportion of women engaged in agriculture varied
sharply from place to place, depending partly on local tradition
(an important force in mid-Victorian years, when field work
was attacked as unwomanly), partly on the alternative forms
of employment available. (In Lancashire, Caird reported in
1851, farmers had to pay out men for singling turnips, because
the women took up employment in the mills.)[43] In the East
Riding 'very few women' worked regularly in the fields except
in the extreme south-west.[44] On the large farms of Norfolk,
when Caird visited it in 1851, the proportion of women to men
among the regular field labourers was 6·25 to 51·4.[45] Much
market-garden work was done by women; in Middlesex,
Tremanheere reported, the number of women employed in it
throughout the year was 'in the proportion of two to one'.[46]
Fruit picking was very largely undertaken by women and girls,

except in the case of apples, which ripened later, when harvest work was over and men were hungry for jobs.[47]

The kind of tasks which women undertook also varied, even as one Suffolk writer remarked depending on the habits of 'narrow localities'.[48] Turnip pulling, for instance, was regarded as 'men's work' in the neighbourhood of Dartford, Kent,[49] but Hardy's Tess and her friend Marian worked long hours at it in the wintry fields of Flintcombe Ash.[50] In many places men and women worked in tandem at potato lifting, the men doing the pulling, the women gathering up, but women might do it alone.

The rise of population produced a shift in the balance of numbers from the landlord-dominated 'closed' village to the more plebeian 'open' villages rising on their flank. In the closed village – Nuneham Courtenay near Oxford is a fine example, with its model cottages symmetrically arranged – building was undertaken by the landlord himself and numbers restricted, so far as possible, to a nucleus of regular staff – 'the shepherd, carter, blacksmith, and a few other superior farm-workers'.[51] Responsibility for their workers, let alone for their dependents, was to be avoided as far as possible. In some cases cottages were deliberately pulled down for fear of creating settlements under the Poor Law, the great engine of clearance, until Union Chargeability in 1865. An extreme case is that of Colwick, Nottinghamshire, a parish which in the 1830s was owned in its entirety by a Mr Masters. It contained 1,250 acres of land, 'but except for the porter's lodge and one cottage occupied by a servant . . . there was not another small house . . .' (Masters drew his labour from Nottingham and from the nearby open villages of Sneiton and Carlton).[52] Dr Hunter in his report to the medical officer of the Privy Council on the state of rural housing in 1864, gives many examples of parishes where numbers had been deliberately reduced. At Preston, Northants, a parish of 1,470 acres, there were only fourteen houses 'of which only 4 were . . . cottages'.[53] At Horton, nearby, with 2,790 acres, there were only fifteen houses 'the number of inhabitants having sunk from 79 in 1831 to 31 in 1861'. 'Of the few cottages now standing only two are available for mere labourers, the cowman, shepherd, and gamekeeper having everywhere to be served first.'[54]

In the open village, by contrast, cottage ownership was

diffused, and new ones could be built as speculations without meeting any impediments from above. Where demand was brisk the number of inhabitants could grow fast. By the middle of the nineteenth century the open village had become the great source of farmers' labour in arable parts of the country. The open village was typically much more populous than the closed. (Denis Mills suggests a population range of from 300 to 500 inhabitants in the case of the open village, compared with 50 to 300 in the closed,[55] but the averages would need to take account of the open hamlets and village 'ends', and the clumps of squatters' cotts on the common or straggling by roadside wastes.) A symbiotic relationship developed between the two, the overflow of population in the one making up for the deficiency of labour in the other.[56] The relationship has been interestingly mapped out for East Yorkshire by June Sheppard, using the manuscript census returns of 1851 for the number of hands employed at individual farms, and comparing it with the resident populations of agricultural labourers.[57]

Open villages (the term first comes into general use in the 1830s: I do not think it is used by Cobbett in *Rural Rides*) are often said to have originated in old freeholders' villages. But in fact some of them were new settlements of the late eighteenth and early nineteenth centuries, by-products of the pressure of population on the land, of urban growth (which led to the formation of extra-parochial clumps of cottages)[58] and of the movement to enclosure (Arthur Young in his *Inquiry into Wastes*, 1801, has a list of some of these).[59] A striking example is Flora Thompson's North Oxfordshire village of Lark Rise, 'the spot God made with the left overs when He'd finished creating the rest of the earth'.[60] Its real name was Juniper Hill and originally it had stood on an open heath. About 1820 it had only six houses;[61] by 1853, when it was subject to the Cottisford Enclosure, forty working men held cottages there, and 'looked upon interference with their "territorial possession" as a measure to be resisted'. When the authorities, at Bicester petty sessions, issued writs for ejectment it was thought that the occupants would resist. In the event a compromise was reached: the occupants were stripped of their land, but given fourteen-year leases at 5s. a year for their residences and gardens[62] (thirty years later most of these cottages had fallen into the hands of Bicester tradesmen and the rent payment of 1s. or 2s. a week was the 'first charge' on the labourer's weekly wage of 10s.).[63]

These new squatters' villages were decidedly shabby in appearance and it is not surprising that in the minds of the rich and respectable they had a bad name. Headington Quarry, for instance, appeared to Edward Elton, the perpetual curate of Wheatley, 'a strange collection of cottages in pits' when he made a visit there in 1861.[64] Lark Rise, in the 1880s, 'consisted of about thirty cottages and an inn, not built in rows, but dotted anywhere within a more or less circular group. A deeply rutted cart track surrounded the whole, and separated houses or groups of houses were connected by a network of pathways.'[65] Another new nineteenth- or late eighteenth-century squatters' village, Bourne, on the edge of Farnham, Surrey, is described by George Sturt its biographer, as 'abnormal':[66]

As you look down upon the valley from its high sides, hardly anywhere are there to be seen three cottages in a row, but all about the steep slopes the little mean dwelling-places are scattered in disorder. So it extends east and west for perhaps a mile and a half – a surprisingly populous hollow now, wanting in restfulness to the eyes, and much disfigured by shabby detail.

Open villages were often found on the doorstep of the towns, inhabited by plebeian independents (like pig jobbers, horse and cart men, milk sellers and so on) and by a class of half-rural labourers who looked both to town and country for their livelihood. At Kinson, Dorset, which Dr Hunter visited in 1865, many of the men were employed in building work at Bournemouth (some came home only weekly, staying in lodgings while away).[67] At Potter Newton, two miles outside Leeds, the labouring population in 1858 was 'mainly employed in agriculture and the getting of stone'.[68] At Radford, Warwickshire, some of the men went into Leamington for work, others did field work round Offchurch. The women of the village were mostly employed in the fields, but supplemented this by taking in washing from Leamington.[69] The inhabitants of Mixen Lane, Casterbridge, which Hardy describes as the 'Adullam' of the surrounding villages, were separated from the town only by a bridge, but their orientation, Hardy tells us, was primarily towards the country:[70]

Mixen Lane . . . was the hiding-place of those who were in
distress, and in debt, and in trouble of every kind.
Farm-labourers and other peasants, who combined a little
poaching with their farming, and a little brawling . . . with
their poaching, found themselves sooner or later in Mixen
Lane. Rural mechanics too idle to mechanize, rural
servants too rebellious to serve, drifted or were forced into
Mixen Lane.

'Improvement' in the countryside was absolutely dependent
on numbers. The agricultural revolution of the eighteenth and
early nineteenth centuries had nothing to do with machinery,
but demanded instead a prodigious number of hands. Cheap
labour rather than invention was the fulcrum of economic growth.
The 'New Husbandry' brought a much intenser level of farming,
with heavier yields and the elimination of fallow. Green crops –
the pivot of the Norfolk system – were labour intensive to a
degree. Turnips in particular 'the soul of the best husbandry',[71]
'the grand base of the present system',[72] demanded an almost
gardenly care. 'Upon no one crop is so large an outlay made,
either in manure or labour. . . .'[73] 'Every operation connected
with it requires great nicety', wrote John Grey of Dilston. The
soil had to be in such a state of pulverization 'as to fall from the
plough like meal',[74] with ploughings, harrowings, rollings,
pickings, and liberal dressings of manure before it was ready
for the seed. Once the crop had begun to appear the earth had to
be continually prodded and poked. 'The more irons are among
the turnips . . . the better' was a common farmers' saying, 'even
if there are no weeds to overcome, the turning back and forward
of the soil, and the free admission of air, have a great effect in
promoting the health and growth of the plants'.[75] The first
hoeing began as soon as the leaf appeared. Then, two or three
weeks after, came a second hoeing and the setting out of the
individual plant 'each hoer having a boy or girl following him to
part and pull up any he may have left . . . to see . . . that they
are not left too thick'.[76] A third hoeing might be necessary if the
weather proved unusually warm and moist: 'the weeds may get
so fast ahead as to render a third hand-hoeing necessary, and
neither this, nor the further expense of getting women and
children to weed out wild mustard, charlock, ketlock, or any
other rubbish which may afterwards spring up should ever be

grudged.'[77] Hoeing time – like haymaking and harvest – was
an occasion when extra labour was taken on. In Monmouthshire, as on Salisbury Plain, it was the occasion for a local
migration. 'In the months of July and August small gangs
of people from Herefordshire, accompanied by dirty and ragged
children, come to this parish for turnip hoeing', runs a report
from Llantillo Crosseney in 1870.[78]

The extension of arable cultivation into heath, fen and upland
pasture, another feature of the 'New Husbandry', also involved
heavy demands on labour. The black lands of the Fens, for
instance, required a great expenditure of toil. To start with there
was dyking, and ditching, and claying to bind the peaty soil.[79]
In Cambridgeshire this was a winter job for the out-of-work
farm labourer, 'heaving the heavy clay from the sides and the
bottom to be spread out later on the land'; they went out into
the Fens with thick, lace-up boots reaching halfway to the
knees, and pieces of sackcloth wrapped round their legs for
additional protection.[80] The newly reclaimed land was difficult
to keep clean on account of the luxuriant growth of weeds.
'The black land is . . . peculiarly infested with twitch', wrote
John Algernon Clarke in 1852; 'great and incessant labour is
required in eradicating its long matted fibres, which spread so
deeply and rapidly in this light soil.'[81] The 'heavy twisted
crops'[82] also called for a great expenditure of labour, and this is
one of the districts to which the travelling Irish harvesters were
still coming in 1911, long after they had disappeared from most
of Eastern England. 'The crops could hardly be got in without
such extraneous assistance, for the modern reaper and binder
often fails to deal with them', wrote A. D. Hall in his *Pilgrimage
of British Farming*.[83] Hand weeding was also still very much in
evidence, according to an account from Wicken Fen in 1902:
'women do work a good deal in the fields at Wicken and in the
neighbourhood, where they get a shilling or more a day for
hoeing and weeding which they prefer to washing or charing'.[84]

The availability of cheap labour was one of the reasons why
the advent of machinery in the countryside was so long delayed.
Another was the force of village opinion in face of the chronic
scarcities of work. According to Henry Tremanheere, this is why
almost no machinery was in use in Middlesex. The only machine
of 'comparatively modern construction' which he noted was
a winnowing machine at Norwood. 'There is a strong prejudice

in this district against the use of all modern inventions for
facilitating or abridging labour, and the dislike to so many
admirable machines, now much used in husbandry, originates
in a conscientious though mistaken solicitude for the welfare
of the labouring classes.'[85] Clutterbuck had very much the same
to say of Middlesex twenty years later, in 1869:[86]

> Mowing by machinery is not so often practised as might be
> expected: some persons keep a machine, rather 'in
> terrorem', to secure themselves against the difficulty of
> unreasonable demands, as to price, and wages, in time of
> pressure, than from preference for this method of cutting
> the grass crop; some will own that they are unwilling to
> risk a collision with their regular staff of labourers who
> look with an evil eye on that which they consider
> (however unjustly) an interference with the rights of labour.

On the large farms of Oxfordshire, Caird reported in 1851,
thrashing machines were employed on the wheat crop, but
barley was still thrashed with the flail, 'both to give employment to the labourers, and because the machines in use cut the
grain too short, and thus injure it for the maltster'.[87] At High
Easter, Essex, most of the barley was still forty years after
Captain Swing thrashed by hand. 'Certain men went into the
barns after harvest, and many were thus employed until late
in the spring . . . on a farm growing forty or fifty acres of barley,
two men would be at this work.'[88]

In harvest work the chief change in early Victorian years,
the replacing of the sickle by the scythe, was taking place within
a hand technology, though reaping machines, it seems, had
been in operation since the 1820s. Not until the 1860s did the
reaper come into widespread use, and a scatter of machine-
breaking incidents (more will no doubt be turned up by
research) suggests 'the foolish prejudice against the introduction
of machinery'[89] may still have been at work. J. S. Fletcher,
writing in 1914 from Yorkshire, had a 'very clear recollection'
of the breaking up of the first self-binding reaper introduced
into his village, 'and of the savage determination of the
labourers to deal out similar treatment to any successor'.[90]
Steam ploughs also faced resistance, as David Morgan shows.
(A ploughing machine appears to have been selected 'as an
especial object of malice' by a group of Kent labourers on

strike in 1878, and it was in attempting to discover the perpetra-
tors of the mischief done to it that Arthur Gillow, the owner,
was murdered.)[91] We know as yet very little about the state of
rural opinion after the crushing of Captain Swing. A rare
glimpse is provided in the manuscript autobiography of Charles
Slater, a farm labourer at Barley, Royston (Herts.), which has
come into the possession of R. A. Salaman. The writer recalls an
argument, some time in the 1870s, about the comparative merits
of hand labour and the machine in hay-making:[92]

> . . . I heard an argument on the way to make the best hay
> some did not believe in machines one man said explaining.
> You first of all take two horses out of the stable with
> their stomachs full yolk them to the machines and then the
> horses dropings about the hay next you take a horse rake
> and drag it all up together put it in a stack and it get
> heated with a nasty smell and you have to starve you
> cattle to eat it. and if you wanted to sell it it wont make
> more than one pound per ton. The hay that has been cut
> with the scythe and as not been trample about and shaken
> up nicely and has had a nice heat on it will make five
> pound per ton. That the hay for the stock. They will do
> as well again on that as they will do on hay cut with the
> machines. youll see what machinery will do. spoil all your
> stuf. starve all your cattle. ruin your land. And farmers
> will lose all their money, everywhere men out of work
> workhouses full of starving people. And England ruined.
> And all through some fool inventing machinery . . . why
> they ought to pass a law to have all those machines
> collected up and took out to sea some miles and droped
> into the sea.

The rural population began to decline in the 1860s, but
the balance of numbers and employment was slow to shift. At
Lark Rise in the 1880s, despite the coming of machinery,
labour (Flora Thompson tells us) was still 'lavishly used':[93]

> Boys leaving school were taken on at the farm as a matter
> of course, and no time-expired soldier or settler on
> marriage was ever refused a job. As the farmer said, he
> could always do with an extra hand, for labour was cheap
> and the land was well tilled up to the last inch.

But not everything was the same. The young women of Lark Rise were now going into service,[94] not into the field. The children were at the village school, and subject not to gangmasters but to the Revised Code of Her Majesty's Inspectors.[95] The men all worked for one employer – in the neighbouring village of Fordlow, a 'closed' village with a thin population a mile and a half away. Flora Thompson tells us that their incomes were the same 'to a penny'.[96]

The general tendency of the later nineteenth-century years was towards a smaller rural population, and a more stable labour force consisting almost exclusively of adult males. The pattern of settlement reflected this, with the spread of tied cottages, on the one hand, and the destruction of squatters' cotts on the other, a work to which the newly formed rural sanitary authorities addressed themselves with vigour (at Headington Quarry they also made war on the cottagers' pigs). Land under cultivation contracted with the onset of the great depression, in 1879, and it was the labour-intensive wheat lands which suffered most. The progress of machinery helped farmers to dispense with the need for extra hands, though whether as cause or consequence is not clear. Steam ploughing reduced the amount of labour in tillage; chemical fertilizers abridged the time that had to be spent on manure; the reaper and binder took the place of women's and children's hands. These changes however were long drawn out and uneven: the horse, as George Ewart Evans reminds us in his splendid books, retained its hegemony in many places down to 1914;[97] in Headington Quarry the freelance labourer did not disappear until the coming of the motor works at Cowley.

Notes

1 E. H. Whetham, 'Sectoral advance in English agriculture, 1850–80', *Agricultural History Review*, 16, 1968, p. 46.

2 The industry produced a remarkable boom in mid-Victorian Cambridgeshire, for which see Rev. Edward Conybeare, *A History of Cambridgeshire*, London, 1897, pp. 259, 268; H. C. Darby, 'The nineteenth century' in *Victoria County History, Cambridge and the Isle of Ely*, London, 1948, vol. 2, pp. 119–20. There is an account

of mission work among the coprolite diggers at Eversden in Lilian Birt, *The Children's Home Finder*, London, 1913. 'The coprolite-diggers earn 17s. or 18s. a week, and at harvest time desert the diggings for the farm. They are in fact, agricultural labourers; but the work is much harder than that of the ordinary farm hand . . . and farm hands who have tried the work often go back to their old occupation at 13s. a week.' Frederic Clifford, *The Agricultural Lock-Out of 1874*, London, 1875, pp. 46–7.

3 Rev. T. Mozley, *Reminiscences, chiefly of Towns, Villages and Schools*, London, 1885, vol. 2, p. 306.

4 Parliamentary Papers (hereafter P.P.) 1893–4 (C. 6894–IV) xxxv, Royal Commission on labour, B–IV, 28.

5 George Ewart Evans, *Where Beards Wag All*, London, 1970, pp. 235–76.

6 *Morning Chronicle*, 1 February 1850, Labour and the Poor: Rural Districts, xviii.

7 P. H. Emerson and W. C. Goodall, *Life and Landscape on the Norfolk Broads*, London, 1886, p. 14.

8 Raphael Samuel, Headington Quarry Transcripts, 1969–70, Ward.

9 Bodleian Library, MS. Top. Oxon., d. 475, History of Filkins, fol. 93.

10 See 'Quarry roughs', p. 195.

11 Owen Alfred Williams, *Villages of the White Horse*, London, 1913, pp. 135–6.

12 Francis G. Heath, *Joseph Arch, a Brief Biography*, London, 1874, pp. 6–7.

13 *The Life of Joseph Arch by Himself*, London, 1898, pp. 62–3.

14 Flora Thompson, *Lark Rise to Candleford*, World's Classics ed., 1971, pp. 9–13.

15 A. Wilson Fox, 'Agricultural wages in England and Wales during the last half century', *Journal of the Royal Statistical Society*, 66, 1903, reprinted in W. E. Minchinton (ed.), *Essays in Agrarian History*, Newton Abbot, 1968, vol. 2, p. 145.

16 William Cobbett, *Rural Rides*, Everyman's Library, 1922, vol. 1, pp. 29, 58–9; Cobbett returns to the theme in a number of places, cf. ibid., pp. 220, 240, 294, 302.

17 Sir Charles Whitehead, *Retrospections*, Maidstone, 1913, p. 23. For some examples, Kent County Record Office, The loose farm account book, 1846–53, cf. also A. D. Hall, *A Pilgrimage of British Farming*, London, 1914, p. 54.

18 Frederick Jones, 'The oak and tan-flawing industry in Sussex', *Sussex County Magazine*, 11, 1928, pp. 176–8.

19 F. G. Heath, *The English Peasantry*, London, 1874, p. 183.

20 P.P. 1868–9 (4202) xiii, *2nd Report of the Commissioners on the Employment of Children, Young Persons and Women in Agriculture*, Appendix pt 11, p. 121.

21 P.P. 1893–4 (C. 6894–I) xxv, Royal Commission of Labour, *The Agricultural Labourer*, B–IV, 57. The village had been largely settled by gypsies, led by a man named Reuben Hicks. There is

an interesting account of it in Florence A. G. Davidson, *The History of Tadley*, Basingstoke, 1913.

22 Henry Wolff, *Sussex Industries*, Lewes, 1883, pp. 151–3 (to be found in Brighton Reference Library).

23 S. J. Marsh, *Ashdown Forest*, privately printed, 1935; East Sussex Record Office, Add. MSS., 3780–4104; Sussex Archaeological Society, RF/2/C, interviews of W. A. Raper with old foresters.

24 P.P. 1868–9 (4202) XIII, Appendix pt 11, p. 240. There is a splendid account of the origin, character and economy of this village in H. M. Livens, *Nomansland, A Village History*, Salisbury, 1910.

25 G. E. Briscoe Eyre, *The New Forest, its Common Rights and Cottage Stock-Keepers*, Lyndhurst, 1883, pp. 54–5.

26 Samuel Jonas, 'Farming of Cambridgeshire', *Journal of the Royal Agricultural Society of England*, 7, 1846, p. 35.

27 Darby, op. cit., p. 121.

28 D. R. Mills, 'The development of rural settlement around Lincoln', in D. R. Mills (ed.), *English Rural Communities*, London, 1973, pp. 87–8, 91.

29 John G. Glyde, *Suffolk in the Nineteenth Century*, London. 1856, p. 360.

30 J. A. Clarke, 'On the farming of Lincolnshire', *Journal of the Royal Agricultural Society of England*, 12, 1851, p. 405.

31 C. Stella Davies, *The Agricultural History of Cheshire, 1750–1850*, Chetham Society, series 3, vol. 10, Manchester, 1960, pp. 83, 91; Frank W. Garnett, *Westmorland Agriculture, 1800–1900*, Kendal, 1912, p. 90.

32 There is an accessible tabulation of the ratio of 'indoor' to 'outdoor' farm servants in J. P. D. Dunbabin, 'The incidence and organisation of agricultural trades unionism', *Agricultural History Review*, 16, 1968, pp. 123–4.

33 James Caird, *English Agriculture in 1850–51*, London, 1852, p. 82. These 'strangers' may have come from North Wiltshire, a region of pasture farming and decayed manufactures where there was a chronic labour glut. Caird says that they came in force for the wheat harvest on Salisbury Plain (ibid.).

34 *British Husbandry*, London, 1834, vol. 1, p. 489.

35 Henry Tremanheere, 'Husbandry and education in five Middlesex parishes', *Journal of the Royal Statistical Society*, 6, 1843, p. 124.

36 Cobbett, op. cit., vol. 1, p. 84.

37 J. Clutterbuck, *On the Farming of Middlesex*, London, 1869, p. 12.

38 Bodleian Library, MS. Top. Oxon., d. 475, History of Filkins, fol. 95^r.

39 Tremanheere, op. cit., p. 125.

40 Rev. Thomas Hutton, 'Agricultural gangs', *Transactions of the National Association for the Promotion of Social Science*, 1864, p. 650. In fact the system was older than that and was extensively documented by the Children's Employment Commission in 1843. Joan Thirsk dates it in Lincolnshire from about the 1820s; see

Joan Thirsk, *English Peasant Farming*, London, 1957, p. 268.
Marx wrote of the gang system, 'For the farmer there is no more
ingenious method of keeping his labourers well below the normal
level, and yet of always having an extra hand ready for extra
work, of extracting the greatest possible amount of labour with
the least possible amount of money . . . The cleanly weeded land,
and the uncleanly human weeds, of Lincolnshire, are pole and
counter-pole of capitalistic production', Karl Marx, *Capital*,
London, 1949, vol. 1, pp. 717–18.

41 Lilias Rider Haggard (ed.), *I Walked by Night, Being the Life and
History of the King of the Norfolk Poachers*, London, 1951, p. 93.

42 William Clift, *Reminiscences of William Clift of Bramley*, Aldershot,
1897, pp. 61–5.

43 Caird, op. cit., p. 284. 'This makes the manual labour on the
turnip-crop nearly double the cost in Lancashire, compared with
other countries.'

44 June A. Sheppard, 'East Yorkshire's agricultural labour force in
the mid-nineteenth century', *Agricultural History Review*, 9, 1961,
p. 44.

45 Caird, op. cit., p. 175.

46 Tremanheere, op. cit., p. 125.

47 Charles Whitehead, *Fruit Growing in Kent*, London, 1881, p. 9;
Charles Whitehead, *Profitable Fruit-Farming, an essay*, London,
1884, p. 88.

48 Glyde, op. cit., p. 364.

49 Trinity College, Cambridge, MS. Diaries of A. J. Munby, XVII,
3 January 1863.

50 Thomas Hardy, *Tess of the D'Urbervilles*, ch. 43.

51 Flora Thompson, *Lark Rise to Candleford*, World's Classics ed.,
1971, p. 37.

52 J. D. Chambers, 'Nottingham in the early 19th century',
Transactions of the Thoroton Society, 46, 1942, p. 29.

53 P.P. 1865 (3484) XXVI, *7th Report of the Medical Officer of the
Privy Council*, Appendix 6, *Inquiry on the State of the Dwellings of
Rural labourers* by Dr Hunter, p. 243.

54 Ibid.

55 Denis Mills, 'English villages in the 18th and 19th centuries: a
sociological classification', *Amateur Historian*, 6, 1965, p. 276.
There is a very clear demonstration of the different rate of growth
in closed and open villages in Alan Rogers (ed.), *Stability and
Change, Some Aspects of North and South Ranceley in the Nineteenth
Century*, Nottingham, 1969. For another recent discussion of the
subject, B. A. Holderness, ' "Open" and "close" parishes in
England in the eighteenth and nineteenth centuries',
Agricultural History Review, 20, 1972.

56 Lincolnshire farmers provided their open village labourers with
donkeys, Caird tells us, in order that they should not wear
themselves out on the six or seven mile journey to work, op. cit.,
p. 197.

57 Sheppard, op. cit., p. 52.
58 Among them Summertown, Oxford, 'A Place which is but of yesterday', founded by James Lambourn, an itinerant horse dealer in 1820. There is a very good account of the village in 1832 in Bodleian Library, MS. Top. Oxon., e. 240.
59 Arthur Young, *Inquiry into Wastes*, London, 1801.
60 Thompson, op. cit., p. 279.
61 Ibid., pp. 73–4.
62 *Oxford Chronicle*, 20 August 1853, p. 8, col. 2.
63 Thompson, op. cit., p. 6.
64 W. O. Hassall (ed.), *Wheatley Records*, Diary of Rev. Edward Elton, 12 April 1861.
65 Thompson, op. cit., pp. 1–2.
66 George Bourne (Sturt), *Change in the Village*, London, 1959, pp. 2–3.
67 Dr Hunter's Report, p. 178.
68 Robert Baker 'On the industrial and sanitary economy . . . of Leeds', *Journal of the Royal Statistical Society*, 11, 1858, p. 429.
69 Dr Hunter's Report, p. 277.
70 Thomas Hardy, *The Mayor of Casterbridge*, Macmillan ed., 1964, pp. 254–5.
71 *British Husbandry*, 111, 1840, p. 29.
72 William Marshall, *The Rural Economy of Norfolk*, 1787, 1, p. 256. For a general discussion of the labour intensive character of the 'New Husbandry', David Grigg, *The Agricultural Revolution in South Lincolnshire*, Cambridge, 1966, pp. 3–4, 40–1, 48, 58; Joan Thirsk speaks of the 'unprecedented demand for farm workers' when the Lincolnshire uplands were ploughed up' (op. cit., pp. 267–8).
73 R. N. Bacon, *Report on the Agriculture of Norfolk*, London, 1844, p. 214.
74 John Grey of Dilston, 'A view of the present state of agriculture in Northumberland', *Journal of the Royal Agricultural Society of England*, 11, 1841, p. 165.
75 Ibid., p. 168.
76 Jonas, op. cit., p. 43.
77 *British Husbandry*, 11, 1837, p. 340.
78 P.P. 1870 (c. 70) XIII, *3rd Report of the Commissioners on the Employment of Children, Young Persons and Women in Agriculture*, Appendix pt 11, p. 9.
79 John Algernon Clarke, 'On the great level of the Fens', *Journal of the Royal Agricultural Society of England*, 8, 1847, pp. 92, 101, 119.
80 Arthur R. Randell, *Sixty Years a Fenman*, London, 1966, p. 6.
81 John Algernon Clarke, *Fen Sketches*, London, 1852, p. 256.
82 Hall, op. cit., p. 75.
83 Ibid.
84 M. Knowles, *History of Wicken*, London, 1902, pp. 8, 11.
85 Tremanheere, op. cit., p. 122.

86 Clutterbuck, op. cit., p. 12.
87 Caird, op. cit., p. 21; cf. also Clare Sewell Read, 'Farming of Oxfordshire', *Journal of the Royal Agricultural Society of England*, 15, 1855, p. 247.
88 Isaac Mead, *The Life Story of an Essex Lad Written by Himself*, Chelmsford, 1923, p. 32.
89 The statement is that of a judge at the Berkshire Lent Assizes, 1853, summing up in a rick burning case 'out of revenge, it was supposed, because a reaping-machine had been introduced into the parish'. Two men were sentenced to transportation for fifteen years, and four to ten years. *Oxford Chronicle*, 5 March 1853, p. 3, col. 2. 'Several cases of incendiarism' were reported from Devon in November of the same year, in two instances being perpetrated on farmers with thrashing machines on their premises. 'It seemed likely that the offenders belonged to that misguided class of men who think that machinery for agricultural purposes injures the labourer and diminishes wages.' *The Times*, 29 November 1853, p. 7, col. 6.
90 Joseph Smith Fletcher, *The Making of Modern Yorkshire*, London, 1918, p. 176.
91 'Strikes and machinery', *Ironmonger*, 14 December 1878, p. 1390. When double furrowed ploughs were introduced into the Yorkshire Wolds in 1872 'in several instances' the labourers and yearly servants refused to work them and were prosecuted under the Master and Servant Act. The plough 'worked by a man and three horses' effected the saving of a man and horsekeeper. *Labour News*, 18 May 1872, p. 3, col. 2.
92 MS. Reminiscences of Charles Slater of Barley, 11, 45–7. The writer is very grateful to Mr Salaman for letting him see a copy of this valuable MS.
93 Thompson, op. cit., p. 41.
94 Ibid., ch. 10, 'Daughters of the Hamlet'.
95 For the visit of one of them to Lark Rise, ibid., ch. 12, 'Her Majesty's Inspector'.
96 Ibid., p. 39.
97 See especially George Ewart Evans, *The Horse in the Furrow*, London, 1967.

Part 2

The place of harvesters in nineteenth-century village life

David H. Morgan

1 The crowded fields

Perhaps the first thing we should say about nineteenth-century harvesting is that it was an immense activity, involving more workers than ever before or since. This was partly because of the growth of population (larger in country districts than it had ever been, even though the towns were growing faster); partly because farms were larger, crop yields heavier, and landless labourers more numerous; above all because the work of the human arm was still of far greater importance than that of the machine. The 1851 census gives a figure of 1,077,627 for agricultural workers in England and Scotland. But the number of people in the harvest fields was certainly more, because at harvest time the Victorian farmer relied not only on his regular workers, but also on their wives and their children, on labourers from the open villages, on migrants from Ireland, and on casual labourers from the towns.

There was more land under cultivation in the middle years of the nineteenth century than ever before or since. Bread was the staple food of the working man, and to meet the demand of a rapidly rising population, the acreage in wheat was continually increased, reaching a maximum of over $3\frac{1}{2}$ million acres in 1869. In Berkshire, for example, land in arable cultivation increased from 255,000 acres in 1831, to 451,210 acres in 1866. It was not only the cultivation of grain that increased, but all the other crops of the summer harvests – the hay harvest in June and July, peas in late July, hops in September.

The nineteenth century was an era of agricultural expansion; but husbandry was still traditional. The methods of harvesting and the tools employed (with the single exception of the threshing machine) were very little different in 1850 from those of 1750. Only towards the end of the nineteenth century did machinery begin to have any real impact either on production methods or on the working lives of country people. The four basic tools in use – the sickle, the reaping hook, the fagging hook and the scythe – were all hand tools. Irish harvesters used the sickle, a light crescent-shaped hook with a serrated edge;[1] the reaping hook, its smooth-edged counterpart, was the preferred tool of the English. 'The reaper passed the curved blade round a portion of standing corn and drew it towards himself; the pull made the ears cluster in a bunch which he gripped, and severed the straws immediately afterwards. Tucking the corn under the left arm, he repeated the action until he had enough to make a sheaf.'[2] In harvest time the work was physically hard, as a passage from Richard Jefferies may remind us:[3]

> Next day the village sent forth its army with their crooked
> weapons to cut and slay . . . More men and more men were
> put on day by day, and women to bind the sheaves . . .
> as the wheat fell, the shocks rose behind them, low tents
> of corn. Your skin or mine could not have stood the
> scratching of the straw, which is stiff and sharp, and the
> burning of the sun, which blisters like red-hot iron. No one
> could stand the harvest-field as a reaper except he had been
> born [to it] . . . Their necks grew black. . . . Their open chests
> were always bare, and flat, and stark . . . The breast bone
> was burned black, and their arms, tough as ash, seemed
> cased in leather. They grew visibly thinner in the harvest-
> field, and shrunk together – all flesh disappearing,
> and nothing but sinew and muscle remaining. Never was
> such work . . . So they worked and slaved, and tore at
> the wheat . . . the heat, the aches, the illness, the
> sunstroke, always impending in the air – the stomach
> hungry again before the meal was over . . . No song, no
> laugh, no stay – on from morn till night . . .

There were many more tasks in the harvest fields than could be performed by the regularly employed farm labour force, and extra hands were needed from the time the corn was cut to the time when the last bolt of straw had been carried to the thatcher and the last rick made safe. Cutting could still be going on in one field, while in another corn already cut was being shocked or carted away. Wheat might be ready to cart in a matter of days; oats it was considered should stand in 'stook' for three Sundays.[4] Oats (if mown) and barley had to be turned like hay in the swathe, because, unlike wheat, they retained sap in the straw, so carrying had to wait on wilting, especially in the case of undersown barley.[5] No single group of workers could perform all the harvest tasks, for their demands inevitably clashed. There was a continuous succession of work for all available hands – children helping to make bands and binding and stooking; men cutting and carting; women raking the ground behind. The younger men pitched to wagon, and from

wagon to stack, for this was regarded as the most strenuous
work; older men often worked at loading the wagons or building
the ricks, where their experience was valued and their strength
less taxed. Young lads and even small boys were generally in
charge of leading the wagons.

Each task was urgent. The corn, once cut, could not be left
unsheaved and unshocked overnight; the shocked corn could
not be left uncarted when ripe for risk of shedding. 'A field of
wheat left uncut a day too long may have two bushels an acre
blown out of it by a high wind . . . barley left uncarted . . .
changed from good malting sample to cheap feeding stuff.'[6]
There was the same urgency at hay time. If grass for hay is cut
too early, yields are less; if too late, it starts to seed; if there is
rain the hay is unfit to carry until forking and raking have dried
it out. A stack made from damp hay will heat, then the hay may
go musty and become unpalatable for stock; the rick can even
catch fire.

The harvest field in the nineteenth century was a hive of
human activity.

J. G. Cornish recalls of Berkshire in the early 1880s that when
harvest time arrived:[7]

most of the villagers migrated to the corn-fields . . . nearly
all the wheat and most of the barley was cut by hand. The
fields were usually about one furlong wide, and perhaps
there might have been eight acres of wheat ready for
cutting and, let us say, eight men engaged on the task.
They would draw lots for their strips in the field, and
then eight families would begin to drive their pathway
into the standing corn. I said eight *families* though
perhaps some of the men who were 'widow men', i.e.
bachelors, must work alone and so be outdistanced by their
more fortunate neighbours. Father with his broad-bladed
fagging hook in his right hand and crooked stick in his
left, slashed through the yellow stalks and left them
gathered by his foot. Mother followed, swept a sheaf
together placed it on 'the bond', drew this tightly and
fastened it by a twist. The children pulled the bonds, the
younger perhaps only able to select six or eight stalks
needed to make one, the elder making them ready for
mother to use.

At Lark Rise, Flora Thompson's village in north Oxfordshire, 'For three weeks or more during harvest the hamlet was astir before dawn.'[8] Across the north-east border, at Ilmington in Warwickshire, 'The farmer would take on as many families as he could . . . each taking their allotted acre or two.'[9] In Buckinghamshire:[10]

> Whole families planned for work in the harvest field: the
> father with the eldest children, to go daily in advance;
> the mother, with those younger, to follow later, with
> provender for the day. The work was done by the piece;
> it was a matter of slaving from the morn to late evening,
> an incessant 'slash, slash,' with the gleaming fagging hook
> at the ripe corn; and then the gathering of the severed
> halm together and the binding of it with a straw band
> laid ready on the ground by one of the children.

Thomas Ratcliffe of Worksop, writing in 1905, described the general situation as it was in midland villages in his childhood thirty years earlier:[11]

> Every man, woman and child went forth into the fields to
> help . . . and win the extra wage for harvest . . . When the
> first corn field was ready . . . the sicklemen or scythemen
> with the gatherers and binders were at the field. The
> gatherers of the sheaves and the binders were generally the
> wives and children of the men, and the whole work of the
> harvest was of the nature of a family outing . . . though a
> hard working one . . . the reapers or mowers fall in one by
> one behind the leader, the women and children as gatherers
> and binders following in their wake. The first stop was
> when the leader wanted to sharpen. He said 'Now', and all
> stopped at the end of his sickle or scythe swing. Then
> came the music of half a dozen tools sharpening as the
> stone rasped the steel blades . . . The sharpening was often
> as not the time of 'lowance' as well, when from the wooden
> kegs or stone bottles came . . . the home-brewed as it fell
> into the horn ale-tots . . . These ale-tots of horn were held
> to be the best for harvest drinking . . . being cooler and
> sweeter than in any other form and far before that of
> 'sucking the monkey' as liquor drunk from a bottle was
> called. The tots were emptied at a drain.

Women were an essential part of the harvest labour force. They were usually employed on the 'lighter' kinds of work, but so long as the sickle was in use, this included reaping as it had done in the days of Wordsworth's *Solitary Reaper*. Mabel Ashby describes the sickle used by the women at Tysoe:[12]

A very neat, small instrument it was; a good worker dropped hardly a straw where the corn stood up well. A dozen or maybe twenty reapers, largely women would work in one field, with men following to tie up the sheaves and another group to set them in shucks . . . there was talk and banter and flirting and yarn-spinning during the meals under the hedge.

Older men, who might find it difficult to get work at other times of the year, were also very generally employed, usually in unloading wagons and helping in rick building. Their names crop up often in reports of harvest accidents. No wonder; working on top of wagons and ricks, and clambering up and down ladders was made still more hazardous by deteriorating reflexes and rheumatic joints.[13]

At Great Tew near Deddington in July 1872 an aged agricultural labourer (seventy-seven) slipped off a wagon load of hay, head downwards, and 'expired about 6 o'clock'.[14] At Deddington four years later an old man of seventy-five, who was working on a straw rick, 'tumbled therefrom to the ground and thereby received such injuries that he died'.[15] At Bampton on 10 August of the same year John Martin, farm labourer aged sixty-one years, had just emptied a load at the rick and was standing on the raves of the cart when the horses suddenly moved and 'he fell to the ground striking his head against a ladder . . . died the same evening'.[16] At Murcot in July 1899 a sixty-two-year-old labourer had a fatal fall when he was climbing down from a hay rick.[17] Falling from a straw rick George Woodward aged fifty-six, a labourer of Appleton, died from haemorrhage of the brain at the end of harvest in 1898.[18] A shepherd aged fifty, employed by Mr Salmon of Luffield Abbey near Silverstone, Buckinghamshire, engaged with others building a rick in 1873, 'overbalanced himself and fell from the top of the rick to the ground, a distance of 27 feet', and died the next day from injuries to his spine.[19] An old man at Chalcombe slipped when climbing on to a wagon and died

from his injuries; a seventy-five-year-old Easington man
collapsed and died climbing back to work on a rick; an aged man
dislocated his neck from a fall off a wheat rick at Overthorpe;
in Cornwall a labourer fell backwards off a ladder while paring
a rick and 'was a corpse in a few hours'. These last fatalities all
occurred in the last week in August 1847.[20]

Children helped in the harvest from an early age. The piecework earnings of the family depended on them, but boys also
were often employed in their own right, especially to lead horses.
Arthur Gibbs describes a boy at work in 1896:[21]

> In the fields beyond the river haymakers are busy with the
> second crop. Down to the ford comes a great yellow
> hay-cart, drawn by two strong horses, tandem fashion. One
> small boy alone is leading the big horses. Arriving at the
> ford, he jumps on the leader's back and rides him through.
> The horses strain and 'scaut' and the cart bumps over the
> deep ruts, nearly upsetting. Luckily there is no accident.
> So much is entrusted to these little farm lads of scarce
> fifteen years of age, it is a wonder they do the work so well.

Isaac Mead, an Essex lad, was fifteen when he took a scythe
for the first time, and went to work in the harvest of 1874.[22]
Arthur Randell recalls how as a much younger child he worked
in the Fen harvest fields at the turn of the century, tying
sheaves:[23]

> My parents had harvested on the same farm for many
> years, and as soon as we children were able to do so we had
> to take our share in . . . making the bands to tie the corn
> and then, as we got older, to tie and shock alongside our
> elders . . . I have often seen the harvest men, during a
> spell of very dry weather, take armfuls of a straw and lay
> them in the bottom of the Hook Drain to soak, otherwise
> the bands, being too dry would have broken as soon as they
> made them.

Walter Barrett, another fenman, was only eight when he first
worked a full day in the harvest fields. He was employed leading
horses, and his day began at 6 o'clock in the morning:[24]

> I was taken to a field of wheat where a six sailed reaping
> machine, with four horses attached, was waiting . . . I was

to ride the offside front horse, keeping it close to the
standing corn, then pull out on reaching the corner and
then swing back . . . The horses were changed at ten,
two and six o'clock; there was no dinner break, one of the
men taking my place while I was eating . . . The two men
were paid one shilling an acre so, by cutting ten acres a
day, they earned five shillings each. Just as dusk was falling
I ended the longest day so far in my young life . . . I
spent three weeks riding the reaping horse, then I was
switched over to leading the horse and shouting 'Hold tight'.

The wife of a Sussex shepherd, who herself worked as a reaper
in the harvest field, describes the way in which even 'toddlers'
could be used. She is writing about the 1870s:[25]

After an early breakfast, I used to start with my children
for one of the Hall fields, carrying our dinner with us . . .
Even the toddlers could help by twisting the straw into
bands and also by helping me tie up my sheaves. But
cutting and binding our sheaves was not the end of our
day's work. We still had to make the shocks. Many is
the time that my husband came round to us when his own
day's work was done, and we worked together setting up
the shocks by moonlight.

Getting the harvest in was a time of involvement, often of
anxiety, sometimes of crisis. The need for labour was never
predictable; no two harvests were alike. If the fields ripened
together, they all had to be cut at the same time, which needed
a much larger labour force than if the crops ripened in stages.
'Upstanding' corn required less labour than corn that had been
flattened by storm.[26] Overnight the situation of the crop might
change. The farmer was not concerned who took his harvest
so long as it was safely gathered. Occupational barriers
disappeared:[27]

The carpenters and wheelwrights left their benches, the
masoners laid down their trowels and all others left their
crafts . . . to get the precious corn in. If they had not gone
. . . the farmers would have withheld their patronage
during the ensuing winter.

In August 1872 two building labourers demanded 7s. 6d. a day
to dig a site for the new gas-holder at Woodstock, because the

harvest was about to begin. They were told this rate was 'exhorbitant' and so went harvesting instead.[28] Earlier in the century, the rick-builders during the harvest at Sutton were said to have been made up of the following professions: one gentleman, two carpenters, two shoemakers, one wheelwright, one collar maker, one miller, one labourer and one land surveyor.[29] Other fields too must have held as motley a collection of harvest workers as those of Tom Strong's 'Stubble Farm' in Berkshire, where there were[30]

> all sizes and ages, men and women, Irish and English, strollers and neighbours, reapers and faggers, good workmen and bad, grandmothers and children, kettle-boilers and tiers, married and single.

Some casual labour came out of the market towns, 'men and women, and girls, glad of the open-air work'.[31] But much more came from 'open' villages such as Headington Quarry.

It was because the fields were so crowded and so much extra labour of all ages was employed that harvest time was an occasion of drama, of distress, and even of tragedy: the arduous work in the summer heat brought deaths from sun-stroke;[32] little children slipped under the wheels of the heavily laden carts.[33] Older men like Henry Burton of Chalgrove, who died on a Friday in September 1895 with 'Oh dear! Master Brown' on his lips as he placed the last sheaf on the last load of the corn harvest,[34] and poor women like Sarah Lawrence, aged seventy-one of Cholsey, who returned home after a long toil of a harvest day in July 1869 to die in her bed,[35] were victims of exhaustion. There were acts of God when lightning struck[36] and sadly the acts of men when young girls left alone in the harvest field were raped.[37]

Excessive drinking at harvest time often led to quarrels, and might have more serious consequences than a mere argument over who should foot the bill – the occasion for a group of labourers appearing before the Aylesbury magistrates in July 1878.[38] Quarrels, fights, even serious physical injury were part of the un-noted disharmony of harvest time. It seems they may have been a way in which unofficial harvest practices were maintained from below, as in a police court case reported in 1882 when a harvest labourer was sent to prison for one month for assaulting a mate who would not 'stand' their gang a quart of beer.[39] A Fulbrook labourer found himself in prison for fourteen days after an argument on a rick with a youth of seventeen on 28 August 1872. He had struck the lad on the head with a prong for not getting 'out of the road' when told.[40] An assault during a disturbance among labourers who quarrelled under the influence of the harvest beer cost a Hornton labourer 21s. at Banbury Petty Sessions on Thursday, 8 September 1859.[41] In the harvest of 1873 at Deddington a complaint of 'the beer being bad' caused a fight between farmer and labourer while they were pitching beans and vetches. The labourer sued unsuccessfully for assault.[42] A dossier of such incidents could be collected from the local newspapers of the period, and many more must have gone unrecorded.

Harvesting was still essentially a communal activity, and it is not surprising that harmony among the crowds of harvest workers was not consistently maintained. The use of sharp cutting tools, the lumbering, horse-drawn, heavily-loaded carts and wagons, the tempo of the work, and the spur of increased earnings, all contributed to increase tension and fatigue. Tempers could fly, the older men over-exert themselves in keeping up the pace, the young children hinder as well as help, even the strongest grow tired and careless. A dispute over choice of positions in binding the corn led to an assault on another labourer and cost a Southmoor man a fine of 1s. and 11s. 6d. costs at Aylesbury County Petty Sessions in August 1899.[43] Two harvesters fought over work in a field at Summertown in September 1874 using reaping hooks.[44] On the Ditchley Estate near Enstone in 1848 with 'Harvest Home' resounding through the woods, three lads 'influenced by beer and feelings of animosity' engaged in an affray during which one was stabbed with a sheep knife, and died.[45] A mower, given unwelcome orders by a bailiff, threatened to stab him with his scythe 'if he did not get out of the way'.[46] (The Winslow Magistrates fined him 10s. and 9s. costs for assault and being 'out of temper'.)

The local inhabitants alone were rarely capable of supplying the total labour required for the safe gathering in of the harvest, and usually they were supplemented by outsiders, whether 'companies', individuals or travelling Irishmen. If farmers viewed 'strangers' as a very necessary pool of labour their presence was never much welcomed by local inhabitants.

Three Ipsden men brutally attacked a harvester from Woodstock in August 1897.[47] In August 1876 John Clements of Saintsbury 'used violence' towards John Sanders ('a reaper and a stranger'), threatening and intimidating him with a view to coerce him and prevent him reaping at Weston Subedge until 'he was bound to give up his reaping and seek protection'.[48] A labourer, dismissed from a Hardmead farm during the harvest of 1889, assaulted his replacement ('being a Chicheley man')[49] and was able to secure the aid of four other labourers in the attack. Harvest earnings were 'preserves' not to be lightly invaded by the stranger, and the outsider who trespassed on a villager's territory was liable to receive short shrift.

2   Harvest earnings

The earnings of the rural worker at harvest time were the key to his survival. The wages he was paid during the rest of the year were often inadequate to maintain a family at even subsistence level. At harvest all the family could earn; wage rates were higher and for the man who was willing to travel there was the possibility of working two or more harvests. The period immediately after harvest, when lump payments were made, was the one time of the year when the labourer and his family could afford to pay for 'extras' (i.e. household necessities other than food) – 'to pay rent, back debts, find shoe-leather and so forth'.[50] Boots were often bought with the extra money. At Haddenham, Buckinghamshire:[51]

> Everyone looked to harvest earnings for the extra money for boots for the family. And the bootmaker knew this and worked to it; the many pairs he made in advance (on that understanding) were a very important part of his livelihood. The village feast fell at a lucky time for all concerned – just on the edge of winter, when back money, due on harvest earnings, had been paid. Gladly mixing business and pleasure, they all assembled at the bootmaker's house to supper, where they feasted together to the honour of the boots that he had made.

The farm labour books of the period show the wide difference in earnings between winter and summer. The labour accounts for Monkton Farm, Tarrant Monkton, Dorset,[52] for the years 1875–6 show the following:[53]

			£	s.	d.
1875	February 22nd	4 weeks Pay	20.	1.	6.
	March 22nd	4 weeks Pay	20.	2.	10.
	April 19th	4 weeks Pay	21.	1.	7.
	May 17th	4 weeks Pay	22.	13.	8.
	June 14th	4 weeks Pay	23.	9.	8.
	July 12th	4 weeks Pay	27.	5.	$2\frac{1}{2}$
		(Hay Harvest)			
	August 1st	3 weeks Pay	24.	0.	0.
	August 7th	1 weeks Pay	7.	18.	6.
	September 6th	Harvest Month	67.	15.	4.
	December 27th	4 weeks Pay	20.	18.	8.
1876	July 31st	3 weeks Pay	28.	6.	10.
		(Hay Harvest)			
		Harvest Labour	61.	10.	$1\frac{1}{4}$

There is a striking difference between the low figure of £20 1s. 6d. (for February) and the harvest month's £67 15s. 4d. If the wages paid during the three months commencing 22 February are set against those commencing 12 July (which included both the hay and corn harvest) there is a difference of £65 13s. 3½d.

On John Barford's farm in 1869 at Fawcett, Oxfordshire, the wage bill for the last three weeks of the 'harvest month' amounted to £38 16s. 0d. The wages for the four weeks from 9 October, on the other hand, amounted to only £20 6s. 0d. The difference between the two was even greater than this, because in addition to the £38 16s. 0d. there were various payments for cutting at piecework rates, amounting in all to £16 1s. 7d.[54]

The 1863–4 figures for Joseph Martin's farm, Ripple, Tewkesbury, Gloucestershire, which are presented in a graph (Figure 1, p. 40) show a similar contrast. The 'dead' month of the year, February, expectedly shows the lowest wage bill £21 13s. 5½d.; in the harvest month the wage bill is £65 11s. 7d., a difference of £40 5s. 7d. July's wage bill was £42 10s. 11d., significantly the month of the hay harvest (payment was in this case for a five-week period).[55]

On Wick Farm, Radley, Berkshire, the first week's wage bill

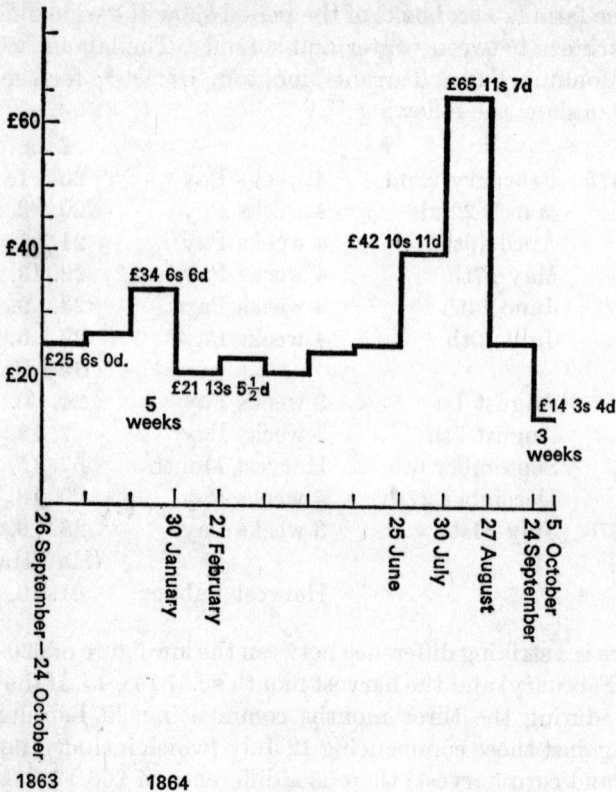

Figure 1 *Joseph Martin, Ripple, Tewkesbury, Glos. Account for labour 26 September 1863–5 October 1864. Total labour bill = £379 0s. 10d.*

in October 1853 was £8 16s. 2d. In the first week of September, during the harvest, it was £36 0s. 5d., a difference of £27 4s. 3d. On the same farm in 1861 the wages paid for the week commencing 30 August amounted to £55 19s. 11d. Three heavy payments for piecework are itemized:

	£	s.	d.
August 30th. Fagging 43 acres wheat at 9/- per acre		19.	7. –
Do 43 acres Barley at 9/- per acre.		19.	7. –
Pulling 20½ acres beans at 10/- per acre		10.	5. –

The wages, in contrast, for the week commencing 18 October came to £8 8s. 8d., a difference of £47 11s. 3d. Again in 1860 at Wick Farm in the harvest week of 7 September the week's wage bill was £54 12s. (£42 1s. 5d. was paid for the piecework fagging of barley and wheat). By 21 September, with the harvest over, wages had fallen to £6 14s. 11d., even with the inclusion of some back payments for turnip hoeing.[56]

The extra earnings at harvest time were made up in various ways: in 'Michaelmas money', through an enhanced day rate; at piecework, through the harvest agreement or contract; in beer money, or indirectly through payments in kind (provision of beer or cider, or sometimes the equivalent in malt and hops, and sometimes meals). Some of these benefits were mutually exclusive; and the amount finally received depended on the conditions of service.

The main difference to be noticed is between the 'hired' labourer, i.e., the regular farm 'servant', who worked for a single employer all the year round; and the 'day' labourer, who was free to work for different employers in the course of the year (or to work on his own account), and who took on harvest work by piecework contract.

Harvest opportunities for the day labourers were as follows: (1) an enhanced day rate; (2) piecework; (3) contract work. Their advantage lay in being able to switch from working by the day to taking piecework without being hindered by other commitments. At piecework not only could they work as many hours as they wished, to complete their work quickly, but their opportunities were not confined to a single farm: they could seek piecework on other farms. Organized into bands they could bargain with the farmers for a profitable rate, especially when labour was in short supply. If the rate was unacceptable a refusal could not incur unpleasant consequences such as might have arisen had they been hired men. Most importantly they could increase the profitability of piecework by enlisting family help.

Harvest extras for the 'hired' labourers (the regular farm servants) were more various and more complicated, though in total amounting to less in money terms. Here are the different forms:

1   Michaelmas money (or 'over money')

Michaelmas money was a lump sum payment made after harvest, and always contracted for at the beginning of the yearly hiring. The amount varied according to age and experience. It was not exclusively a harvest payment but contained a general allowance for longer hours worked before 'dawn' and after 'dusk', the traditional span of a working day. The sum of money was substantial – a hiring agreement for Wick Farm, Radley, Berkshire, in 1838, specifies '£3 at Michaelmas'. Often the labourer could only pay his rent after the receipt of Michaelmas money: in some hiring agreements a cottage was given rent free instead of Michaelmas money.[57]

2   An enhanced day rate

The amount varied; generally it was up to double the normal day rate depending on the difficulty of the work, the length of the working day, and the status of the workers. At Hill Farm, Stokenchurch, Buckinghamshire, in 1860, where the ordinary rate for the regular labourer was 10s. a week, some were being paid a rate of 15s. a week during harvest, and some a double rate of £1 3s. 0d.[58] In 1879, at Lodge Farm on the Ditchley Estate, Oxfordshire, rates for regular farm servants were increased at harvest time from 2s. 4d. to 3s.; 2s. 2d. to 3s.; 1s. to 1s. 6d.; 10d. to 1s. 3d.[59] As well as this there was a harvest payment of 'beer money' – £1 each to the men, and 10s. to a lad or boy. At Fawcett, Oxfordshire, up to double the day rate was paid during harvest, though this was somewhat curtailed by the employment of two 'harvest companies', Joshua Allen '& Brothers', who were paid £1 14s. for reaping at 13s. per acre; and Mark R. South '& Company', who were paid £2 19s. 8d. for the same. This was the practice over a period from 1865 to 1884; no Michaelmas money was paid.[60]

3   Piecework

This was very limited for the regular farm servant because of his ordinary, day-to-day commitments. A little piecework – cutting, reaping or fagging – might come his way, but not much of it. The carter would have to feed and groom his horses, in harvest as at other times; the shepherd would have to tend to his sheep. What really made piecework profitable at harvest time was the extended working day, starting very early in the morning and finishing late at night. Only the unattached outsider, who came in just for the harvest, could manage this.

4 The harvest 'extra'

This was a lump sum paid for the weeks of the harvest, on top of the ordinary day rate. The amount usually equalled an enhanced day rate paid over the harvest period, but the two payments were mutually exclusive. Michaelmas money and the harvest 'extra', however, sometimes went together. For instance, at Wick Farm, Radley, Berkshire, William East was hired as a carter in October 1861 at 11s. per week with £2 10s. at Michaelmas, and 10s. extra for the harvest; 'earnest' was paid, but there were no other extras.[61]

5 Overtime

Work done after normal working hours might be paid by the hour instead of at the ordinary day rates. But this was relatively unknown until the 1870s, when farm workers began successfully to assert that the working day should be limited to a definite number of hours, instead of the vague formula (open to so much exploitation by the farmers) of 'dawn to dusk'. (The demand for a fixed working day was one which Warwickshire labourers were making on the eve of Joseph Arch's Wellesbourne meeting in 1872.)[62] During most of the year it was to the labourer's advantage to have the length of the working day fixed, and have overtime pay; but at harvest time he probably stood to gain more by the traditional enhanced day rate.

6 Beer money

Beer was usually supplied free to all fixed-rate workers, during harvest, but generally not to pieceworkers; sometimes however if piecework was taken at a lower rate beer was also provided. If no beer was supplied a cash equivalent (usually £1) was paid at the end of the harvest period, but never to pieceworkers.

7   Harvest home supper ('Horkey' in East Anglia and the Fens)

This was a supper provided by the farmer for the workers and their families to celebrate the completion of harvest. After the 1860s a practice of commuting the harvest supper into a money payment was gradually introduced and the sum of 2s. 6d. was paid to each worker (*pro rata* for women and lads, usually 1s.). The provision of harvest supper at Hill Farm, Stokenchurch, Buckinghamshire, cost £1 6s. in 1850.[63] At Fullwell Farm on the Ditchley Estate, at the end of the harvest in 1878, eight men and two ploughboys received £1 each for beer allowance and 2s. 6d. harvest home money; two day men received £1 beer allowance and 6d. harvest home money; one ploughboy received 8s. harvest home money, two others 7s. each, three women received 1s. each, and two casual workers were paid 16s. 6d. and 14s. 6d. respectively.[64]

8   Payments in kind (beer, tea and provisions)

These were usually supplied only to day workers whether paid at day rates or at enhanced day rates; sometimes to piece-workers when the piece-rate was lower. Free drink and meals were sometimes the *only* payment made at hay time to those working by the day. The cost of such perquisites on a farm at Holton, Oxfordshire, in 1886 was: beer, tea and provisions supplied during hay making, corn harvest and for the harvest home supper, £18 13s. 6d.; in 1887 it was £17 11s. 6d.; in 1888 it was £11 14s. 6d.; in 1889 it was £10 5s. 6d.[65]

These payments, if totalled together, seem to suggest that a substantial sum could be earned at harvest time by the regular farm 'servant'. This was not the case. Some were mutually exclusive; some had to be paid almost immediately. Piecework, the enhanced day rate and the harvest 'extra' were *alternative* methods of payment; a labourer could receive cash from a combination of the first two, though more generally his choice rested between an enhanced day rate or working for ordinary rates with a lump sum (the 'extra') paid at the end of harvest. His final harvest earnings differed very little, whatever the method of payment. If the harvest 'extra' was paid, this usually precluded the payment of Michaelmas money. Michaelmas money itself almost invariably went straight back to the farmer, as payment for cottage rent. Harvest money in fact probably meant less to the regular farm servant than to any other group. The day labourer, by contrast, like the casual labourer, the older men, the out-of-work, and very often village women, depended upon the harvest absolutely. It gave them their chief – and in some cases their only – earnings of the year.

3   The harvest contract

The harvest altered the nature of the rural labour market and the circumstances of competition. It provided work for all; it restored family earning power. The labourer did not have to beg for work; he was badly needed and could state his terms. Even the hired men – the regular farm servants – were affected as the harvest month approached. 'The holy time was the harvest', an old labourer in Akenfield recalled, 'the farmer would call his men together and say "Tell me your harvest bargain."'[66]

The change of mood and social relationships can be seen in the making and carrying out of the harvest contract – the agreement under which the day labourer undertook his harvest work. The contract was in the nature of a bargain, in which the labourer stood face to face with the farmer, on terms of rough equality, using his strength and skill to get a good price for his work. Basically the harvest contract was a system of organized piecework. Sometimes it was made by individuals, sometimes by harvesting companies, but in either case the element of bargaining remained. If the farmer did not pay a decent rate they could take themselves elsewhere. There is a sense of this transformation in the labourer's status in the following description of a harvest agreement:[67]

We were allus hired by the week . . . except at harvest. Then it was piece-wukk. I dessay your've heard of the 'lord', as we used to call 'im? Sometimes he was the horseman at the farm, but he might be anybody. His job was to act as a sort of foreman to the team of reapers – there was often as many as ten or a dozen of us – and he looked after the hours and wages and such-like. He set

the pace, too. His first man was sometimes called the
'lady.' Well, when harvest was gettin' close, the 'lord' 'ld
call his team together and goo an' argue it out with the
farmer. They'd run over all the fields that had got to be
harvested and wukk it out at so much the acre. If same
as there was a field badly laid with the wather, of course
the 'lord' would ask a higher price for that. 'Now there's
Penny Fields', he'd say – or maybe Gilbert's Field – or
whatever it was; 'that's laid somethin' terrible', he'd say.
'What about that, farmer?' And when the price was named
he would talk it over with his team to see whether they'd
agree. The argument was washed down with plenty of
beer, like as not drunk out of little ol' bullocks' horns;
and when it was all finished, and the price accepted all
round, 'Now I'll bind you', the farmer 'ld say, and give
each man a shilling.

Arthur Randell recalls the making of a harvest contract in
the Fens:[68]

It was quite a business when the harvest men met the
farmer each year to fix the price per acre for tying,
shocking and carting . . . Often they would argue for as
much as half a day but in the end they always came to
some agreement and then the farmer would send for some
beer to seal the bargain and a start could be made on the
work.

Harvest work was divided into two great departments. One
(cutting, shocking and tying) was invariably done as piecework
and on a contract basis, and mostly by outsiders; the other was
done on a time-work basis and usually under the direction of
the farmer's 'own' men, with a lot of casual help recruited
locally in the home village. The broad division held even where
a harvest 'company' was engaged; usually the company would
contract to do the first part of the work, the cutting, shocking
and tying, where speed mattered most, and leave the more
protracted part of the work to local labour.

In the first part of the work the time factor mattered most,
and the workers' bargaining position was at its strongest. There
was an optimum point when the crops were ripe enough to
cut, and once that point had been reached speedy cutting was

essential. Shocking also had to be done at high speed, especially
if the weather conditions were uncertain. Once the crop was
in shock, it could no longer be flattened by storms. The very
method of forming the shocks gave them protection. In the
wetter counties, and elsewhere when the weather was doubtful,
'hooding' was practised; two of the sheaves were placed ears
downwards on the top of the shock for covering.

Earnings at this stage depended on the bargain which individuals or the company had made and the speed with which they
could carry out its conditions. There was neither supervision
nor co-ordination. They depended entirely on themselves. The
only disciplines at work were those which the individual
pieceworkers agreed amongst themselves, and these related
principally to 'fairness'. Earnings on piecework depended upon
the state of the crop, and this was taken account of, in a general
way, when a price was bargained for the job. But the local
distribution of work in the fields, between the 'rough' and the
'smooth', would be a matter for decision amongst the workers
themselves, usually by drawing lots. Strips in the headlands
were quicker to work, because the crop grew less thickly. In
some parts of a field the crop might be more upstanding than
in others and therefore easier to cut; the crop that had been
badly 'laid' (blown by wind or flattened by storm) was harder
and slower to work in. James Cornish recalls that on the
Berkshire Downs heavy crops of barley were 'fagged' with the
broad hook, but light crops were mown with the scythe and
left to dry on the ground. Extra effort was needed to cut 'laid'
corn but a 'poor plant' was easy to clear. None of the labourers,
however, had a right to grumble at the luck of his neighbour if
the harder task came his way for 'us drawed cuts for he'.[69]

Because harvesters usually cut down the whole length of the
field, following the ploughed 'lands', strips were often used as a
guide to the acreage cut. On Stubble Farm this important
economic aspect of harvesting was already taken care of before
the harvest began:[70]

All the wheat and oat lands had been previously measured,
planned, and numbered in a book, and the acreage marked,
so that Mr. Strong had only to agree about price and then
let them on to a small cut or large one, according to the
strength of the reapers.

The measurement of the work, however, was sometimes not in the hands of the farmer or one of his servants but was delegated to an outsider, jointly paid by the farmer and the workers themselves.[71] Sometimes he was a professional taking any kind of measuring; usually he was a respected man in the village who had learned to read, write and cast up figures (a carpenter, a wheelwright, a shopkeeper, sometimes even the local schoolmaster).

In the second department of harvesting work (carting and stacking) continuous organization and co-ordination took the place of self-regulation. The work was essentially teamwork, and the farmer, or one of his leading servants (usually the carter) directed the operations. The carting of the corn depended upon the general deployment of wagons about the fields. The building of ricks, though requiring skilled extra workers, was carried out under the control of a chief rick builder (again, usually the carter). Extra labour was taken on for carting and stacking, but payment was on the basis of time not piece, and though an enhanced day rate was paid, there was not the same big money to be earned as in work by the piece.

In the corn-growing counties of Oxfordshire, Buckinghamshire, and Berkshire the first department of work (cutting, shocking and tying) was usually taken on by *individual* piecework contract. The bargain was made by word of mouth, the terms depending on the quality and 'lay' of the crop. The pieceworker would expect a higher rate for heavy or badly-laid crops; he would be ready to take a lower one for crops that were lighter than average and therefore easier to cut. Sometimes he would take the cutting 'rough and smooth' weighing the gain if the weather held, against a loss should a sudden storm make his task harder and longer to complete. Piecework earnings in these counties were high not because of the rates themselves, but because of the 'hidden help' of the family. Earnings depended above all on the quantity of work that could be done, and the man with 'followers', i.e., wife and children, earned very much more than the 'widow' man who worked alone, with no one to help in the shocking and tying. These individual contracts were most frequent in counties which retained a large agricultural population, much of it unattached and living in 'open' villages (see Figure 2). The situation was very different in the eastern counties, where there was a chronic shortage of labour, even in winter time, and where much of the harvest was gathered by travelling companies.[72]

Harvest was the time of the year when the day labourer came

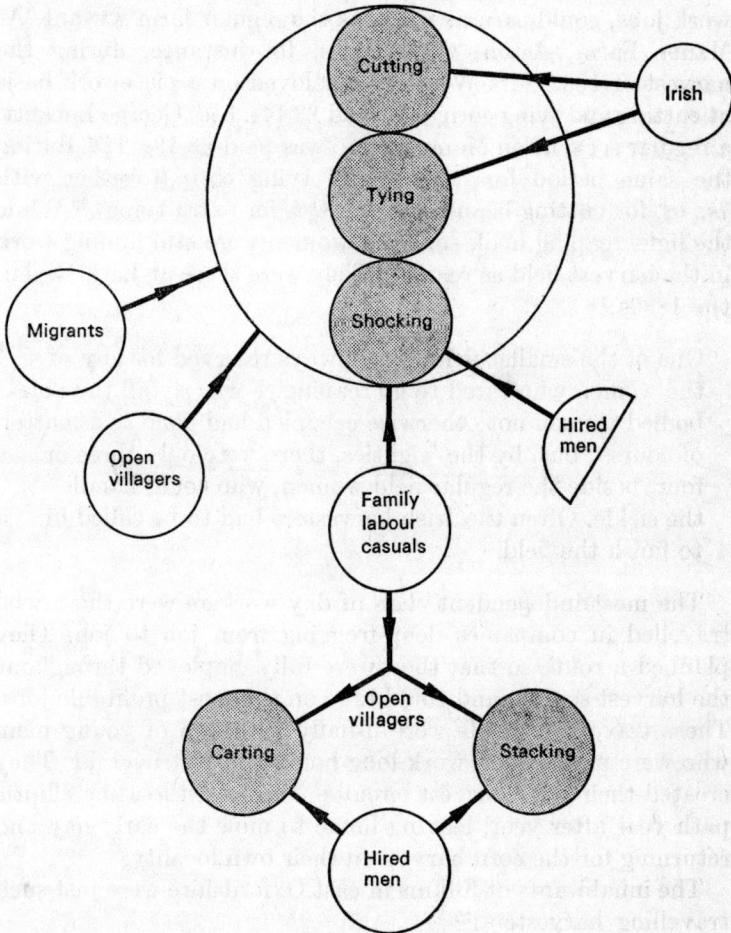

Figure 2   *Harvest work force*

into his own. During the rest of the year the apparent advantage rested with the hired man, the regular farm servant: he had security, a regular weekly wage, often a cottage. The day labourer, on the other hand, was often hard put to it to find any work, especially in winter. In the harvest months, however, his earnings outstripped even the élite, carters, cattlemen and shepherds, whose harvest earnings were built into the annual hiring agreement.

At harvest time even the women, when they took on piece-work jobs, could earn as much as the regular farm servant. At Manor Farm, Aston, Oxfordshire, for instance, during the harvest of 1883, Mrs Wearing, employed on a piecework basis at cutting and tying corn, was paid £3 14s. 3½d. George Luckett, a regular servant on Manor Farm, was paid £3 18s. 1½d. during the same period for cutting and tying corn (together with 7s. 1d. for cutting beans, and 2s. 8½d. for extra tying).[73] While the light reaping hook survived women were still finding work in the harvest field as reapers. They were there at Lark Rise in the 1880s:[74]

> One of the smaller fields was always reserved for any of the women who cared to go reaping. Formerly all the able-bodied women not otherwise occupied had gone as a matter of course; but, by the 'eighties, there were only three or four, beside the regular field women, who could handle the sickle. Often the Irish harvesters had to be called in to finish the field.

The most independent class of day workers were those who travelled in companies, leap-frogging from job to job. They planned a route so that they were fully employed throughout the harvest season, and could take on the most profitable jobs. These travelling bands were usually made up of young men, who were prepared to work long hours and to travel far. They created their own 'harvest circuits', and trod the same elliptic path year after year, leaving home to mow the early hay and returning for the corn harvest in their own locality.

The inhabitants of Filkins in east Oxfordshire were just such travelling harvesters:[75]

> They used to go to London mowing the parks and fields with the scythe; then helped to make the hay and put it into ricks. When the haymaking was done they worked their way back by doing hoeing for market gardeners. After working a week in one place, they walked on Sunday a few miles nearer home, and by the time they got to

Wantage, the harvesting was ready as it was earlier on the downs. After cutting the corn with their fagging hooks, the harvest at Filkins itself was ready; then they would go on to Northleach where the harvest was later still.

The last journey to these hayfields was made in 1912. From the borders of Wychwood Forest, too, labourers travelled to London for the hay harvest. Some of them were morris dancers and during their tour they would give exhibitions of dancing and singing, and strange villages would hear the songs they sang – 'Green Garters', 'The Maid o' the Mill', 'Trunk Hose', 'White Sock', 'Moll o' the Whad' – perhaps for the first time. And in this way they would increase their harvest wages.[76] Edwin Turner of Finstock was one of these travelling harvesters in the 1860s:[77]

He and others used to go up to London every summer for haytime and would often go up a month sooner than necessary in order to morris in the streets, would go out day by day in different parts of London – Clerkenwell was the only name he could remember – Often made 10 or 11 shillings apiece per diem. Once a fiddler from Churchill ('we took him with us; thought it would do him good') stole the takings.

Edwin Turner went dancing and haymaking nineteen consecutive summers. There were other Oxfordshire villagers who met up in the hayfields of Middlesex, labourers from Asthall and Ducklington, for instance, who went taking their 'Pipe and Taber', their whittle and club, and sometimes were accompanied by their wives.[78]

Harvesters from other counties would be there too, such as the villagers from Haddenham in Buckinghamshire, who used to travel 'uppards':[79]

Each hay season . . . wandering labourers flocked there from London and the country around. Men of our village went regularly and always found employment at once; for the men of Bucks were known, and preferred to those from the town. They started out on a Monday morning, men in groups of three or four who had agreed together to take

mowing by the piece, in co-operation. They knew one
another's capabilities, each would be able to maintain the
pace, and at the same time to cut a swathe of the normal
width . . . They called this migration *going uppards*. If
anyone asked for them . . . the reply would be 'Gone
uppards', for everyone was sure to know what that meant.

They carried their scythes with them; blades of proven
steel, ground ready, wrapped in old sacking . . . they knew
its 'right hang' to a nicety, the angle at which it would cut
the heaviest swathe with the least effort . . .

They slept on shakedowns of straw or hay in the
outbuildings of the farmsteads. Beer was supplied free
and in plenty . . .

Jack Lenten, a Warwickshire thatcher, the 'cleverest labourer
in the village', was another who 'went off towards Lunnon'
whenever the haymaking came on. He made 'a mort o'money',
but he found that he could not get regular employment when
he returned. The farmers told him 'he might go in the winter
where he had been in the summer':[80]

He had to get another place but they would never let Jack
gain a settlement, so in bad times Jack was sent to his own
parish to find that his cottage was pulled down. He had to
live miles away and tear his heart's blood out walking to
and from his work night and morn . . . When the railways
came Jack got work as a ganger.

The men of Hazlewood, Derbyshire, who were celebrated as
mowers, travelled even further. The village rector, the Rev.
J. H. Jenkin, affirmed in 1867 that they had been known to
travel as far as London, working all the way. The farms in
Hazlewood were small and the tenant farmers avoided as much
as possible giving employment to labourers. In winter many
were out of work, and they looked to harvest as the time of
compensation.[81]

The picture of the rural worker in the nineteenth century as
imprisoned within a village community subjected to the
pressures of a rigidly hierarchical society has some foundation.
The annually hired farm servant sacrificed any possibility of
freedom in return for a modicum of security. But their numbers
until the turn of the century never amounted to even one half of

the enumerated agricultural workers in the country. If independence had not been so highly valued the harvests of the
nineteenth century would not have been gathered, for it was the
mobility of labourers, not their servility, that brought them into
the harvest field. So long as the structure of harvest work provided the opportunity of economic survival their instinct was to
accept the challenge.

The day labourer was a creation of the early years of the
nineteenth century; upon his labour and the continuing
peasant practice of family participation depended the successful
gathering of the century's harvests. This changed towards the
close of the nineteenth century when the reaper-binder took
over the early stages of harvesting which had previously
provided the day labourers' most lucrative work. Both family
earnings and the number of day labourers declined. It was in the
nineties that the erstwhile independent labourers or their
sons finally deserted the countryside, and that a more modern
pattern of farming based on hired labour, harvest machinery
and the tied cottage began to emerge.

4   *Gleaning*

At the end of harvest, gleaners (usually women and children)
took over the fields to gather any grain left lying in the stubble.
At Tysoe each woman took a 'land' or ploughing ridge, laid
out a sheet with a stone at each corner, and then the whole
company began to move slowly up the ridges, 'all the figures
bending, hands deep in the stubble, "leasing" fallen ears'. Each
gleaner had a linsey-woolsey bag hanging from her waist. Tiny
boys and girls had tiny bags.[82] After the harvest at Lark Rise:[83]

the women and children swarmed over the stubble picking
up the ears of wheat the horse-rake had missed . . .
Up and down and over and over the stubble they
hurried, backs bent, eyes on the ground, one hand
outstretched to pick up the ears, the other resting on the
small of the back with the 'handful'. When this had been
completed, it was bound round with a wisp of straw and

erected with others in a double rank, like the harvesters
erected their sheaves in shocks, beside the leazer's
water-can and dinner basket. It was hard work, from as
soon as possible after daybreak until nightfall, with only
two short breaks for refreshment; but the single ears
mounted, and a woman with four or five strong,
well-disciplined children would carry a good load home on
her head every night . . . When the rest-hour came, the
children would wander off down the hedgerows gathering
crab-apples or sloes, or searching for mushrooms, while the
mothers reclined and suckled their babes and drank their
cold tea and gossiped or dozed until it was time to be at it
again.

At the end of the fortnight or three weeks that the
leazing lasted, the corn would be thrashed out at home and
sent to the miller, who paid himself for grinding by taking
toll of the flour. Great was the excitement in a good year
when the flour came home – one bushel, two bushels, or
even more in large, industrious families. The mealy-white
sack with its contents was often kept for a time on show on
a chair in the living room and it was a common thing for
a passer-by to be invited to 'step inside an' see our little
bit o' leazings'.

It is difficult to appreciate that the effort of so many days of
back-breaking work was thought worth while but to the
gleaners the gathered grain represented one of the mainstays of
the home – a safeguard against the threatened privations of
winter. In the case of wheat, gleanings provided flour for the
cottager's loaf. Barley gleanings were fed to the chickens or the
pig. For the family who were able to supply themselves with a
winter's stock of flour, gleaning might be the most lasting of the
harvest 'extras'. Bread (or flour) was an absolutely major item
in the labourer's budget – even in the 1890s, when bread prices
had dropped, as much as 6s. in a weekly farm labourer's
budget of 14s. 4½d. could be spent on it. Examples follow from
some farm labourers' budgets collected by the Labour
Commissioners in 1893–4.[84]

ALDWORTH

Farm labourer, man, wife, and five children, four under
eleven years of age. Man's wages 10s. weekly, one boy
earning 4s. 6d. weekly. Harvest money about 51s.,
Michaelmas wage 21s.

	s.	d.
Bread	6	5
Bacon	2	1½
Butter	1	8½
Sugar	1	8
Tea	0	5½
Soap, soda, &c.	0	6
Oil and candles	0	3
Tobacco	1	0
Wood and coal	2	0
Rent, house, and garden	1	0
	17	1½

LETCOMBE REGIS

Man, wife, and seven children, wages 10s. weekly; one boy
5s. weekly.

	s.	d.
Bread and flour	6	0
Butter	1	0
Cheese	0	7
Bacon	1	3½
Sugar	0	6
Tea	0	5½
Salt and pepper	0	1½
Lard	0	8
Firing and oil	1	6
Rent	1	6
Tobacco	0	3
Soap, soda, starch, blue	0	6
	14	4½

BRIGHTWALTON

Farm labourer, wife, and seven children, wages 10s. weekly; harvest about 81s.; allotment 5s. a year. In Compton Club.

	s.	d.
Bread	6	5
Cheese	0	8
Bacon	2	8
Sugar	0	11¼
Tea	0	11
Butter	1	7½
Lard	0	8
Oil and candles	0	4
Soap, soda, starch, blue	0	6
Tobacco	0	7
Wood and coal	2	0
Club	0	5
Insurance	0	4
Rent, house, garden and allotment	1	1
	19	1¾

Gleaning was a universal practice in the corn-growing counties of nineteenth-century England, despite the fact that farmers and landowners, at different times, had attempted to put it down, or to bring it under tighter control. It was an ancient common right, embodied in the Mosaic Law, that harvest gleanings should be left 'unto the poor and the strangers'. It continued to be practised at a time when many other common rights were under attack. In 1787 the right to glean 'indefinitely' by 'poor, necessitous, and indigent persons' had been denied on the grounds that it was 'inconsistent with the nature of property', 'destructive of the peace and good order of society', and 'amounting to a general vagrancy'.[85] This judgment was reinforced and re-stated in more comprehensive terms a year later by Lord Loughborough, the Lord Chief Justice, and two of his fellow judges. In the nineteenth century, when farmers instituted prosecutions before the local courts, magistrates repeated these condemnations. But rights so deeply rooted in the needs and practices of the local communities could not be extinguished on the mere say-so of a High Court judge. And when a case was brought before the Oxford County Court in 1809, after four Kirtlington villagers had been indicted for leasing corn, the magistrates were forced to recognize this:[86]

> As it appeared to the Court that the parties were not aware they were committing a felonious act, they strongly recommended an acquittal: but they were clearly and decidedly of opinion that no person has a legal right to lease without the consent of the occupier of the land; that the practice of leasing is an indulgence founded on benevolence, and ought, when permitted, to be exercised with gratitude and respect. That leasing should never be attempted or permitted before the bulk of the corn is carried from the ground: and that then it would be highly discreditable to any person to endeavour to prevent or interrupt it.

The numerous court cases in the nineteenth century illustrate the considerations that led farmers to object to gleaning. It seems clear from the almost complete absence of cases involving wheat that there was rarely any objection to gleaning this crop. In farming practice there was no reason to forbid the gleaning of wheat – in fact there was a sound reason for allowing it, because in a four or five course crop rotation gleaning could be considered a 'cleaning' operation in preparation for winter ploughing. With barley and beans it was far otherwise, and almost all the nineteenth-century court cases refer to them. Barley and beans were used as livestock feed, especially for pigs, and farmers feared that gleaning might encourage their labourers to keep stock: once the supply of harvest gleanings was exhausted this might lead to subsequent pilfering from their granaries. On some farms labourers were actually prohibited from keeping pigs and poultry at all (particularly the carter, who held the keys of the granary). In addition there was the matter of grazing. Barley was often undersown with grass to provide grazing for sheep or cattle in the few short weeks between harvest and the early autumn frosts – a practice which was impossible for farmers while the gleaners were still in the fields.

Farmers did not often attempt to prohibit gleaning, but they tried to restrict it so far as they could. One way was by attempting to keep the gleaners out of the bean and barley fields. Another was to limit the privilege to those who had worked for them at the harvest on individual fields. All others were excluded or only allowed to glean when the farmers' labourers were free to glean themselves.[87] 'Why will you not allow the poor to lease your fields?' a Dinton farmer was asked in 1840 when prosecuting a labourer for attempting to glean in a field which had already been cleared of corn. 'I thought my own labourers should have the first chance of picking up what corn might be left on the ground, and they were carrying off barley at the time. If they could have gone, I should not have objected. . . .' The labourer received a firm reprimand ('You know that leasing is robbery') but no penalty.[88] Farmers often tried to insist that no gleaning should start until a field was completely cleared, for both the temptation to rob the sheaves and the risk of loss would be too great. In 1853 a Dorchester farmer printed a notice warning gleaners not to enter his fields until they were cleared of their crops, 'because of the loss and annoyance to the farmers of the neighbourhood'. The notice had little effect and he was charged with assaulting a woman who had refused to give up the barley she had gleaned. He was acquitted as he 'had acted in defence of his right' but could obtain no redress for his 'stolen' barley unless he was prepared to bring an action for trespass.[89] In the case of barley, outright prohibition was sometimes attempted. In 1859 a Brill labourer was prosecuted for gleaning barley by a farmer who had bought extra pigs to feed on the stubble. The case was dismissed with a caution.[90] In 1862 five Blackwell women were charged with stealing one gallon of barley valued 6d. at Shipston-on-Stour. They claimed they had permission to glean, but they had to pay a fine of 2s. each. The fine was unusual but the gleaning took place in an open field where some barley was still uncarted and 'as the law in open field farming is very stringent' the magistrates felt they could not be lenient.[91] In 1890 at Sutton Courtenay two boys had to pay the harsh fine of 5s. each for gleaning beans after they had been previously cautioned. The farmer explained 'We allow them to glean wheat on sufferance . . .' but 'not beans or barley'.[92]

If farmers on their side tried (not always successfully) to
impose restrictions on gleaning practices, the villagers had their
own ways of attempting to regulate it, deciding for themselves
when gleaning should be allowed to start, keeping out strangers
(when they threatened to make an appearance), and deciding
who had a right to glean in certain fields. A 'gleaners' bell' was
rung in some villages to denote the time to start and finish
gleaning for the day so that all should have a chance of fair
shares. In 1860 at Tibenham in Norfolk, and at Aldeby (also in
Norfolk but within three miles of Suffolk), no one was allowed to
commence gleaning before the morning bell or to remain in the
fields after the evening ringing, though it was not considered a
usual Norfolk custom. At the same period the gleaners' bell
was reported as being rung in the parish of Churchdown,
Gloucestershire, and in the neighbouring parish of Sandhurst
until 'within the last few years'. The use of it was 'that all the
gleaners might have a fair start'.[93] At Tadmarton and Swal-
cliffe near Banbury and in some other Oxfordshire parishes the
custom still prevailed at this time and the gleaners were 'very
particular in attending to its warnings'.[94] At Driffield in
Yorkshire a 'harvest bell' had been rung from time immemorial at five o'clock each morning and at seven each evening, but the gleaners' bell was a late introduction, and by
1901 it had disappeared.[95] A. H. Cocks, writing in 1897,
claimed that gleaning bells were 'no longer rung anywhere in
the country'.[96] But as late as 1911 at Upton St Lawrence,
Gloucestershire, a bell was rung at 5 a.m. to let people know they
might go to glean or leaze; and in spite of the early hour, 'Many
would be ready to start.'[97] So it seems that the custom
survived fairly late in the nineteenth century. At Aston Abbots
in Buckinghamshire, where it was called the 'leasing bell', it
was rung at 8 a.m. and 7 p.m. and was only discontinued about
1883. At Olney it appears only to have rung for thirty or forty
years and was discontinued in 1885 or 1886; here it rang at
7 a.m. and 7 p.m.[98]

At the turn of the century 'everyone' at Garsington gleaned,
but only wheat. 'If someone went to glean the barley stubble –
you still wouldn't stop them. Oh no [a local farmer told me],
the country people in those days, they knew when to go, when
not to go.'[99] A colourful illustration of how seriously country
people took the practice of gleaning was the revival at

Rempstone in Nottinghamshire in 1860 of the old custom of proclaiming a 'Queen of the Gleaners':

> The village crier having 'proclaimed the Queen', nearly 100 gleaners assembled at the end of the village. Women with their infant charges, boys with green boughs, and girls with flowers, the whole wearing gleaning-pockets; children's carriages and wheelbarrows, dressed in green and laden with babies, etc. were in requisition . . . [A] royal salute was shouted by the boys, and the crown brought out of its temporary depository. This part of the regalia was of simple make; its basis consisting of straw-coloured cloth surrounded with wheat, barley and oats of the present year. A streamer of straw-coloured ribbon, dependent on a bow at the crown, hung loosely down; a leaf of laurel was placed in front, while arching over the whole was a branch of jessamine, . . . The ceremony of crowning was now performed; after which the Queen, enthroned in an arm-chair decorated with flowers and branches, moved . . . [to] the 'first field to be gleaned'.

At the scene of labour her Proclamation Speech was read:

> You have made me Queen of the Gleaners till the harvest is finished. I will try to rule by right and in kindness, and I trust to your obedience that I may not have to exercise my power. I will now tell you my laws, which shall farther be made known by the crier of the village.
> 1st. My attendant shall ring a bell each morning, when there are fields to be gleaned.
> 2nd. Half-past 8 o'clock shall be the hour of meeting, at the end of the village, and I will then accompany you to the field.
> 3rdly. Should any of my subjects enter an ungleaned field, without being led by me, their corn will be forfeited and it will be bestrewed.

Then following a brief address from the Queen of the Gleaners and a suitable song, the 'whole commenced their labours in the barley field of Mr James Moor, the first field to be gleaned'.[100]

During the period of gleaning the fields no longer belonged to the farmers but to the villagers. The law decreed one thing, but the labouring poor went their way regardless, and the

weight of village opinion was on their side. In an age when
property rights were sacrosanct, and when the Game Laws were
being enforced with the whole paraphernalia of the police
behind them, this mass invasion of property went on year by
year. It must be seen as a manifestation of the belief that
common access to the soil was an enduring right. The gleaning
bell confirms this: from the parish church itself came a formal
recognition – even celebration – of this annual suspension of
property rights. In gleaning, the final stage of harvest, one sees
the clearest expression of the psychological advantage which the
village labourer and his family enjoyed in the few brief weeks of
harvest.

5 The coming of the machine

Mechanical aids to harvesting were slow to be accepted in
English agricultural practice, and the extensive use of hand
tools continued right up to the end of the century. The mechanical reaper was the first to come into general use, from the
1870s, but was by no means universal even at the turn of the
century. On many a smaller farm the nails on a barn wall or the
corner of some shed might still have accommodated the tools
of harvesting.[101] But by the 1880s all the aids of modern
machine harvesting (with the exception of the combine-
harvester) were in production. The self-sheaving reaper-binder
(with the problem of an efficient knotting device finally solved)
was now available.[102] Farmers had also the choice of a variety
of horse-drawn machines, quite apart from the mechanical
reaper. Mowers, 'kickers', 'tedders' and 'swathe turners' for
tossing and turning the hay, horse-rakes to windrow and rake
the fields clean, stacking machines and elevators, all worked by
horse power, were by now commonplace and 'all but sufficiently
perfected to prove a boon'.[103]

Despite the fact that mechanical reapers of many kinds were
invented in the earlier decades of the century it was not until
the late 1850s and early 1860s that they began to be considered
as alternatives to hand tools.[104] A revealing survey framed in
terms of questions and answers put to farmers regarding
harvest practices by the *Agricultural Gazette* in 1867 suggests

that the use of machinery was still in the embryonic stage –
'it is still difficult to cut by machinery'; 'used little at present';
'none has been seen yet that will cut a layered crop perfectly'.
The main cutting tool in Oxfordshire and Berkshire was the
fagging hook. Drawbacks to mechanical reapers were many:[105]

> they were liable to break down, they consistently could not
> deal with heavily laid crops, they often could only be
> worked one way, down or up the ridges, and certainly
> rarely across heavily ridged and furrowed land, they
> represented capital investment and if by the late seventies
> improvements in design had converted farmers to favour
> their adoption, their pockets kept them in two minds.

Rider Haggard in 1899 was still echoing the objections to the
reaping machine that farmers had expressed in 1867. It was a
'mistake to suppose' that the reaper would cut corn 'in every
case and every season'; if the corn was badly laid and twisted it
'does more harm than good'; as for barley: 'treading of the
horses is too destructive'.[106] It was not until the early years of
the twentieth century that reaping by hand became an
anachronism.

Machines were not necessarily more economic for the farmer
than the continued employment of hand labour, so long as it
was readily available and comparatively cheap,[107] and when
they were introduced they did not supplant hand-cutting.
In Lark Rise in the 1880s the mechanical reaper was still
considered as an auxiliary,[108] a farmer's toy. At this stage it
was an adjunct rather than an alternative to hand-cutting –
one field might be cut by a mechanical reaper; another field of
wheat might be fagged; a field of barley scythed. In 1900
hand-cutting still remained a very necessary complement to
mechanical cutting when crops were badly laid, in very wet
seasons, in a field of barley, and in cutting a road round the
headlands. The 1901 labour book for a farm at Little Witten-
ham, Berkshire, shows machine-work and hand-work side by
side. The reaper-binder was in use on the farm, and in the fortnight commencing 31 July was used to cut 36 acres of wheat.
But handwork and piecework payments were by no means
eliminated. The shocking was still taken at a piecework rate
of 1s. 6d. per acre. A limited amount of hand-cutting is recorded

('cutting round 20 acres of wheat', 'cutting round 16 acres of wheat', 'women on reaping'). Though the entries refer to 'reaping', the hand tool in use was in fact the fagging hook, and the price paid for cutting, tying and shocking some ten acres of wheat was 14s. per acre in addition to 16s. paid for cutting round the 36 acres in readiness for the binder. The small payment of 5s. to a woman 'on reaping' is of interest, suggesting the late survival of the reaping hook on the odd occasion.[109]

The mechanical reaper certainly displaced hand-labour in the cutting process, but because it speeded up the cutting so much it produced an even more concentrated and urgent demand for hand-labour in the shocking and tying. Richard Jefferies's opinion was that machinery in the field did not reduce the number of men employed. But they were employed in a different way. 'The work all comes now in rushes . . . acres are levelled in a day . . .'[110] The cut corn demanded immediate attention.

All the indications suggest that if machine reaping was gaining ground south of Caird's line in the late 1860s, its general adoption was to be slow rather than fast until the turn of the century. If farmers were beginning to have doubts about the scythe, and to think in terms of possibly buying a machine, the shock of seeing a Rochester 8-horse-power road locomotive, with a Crosskill reaper with a cut twelve feet wide mounted in front of the engine, 'charge' into a piece of bright-strawed wheat (one of the features of a machinery show at Leamington in August 1876) might have been enough to put them off. The Britannia Works at Banbury were said to be turning out a 'remarkable number' of reaping machines in the peak year of 1872,[111] but a perspective on the extent to which such machines were in use is given by G. E. Fussell, who claims that in 1892 rather less than 1 per cent of agricultural holdings had a reaper.[112] Indeed the depression in agriculture had so greatly affected the Great Hasely Iron Works by 1893 that John Venables Gibbon, its owner and an inventor of several agricultural machines, committed suicide.[113]

Research is needed before it is possible to say how far the hesitations of the farmers were reinforced by the hostility of labourers who saw the introduction of the mechanical reaper, like that of the threshing machine in earlier years, as a threat to their livelihood. There were certainly places where this happened. On Stubble Farm in Berkshire, in the early 1880s, when labourers saw their master assembling his new combined mowing and reaping machine, at the beginning of hay harvest, they felt bound to protest: 'Well, master, you wants we to go and cut all them meadows where the grass is laid, and you're going to cut all the uplands with that there machine, and we don't think it jestly right. Them as cuts the one, ought to cut t'other.' The farmer's answer was uncompromising: 'If you think I am going to be dictated to ... because Joseph Arch ...

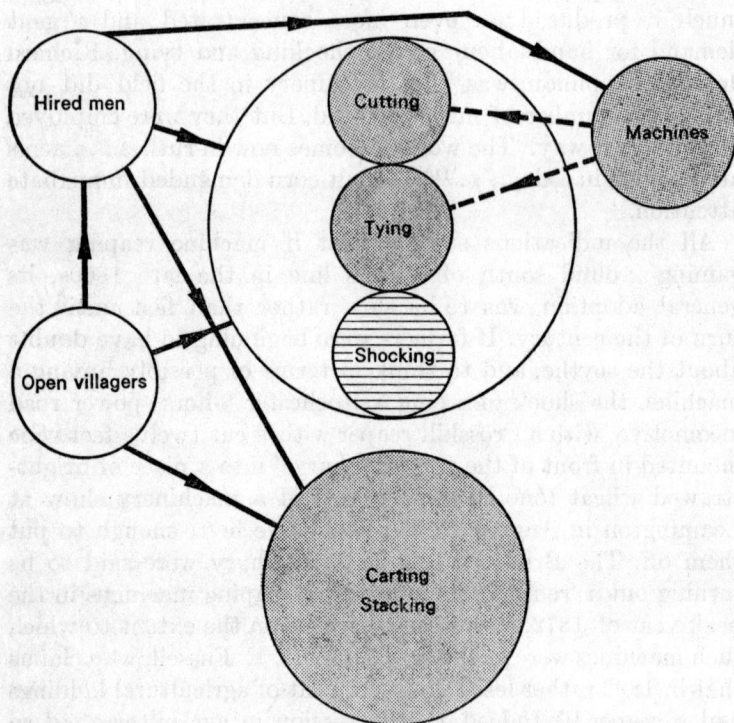

Figure 3   *Machinery and harvest work*

With the coming of the reaper and binder more of the work at harvest time could be done by the regular farm servant, the man who worked for the same employer all the year round. The machine took over the two most labour intensive parts of harvest work: cutting, which had often been a work for open villagers and travelling harvesters; and tying, which had been the work for which women and children came into the harvest field.

. . . lectured you last night . . . you have the wrong man to deal
with.' The men however were equally uncompromising. With
'then you cut the meadows yourself' as their last words, they
left his farm to 'go "uppards" ' . . . where . . . stout mowers
could find work in abundance, at a much higher rate of pay'.
Later the machine was found broken up in the field where it had
been left overnight. There was further trouble for the farmer
when corn harvest came round; reapers were scarce and those
who assisted with the making of the stacks not only demanded
4*s.* per day and beer money but: 'When six o'clock came, they
stuck up their prongs, no matter that the corn was fit to carry
and the rain threatening, and declined to work any more unless
they were paid overtime.'[114]

The gradual introduction of the machine mower and the
machine reaper with its 'splendidly painted sails' was in
principle no different from the continuous process of speeding
up the harvest which had been going on for many years; it was
in line with the changes in hand technology and the replacement of the sickle by the fagging hook. It changed the balance of
the work in the harvest field, but only partially. Labour in the
first stage of harvest – the piecework cutting which had usually
been in the hands of outsiders – was drastically curtailed. But
there was still ample work available at haymaking and carting
in the hay harvest, and at tying, shocking and carting in the
corn harvest. There was much less work for travelling harvesters
but the employment of women and children and extra hands,
drawn from the locality, was not affected. Nor was gleaning.
Moreover the introduction of the machine mowers and reapers
coincided with, though it did not cause, the beginning of rural
depopulation, so that its impact on the rural labour market was
to some extent cushioned.

The mechanical reaper-binder effected a much more drastic
change. It eliminated the branches of harvest work that had
been the chief work of women and children – the making and
tying of the sheaves. It also put an end to gleaning, since the
harvesting no longer left a trail of waste. At a stroke it destroyed
the 'double wage' – the family working unit that had been the
basis of high piecework earnings. Henceforth piecework was
only called for in shocking the sheaves or when machines could
not cope with badly-laid crops. The reaper-binder presented a
threat to a pattern of family participation which had existed

from time immemorial. And it was this threat, not the threat of strangers or Irishmen to their livelihood, that brought the villagers out into the streets of East Hendred at the turn of the century when such a machine was first introduced in the Allin Estate. The farm workers held torchlight protests – and even set a thatched building ablaze.[115] (For a model of the effects of machinery on harvest work, see Figure 3.)

The introduction of the mechanical reaper and binder transformed the harvest situation to the advantage of the regular farm servant. As regards the ordinary staff of the farm no labour was dispensed with, but for the unattached labourer – and for all those villagers who had been accustomed to take up field labour at harvest time – it was quite otherwise. Casual labour, whether specialist or local, was no longer wanted; there was no longer a need for a migrant labour force, or for the village population at harvest time to take to the fields. Farmers were able to put the opportunity of extra harvest earnings in the way of their regular employees, and the labour books begin to record special payments against their names instead of against those of outsiders.[116] Overtime payments took the place of piece-rate jobs. Regular farm servants were now used in all stages of the harvest. Family labour was dispensed with. The farm labour force became more fixed. The independent villager's position was undermined. There was more regular employment, but it went with a growing dependence on the farmer all the year round, with the spread of the 'tied' cottage, and with the disappearance from the countryside of independent men. As a Britwell Salome villager put it at the turn of the century: 'You didn't dare say a word as big as a clover seed or you might lose your job. There was always someone else waiting for it.'[117] This was as much an expression of a new social grievance as an old economic one.

Glossary of harvest terms

Berkshire

arnest   Earnest. The 'arnest' or 'arnest money'.
earnest (Oxon.)   was a shilling given on hiring a servant and completed the contract.

aftermath/lattermath The second crop of grass, i.e. aftermowth.

barleycleys The beards of barley.

dummle In corn or hay, damp.

ell raakye or *hel-rake* (Oxon.) The large-sized rake used for raking hay left behind where 'cocks' have been 'pitched' into the wagon.

graains The forks of a prong, thus: a dung prong is a three-graained prong. (Malt after all the goodness is extracted in brewing – brewers' grains.)

grist Corn brought to the mill for grinding.

haam or *haulm* Stubble or straw of vetches, peas and beans. The 'haam' rick in the Vale of Berkshire is of beans or wheat straw – vetch 'haam' rick in the hill part of the county.

hack To fag or reap vetches, peas or beans.

harvest whoam The festival which winds up harvest work.

ley Growing grass.

me-ad A meadow.

mow or *mou* (Oxon.) Corn or straw stacked in a barn.

mullock Wet straw.

pollards The ground husk of wheat, medium size; the coarsest size being 'bran' and the finest 'topping'.

prong The metal part of the implement for moving hay, straw, etc. The wooden part is the 'prong-handle'. The ordinary prong has two forks, whilst the dung prong has three.

rick/wrick 'Rick' is always used for stack, hay-rick, barley-rick, etc.
A rick cloth is a waterproof sheet placed over the top of a rick to keep out the wet until such time as the rick may be thatched.

rick yard Place where ricks are made.

rip-hook A sickle.

scoop A wooden shovel as used for shovelling corn after it is threshed.

shock A few sheaves of corn placed together in the field so that the ears and straw may dry in the sun before the rick is formed.

to shock-up To form sheaves into shocks.

strapper A journeyman labourer coming for work at harvest time or haymaking.

stubs Stubble. A field lying in stubble is called a 'pe-us o' whate-stubs' or a 'peus o' wut-stubs' (oats).

tuck To trim. A rick is said to be 'tucked' when raked down so as to take off loose surface straws and leave the others neatly lying in the same direction.

upperds or *uppards* (Bucks.) Upwards.

vraail A flail

yarnes 'Yarnest' money.

yead-lan   A headland. Part ploughed at the head or top of the
main plough.

yelm   To straighten straw in readiness for threshing.

swathes   Rows of hay when first cut.

swingel   The top part of the threshing flail.

Oxfordshire

backaive   To winnow corn through a fine sieve, called a
backheaving sieve.

blind   When spring corn does not thrive or grow well, it is said to
'look very blind'.

crass crappin   Sowing the crops out of the accustomed order.

earnest money   A shilling given at a hiring fair to a servant to
'bind the bargain'.

faggin   Cutting corn with a heavy hook and a hooked stick
called a faggin stick.

four o'clock   A tea in the hay field – Holton, Islip, Yarnton.

frail   A flail.

grinsard grounds   Pasture fields.

haams   Stubble cut after the corn is carried – straw of white
crops only.

hackle   To rake hay into rows after it has been 'tedded'; usually
called to hackle in or up (to leet – Holton).

hadlans   The top and bottom lands which are ploughed the
reverse way to the others.

hayn up   To reverse grass for hay.

land   A ridge and furrow.

rakers-arters   The people who rake after the wagons in the hay
field.

run-away-Mop   The third Mop or hiring fair said to be composed
of servants who have been hired at the previous fairs and have
run away from their situation.

tie up   To bind up sheaves of corn in a band (called a bond) of
corn stalks. 'My ole dooman's a gwain tiein up for ma [me].'

Sources: B. Lowlsey, *Berkshire Words*, 1888; Mrs A. Parker,
Supplement to Glossary of Words in Oxfordshire, 1881.

Notes

1 E. E. Evans, *Irish Folk Ways*, London, 1957, p. 157; George Eland, *In Bucks*, Aylesbury, 1923, p. 70.
2 Walter Rose, *Good Neighbours*, Cambridge, 1942, p. 28.
3 Richard Jefferies, *Field and Hedgerow*, London, 1889, pp. 131–2.
4 G. E. Moreau, *The Departed Village*, Oxford, 1968, p. 77.
5 H. Rider Haggard, *A Farmer's Year*, London, 1899, p. 309.
6 *Agricultural Gazette*, quoted in *Bucks Herald*, 17 August 1889.
7 J. G. Cornish, *Reminiscences of a Country Life*, ed. V. Cornish, London, 1939, pp. 81–2.
8 Flora Thompson, *Lark Rise to Candleford*, London, World's Classics ed., 1968, p. 255.
9 John Purser, MSS. reminiscences, kindly lent to me by E. P. Thompson.
10 Rose, op. cit., p. 27.
11 *Notes and Queries* (hereafter *N & Q*), 26 August 1905, pp. 164–5.
12 Mabel K. Ashby, *Joseph Ashby of Tysoe 1859–1919*, Cambridge, 1961, p. 25.
13 Richard Heath, *The English Peasant*, London, 1893, p. 224.
14 *Jackson's Oxford Journal* (hereafter *JOJ*), 3 August 1872.
15 *JOJ*, supplement, 30 September 1876.
16 Ibid., 19 August 1876, p. 8.
17 Ibid., 22 July 1899, p. 7.
18 Ibid., 1 October 1898, p. 10.
19 Ibid., 18 October 1873, p. 8.
20 Ibid., 28 August 1847.
21 J. Arthur Gibbs, *A Cotswold Village*, London, 1898, p. 369.
22 Isaac Mead, *The Life Story of an Essex Lad Written by Himself*, Chelmsford, 1923, p. 25.
23 Arthur Randell, *Sixty Years a Fenman*, ed. E. Porter, London, 1966, pp. 22–3.
24 W. H. Barrett, *A Fenman's Story*, London, 1965, pp. 3–4.
25 Alice C. Day (ed.), *Glimpses of Rural Life in Sussex*, Idbury, Kingham, 1927, pp. 20–1.
26 E. L. Jones, *Seasons and Prices, the Role of Weather in English Agricultural History*, London, 1964, ch. 5.
27 Rose, op. cit., p. 27.
28 *JOJ*, 3 August 1872.
29 *Banbury Guardian*, 14 September 1848.
30 Anon., *Stubble Farm, or Three Generations of English Farmers*, by the author of *Earnest Struggles* (H. Simmons), ii, p. 17.
31 Richard Jefferies, *Chronicles of the Hedges*, London, 1948, p. 184.
32 *Windsor and Eton Express*, 18 July 1868.
33 *Oxford Chronicle* (hereafter *OC*), 10 September 1869.
34 Ibid., 21 September 1895.
35 Ibid., 3 July 1869.

36 *Warwick Advertiser*, 4 August 1860.
37 *Oxford Times* (hereafter *OT*), 7 September 1889.
38 *Bucks Herald*, 13 July 1878.
39 *Reading Mercury*, 14 October 1882.
40 *JOJ*, 21 September 1872.
41 Ibid., 17 September 1859.
42 *Bucks Herald*, 4 October 1873.
43 *JOJ*, 19 August 1899.
44 *OT*, 14 September 1874.
45 *Banbury Guardian*, September 1848.
46 *Bucks Herald*, 26 July 1856.
47 *OT*, 13 August 1897.
48 *JOJ*, 19 August 1876.
49 *Bucks Herald*, 6 August 1889.
50 Jefferies, op. cit., p. 93.
51 Rose, op. cit., pp. 93–4.
52 Reading University Library, *Historical Farm Records Coll.*,
    BER 20/2/1.
53 Ibid., BER 20/2/1, farm account book, August 1874–7, February
    1877.
54 Ibid., OXF 2/2/4.
55 Ibid., GLOS 2/2/2.
56 Ibid., BER 13/5/3.
57 Ibid., BER 13/5/2.
58 Ibid., BUC 7/1/1.
59 Oxfordshire Record Office, DIL 1/q/9b.
60 *Hist. Farm Records*, OXF 2/2/4, fols 22–177.
61 Ibid., BER 13/5/5.
62 F. G. Heath, *The English Peasantry*, London, 1874, p. 197; G. E.
    Fussell *From Tolpuddle to T.U.C.*, Slough, 1948, p. 68. But note a
    warning article in the *Labourers' Union Chronicle*, 7 June 1873,
    that it was 'a mistake to ask for increase in wages and decrease
    in hours at the same time'.
63 Ibid., BUC 7/1/1 f21, 19 September 1850.
64 Oxfordshire Record Office, DIL 1/q/9c. See also *Hist. Farm
    Records*: BER 28/3/1, Chievely Farm, 1869, harvest home money –
    18 men 2s. 6d. each, 10 women, 3 lads 1s. 6d. each; BUC 7/1/1,
    Hill Farm, Stokenchurch, 18 October 1872, harvest home money
    paid – £2; 23 October 1875 – £1 7s. 6d.
65 Ibid., OXF 14/3/5–10; ibid., BUC 7/1/1, Hill Farm, 28 August
    1849, provisions for men, 3s.; 24 August 1850, provisions for
    men carting, 5s. 2d.; 19 August 1851, men's beer, 4s.; 30 August
    beer/extra hands 6s. 4d.
66 Ronald Blythe, *Akenfield*, London, 1969, p. 55.
67 C. Henry Warren, *Happy Countryman*, London, 1939, p. 119.
68 Randell, op cit., p. 23.
69 Cornish, op. cit., p. 82.
70 *Stubble Farm*, pp. 16–17; *Hist. Farm Records*, OXF 2/2/4, Fawcett
    farm labour book, fol. 22, August and September 1869.

71 Oxfordshire Record Office, DIL 1/e/2c, Ditchley Est., farm account book, 1863.

72 In Berkshire, at the time of the 1851 census, there was a ratio of fourteen labourers to each farm; in Cambridgeshire the ratio was eight to a farm.

73 *Hist. Farm Records*, OXF 6/1/3.

74 Thompson, op. cit., pp. 257–8. Cf. also *Hist. Farm Records*, BER 28/3/1, 3 women and 7 men reaping wheat at 12s. per acre. In the 1869 harvest one Ann Church reaped more wheat than any other worker on the Bradley farm estate, Chievely.

75 Bodleian Library, MS. Top. Oxon. c. 220, Notes of Thomas Banting of Filkins, 1887, fos 65r, 96r (I have slightly abridged this quotation).

76 Percy Manning, 'Some Oxfordshire seasonal festivals', *Folklore*, 8, 1887, pp. 318–19.

77 Clare College Library, Cambridge, Cecil Sharp MSS., 'Folk Dance Notes', ii, pp. 129–30.

78 Ibid., pp. 95, 100.

79 Rose, op. cit., p. 79.

80 J. T. Burgess, 'Life and Experiences of a Warwickshire Labourer', quoted in A. W. Ashby, *One Hundred Years of Poor Law Administration in a Warwickshire Village*, Oxford, 1912, pp. 79–80.

81 P.P. 1867–8 (4068) XIII, *Employment in Agriculture*, App. P, p. 425.

82 Ashby, op. cit., p. 25.

83 Thompson, op. cit., p. 14.

84 P.P. 1893–4 (C6894–11) XXXV, Royal Commission on Labour, *Chapman's rep. on the Agricultural Labourer*, B–11. Wantage, App. B.

85 *The English Reports*, vol. cxxxvi, Common Pleas IV, p. 32.

86 Ibid., p. 37.

87 Gertrude Jekyll, *Old West Surrey*, London, 1904, p. 188.

88 *N & Q*, 4th series, 11 September 1869.

89 *Aylesbury News*, 29 August 1840.

90 *JOJ*, 17 September 1859.

91 *JOJ*, 4 October 1862. Cf. ibid., 27 September 1862.

92 *OT*, 11 October 1890.

93 *N & Q*, 2nd series, x, 15 December 1860, p. 476.

94 Ibid., 3 November 1860, p. 356.

95 Ibid., 9th series, vii, 7 September 1901, p. 268.

96 A. H. Cocks, *The Church Bells of Buckinghamshire*, London, 1897, p. 279.

97 *Folklore*, 22, 1911, p. 237.

98 Cocks, op. cit., pp. 279, 303, 392, 543, 556, 564.

99 Personal communication, Walter King, Garsington, Oxfordshire.

100 *N & Q*, 2nd series, 13 October 1860, p. 285. Cf. also Enid Porter, *Cambridgeshire Customs and Folklore*, London, 1969, p. 124.

101 Jekyll, op. cit., p. 182.

102 J. Hannon, 'Report on . . . Self-Binding Reapers at Aigburth',
     Journal of the Royal Agricultural Society of England, 2nd series,
     14, pt 1, 1878, pp. 131–4; Norman E. Lee, *Harvests and Harvesting
     through the Ages*, Cambridge, 1960, pp. 168–71; Primrose
     McConnell, *The Complete Farmer*, 1910, pp. 395–7.

103 John A. Clarke, 'Practical agriculture,' *Journal of the Royal
     Agricultural Society of England*, 2nd series, 14, pt II, 1878, p. 642.

104 *Year-Book of Facts*, London, 1853, pp. 114–15. Two thousand of
     McCormack's mechanical reapers were being sold in the United
     States every year at this time.

105 See *Ag. Gaz.*, 20 August 1860, for early objections; *McConnell's
     Agricultural Note Book*, London, 1883, p. 33, and McConnell,
     op. cit., p. 394 for later objections.

106 H. Rider Haggard, *A Farmer's Year*, London, 1899, p. 274. By
     far the best discussion of the change from hand tools to
     machinery is E. J. T. Collins, unpublished Nottingham Ph.D.
     thesis, 'Harvest Technology and Labour Supply'. For a brief
     discussion of his findings see *Economic History Review*, 2nd series,
     22, November 1969, and *Sickle to Combine*, Museum of English
     Rural Life, Reading, 1968.

107 Rose, op. cit., p. 27.

108 Thompson, op. cit., p. 44.

109 *Hist. Farm Records*, BER 10/2/2.

110 Richard Jefferies, *Hodge and His Masters*, London, 1880, vol. ii,
     pp. 267–8.

111 William Potts, *A History of Banbury*, Banbury, 1958, p. 224.

112 G. E. Fussell, *Farming Techniques from Prehistoric to Modern
     Times*, London, 1965, pp. 198–9.

113 *Reading Mercury*, 19 August 1893.

114 *Stubble Farm*, pp. 209–11.

115 Edwin Manley, *A Descriptive Account of East Hendred*, East
     Hendred, 1969.

116 *Hist. Farm Records*, BER 10/2/2, for example.

117 Moreau, op. cit., p. 66.

Part 3

Country work girls in nineteenth-century England

Jennie Kitteringham

1 The country work girl

Country girls of the nineteenth century were by nature and necessity more hardy and practical than I was as a child. For instance the attitude my younger sister and I had to animals on the farm was that they were pets. We always had chickens which we used to rear from day-old chicks with the aim of them being the 'Sunday joint'. But it was fatal for us to get to know them – how could you eat something that you had reared and played with and liked? As soon as the weekend came round and there was the prospect of 'Carole' or 'Margaret' chicken being killed, Liz and I would start our pleading for her to be spared and a joint bought. For us there was that alternative; our predecessors would have had none. Killing was always done by my father, be it the chicken for dinner or newborn kittens.

A good example of the contrast in attitudes between today and then, is the killing of 'the pig'. Due to the lowness of wages, farmers sometimes allowed their labourers to keep a pig for which they would supply some food, ground, etc. (this varied with the farmer). Possession of a pig, with its promise of future meat and bacon, was a great advantage for the labourer and his family; it was a walking investment for the harsh winter months, or, as F. G. Heath put it, a 'live savings bank'. It was fed all left-overs from meals, along with potato peelings, barley gleanings and acorns. In the North Oxfordshire village where Flora Thompson spent her childhood, and which she vividly evokes in *Lark Rise to Candleford*, all the family would be prepared to go without for the sake of the pig, and time would be spent collecting food for it. Leaves would be collected for its litter. As Flora put it:[1]

> The family pig was everybody's pride and everybody's business . . . The children, on their way home from school, would fill their arms with sow thistle, dandelion, and choice long grass, or roam along the hedgerows on wet evenings collecting snails in a pail for the pig's supper. These piggy crunched up with great relish . . .

There would be a 'pig tub' at the back door, as Edwin Grey describes in his *Cottage Life in a Hertfordshire Village*,[2] into which all scraps would be thrown, and even the slops from the

DVL

cooking and washing-up. (In some villages a local farmer
would provide a communal tub to furnish swill for his own pigs,
and the village pigless would contribute to it in return for a
share of the pork when killed, or for payment – 'We mayn't
keep a pig, but instead of this master gives us 6d. a week for
the wash', a Dorset labourer's wife told the Commissioners.)[3]

The killing of the pig was an important occasion, at once
solemn and festive. Its death was a celebration – it was accepted
that in order for them to live, the pig, no matter how much a
friend, had to die. Its death was prepared with care. As Flora
Thompson recalled:[4]

> When the pig was fattened – and the fatter the better –
> the date of execution had to be decided upon. It had to
> take place some time during the first two quarters of the
> moon; for, if the pig was killed when the moon was waning
> the bacon would shrink in cooking, and they wanted it to
> 'plimp up'.

This belief was also held in Dorset. I was told by Ruth Carey,
who was born in 1882 the daughter of a tenant farmer, and
later was a farmer's wife, spending most of her long and hard-
working life in Dorset, that pig-killing had to be carried out
whilst 'the moon was growing', otherwise the meat would
shrink. Her father would do the cutting of the meat and the
females of the family would do the cooking and preserving but
on no account was a female allowed to touch the meat whilst
she had a period as this would have given it a 'peculiar taste',
a taste which was easily discernible, as Ruth affirmed. Such
attitudes indicate the gross importance of the quality and
quantity of the meat to these workers and their families.

In Flora Thompson's village the killing was done by 'the
travelling pork butcher, or pig-sticker', who by day was a
thatcher and so could only come at night. This made the whole
affair still more dramatic, 'the scene being lighted with lanterns
and the fire of burning straw which at a later stage of the
proceedings was to singe the bristles off the victim'.[5] Ruth
Carey remembered the pig killing as rather a nasty affair, in
which the pigs would scream a lot: and Flora Thompson too
described it as 'a noisy, bloody business'. In her account the
animal[6]

was hoisted to a rough bench that it might bleed
thoroughly and so preserve the quality of the meat. The
job was often bungled, the pig sometimes getting away and
having to be chased; but country people of that day had
little sympathy for the sufferings of animals, and men,
women, and children would gather round to see the sight.

After the carcass had been singed, the pig-sticker
would pull off the detachable, gristly, outer coverings of
the toes, known locally as 'the shoes', and fling them among
the children, who scrambled for, then sucked and gnawed
them, straight from the filth of the sty and blackened by
fire as they were.

The whole scene, with its mud and blood, flaring lights
and dark shadows, was as savage as anything . . .

But . . . there was another aspect of the pig-killing.
Months of hard work and self-denial were brought on that
night to a successful conclusion. It was a time to rejoice,
and rejoice they did, with beer flowing freely and the first
delicious dish of pig's fry sizzling in the frying-pan . . .

The attitude towards such a ritual, and quite gruesome it must
have been at times, was one of acceptance and practical
necessity. To many of those in other social classes, this situation
was held to epitomize the degradation and low character of
those within the labouring class. Hardy shows quite clearly the
attitude via Jude in *Jude the Obscure*. Jude is repelled by what
he considers Arabella's coarseness and lack of feeling over the
slaughter of the pig. To her pig-killing was an art: it had to be
carried out in such a manner as to provide the best quality meat,
and the greatest amount of blood for puddings, and the pig
could not be given any consideration as regards the quickest
death. It had lived well and now must die in order that those
that had fed it might continue to live. Jude's scruples and
inexperience result in a bungling which makes the affair still
bloodier.[7]

Arabella had joined her husband, and Jude, rope in hand,
got into the sty, and noosed the affrighted animal, who,
beginning with a squeak of surprise, rose to repeated cries of
rage. Arabella opened the sty-door, and together they
hoisted the victim on the the stool, legs upward, and while
Jude held him Arabella bound him down, looping the cord

over his legs to keep him from struggling.

The animal's note changed its quality. It was not now rage, but the cry of despair, long-drawn, slow and hopeless.

'Upon my soul I would sooner have gone without the pig than have had this to do!' said Jude. 'A creature I had fed with my own hands.'

'Don't be such a tender hearted fool! There's the sticking-knife – the one with the point. Now whatever you do, don't stick un too deep.'

'I'll stick him effectually, so as to make short work of it. That's the chief thing.'

'You must not!', she cried. 'The meat must be well bled, and to do that he must die slow. We shall lose a shilling a score if the meat is red and bloody! Just touch the vein, that's all. I was brought up to it, and I know. Every good butcher keeps un bleeding long. He ought to be eight or ten minutes dying, at least.'

. . . Scraping the bristles from the pig's upturned throat, as he had seen the butchers do, he slit the fat; then plunged in the knife with all his might.

'Od damn it all!' she cried, 'that ever I should say it! You've over-stuck un! . . .'

'Do be quiet, Arabella, and have a little pity on the creature!'

'Hold up the pail to catch the blood, and don't talk!' . . .

The blood flowed out in a torrent instead of in the trickling stream she had desired. The dying animal's cry assumed its third and final tone, the shriek of agony; his glazing eyes riveting themselves on Arabella with the eloquently keen reproach of a creature recognising at last the treachery of those who had seemed his only friends.

'Make un stop that!' said Arabella . . . Picking up the knife from the ground whereon Jude had flung it, she slipped it into the gash, and slit the windpipe. The pig was instantly silent, his dying breath coming through the hole. 'That's better,' she said. 'It is a hateful business!' said he. 'Pigs must be killed.' The animal heaved in a final convulsion, and despite the rope kicked out with all his last strength. A tablespoonful of black clot came forth,

the trickling of red blood having ceased for some seconds.
'That's it; now he'll go.' said she. 'Artful creatures –
they always keep back a drop like that as long as they
can!'

The last plunge had come so unexpectedly as to make
Jude stagger, and in recovering himself he kicked over
the vessel in which the blood had been caught.

'There!' she cried . . . 'Now I can't make any blackpot.
There's a waste, all through you!'

Jude put the pail upright, but only about a third of
the whole steaming liquid was left in it, the main part
being splashed over the snow, and forming a dismal,
sordid, ugly spectacle – to those who saw it as other than
an ordinary obtaining of meat. The lips and nostrils of the
animal turned livid, then white, and the muscles of his
limbs relaxed.

'Thank God!' Jude said. 'He's dead.'

'What's God got to do with such a messy job as a
pig-killing, I should like to know!' she said scornfully.
'Poor folks must live.'

Society has so 'evolved' that hard physical labour by girls
(or women, for that matter) is neither expected nor approved.
But the girls who I am going to write about grew up in a
situation where it was taken for granted. They were not reared
to be fragile, helpless beings – at an early age they were thrust
out into the world of the open fields, biting winds, aching backs,
and strained muscles.

A traveller in England of the 1860s would have found them
hard at work. For instance, in East Anglia large numbers of
young children would be seen performing numerous (all
arduous) agricultural tasks in gangs; along the shores of the
Wash and also in coastal parts of Lancashire children and
women would be seen making for the shores in gangs to go
musselling and cockling; in Northumberland the 'bondaging'
system prevailed, whereby girls and women laboured at all
kinds of outside farmwork; whilst in the more pastoral region
of say Gloucestershire, Leicestershire, Cheshire, and Wiltshire,
female servants were commonly found who lived with their
employers, doing domestic work indoors and dairy work out.
The hop counties, Kent and Worcestershire especially, provided

work for girls and women in the hop fields at tying and picking, and also in their orchards and market gardens; and in market-gardening counties like those around London, children's deft fingers planted, picked, prepared, and packed the vegetables and fruit. In the vicinity of Bedfordshire and Buckinghamshire their skilful fingers executed intricate and elaborate patterns in lace and in straw plait, furnishing materials for the millinery and dress industries. Along the shores of the fishing coasts, children and women would be found squatting hunched over nets, which they braided and repaired to ensure as great a catch as possible. And in all regions, besides working at the local specialities, children and girls were engaged in the more general and common forms of agricultural work as well, according to the season.

For girls like this endurance and stamina were the very conditions of survival. The country work girl accepted her lot and did not think much of those who moaned and complained. Hardy gives two sharp outlines of this type of attitude in his books *The Woodlanders* and *Tess*. In *The Woodlanders*, Marty's father was ill but in order to keep going it was necessary for his work to be done. Hardy describes how Marty works late into the night making spars for thatching:[8]

> With a bill-hook in one hand and a leather glove much
> too large for her on the other, she was making spars . . .
> On her left hand lay a bundle of the straight, smooth
> hazel rods called spar-gads . . . in front a pile of the
> finished articles. To produce them she took up each gad,
> looked critically at it from end to end, cut it to length,
> split it into four, and sharpened each of the quarters with
> dexterous blows, which brought it to a triangular point
> precisely resembling that of a bayonet.

With blistering and red palm she worked on into the night and finally when she had the number required, she carried them to the shed outside and stacked them for collection in the early morning. Marty's life was one that bred improvisation and adaptability. Even when she felt unwell she knew that there were certain jobs that had to be performed in the countryside. The planting of the young trees was necessary for the continual cycle of nature and so she went out to work regardless of her own physical state, and without martyrdom but with calm

acceptance that life would go on even if she was unwell:
pandering to her own physical state was a weakness when things
were to be done. Again, in *Tess*, Hardy describes how she and
her friend Marian spend the day in a swede field hoeing:[9]

> They worked on hour after hour, unconscious of the
> forlorn aspect they bore in the landscape, not thinking
> of the justice or injustice of their lot . . . In the afternoon
> the rain came on again . . . It was so high a situation, this
> field, that the rain had no occasion to fall, but raced along
> horizontally upon the yelling wind, sticking into them like
> glass splinters till they were wet through. Tess had not
> known till now what was really meant by that. There are
> degrees of dampness, and a very little is called being wet
> through in common talk. But to stand working slowly in
> a field, and feel the creep of rainwater, first in legs and
> shoulders, then on hips and head, then at back, front, and
> sides, and yet to work on till the leaden light diminishes
> and marks that the sun is down, demands a distinct
> modicum of stoicism, even of valour.

For many country children in the nineteenth century,
schooling was something that happened only in the winter time
when the ground was too hard to work on – or when the market
for the gloves, lace or plait that they had spent hours making,
was low. Work came first. Where schooling was available, the
hours were often such as to allow for children to do work
before and after school: 10 a.m. until 12.30 p.m. and then
1 p.m. until 3 p.m., in an example given to the Newcastle
Commission in 1861.[10] Though the three R's were taught to all,
during recreation time it was considered that the girls should
not take part in unsuitable athletic sports such as football,
cricket, etc., but that they should '. . . find a little wholesome
physical exercise . . . in cleaning out the school'.[11] The parents
often could not afford to send their children to school; wages
were low, and every possible contribution to the family budget
was needed. Where schooling tipped the balance from subsistence to starvation, school was easier to give up than food.
An entry in the school log book from Braunton, in Devon,
commented, 'The poorer parents with long families think it hard
if they cannot keep home their elder children two or three days
in the week to earn a little to support the family generally', and

at Ermington, also in Devon, another schoolmaster found it
'hard to snatch a few pence from a parent's weekly income' by
enforcing attendance.[12] Employers were often opposed to
schooling for the labouring classes, and made it difficult for farm
girls or boys to attend lessons, for instance, by making the
working hours so rigid that they were not able to finish early
enough to get to night school.

School log books from the latter half of the century, show how
children were inextricably involved in the survival of their
families and were called upon at particular seasons of the year
to work and earn money at agricultural and rural forms of
labour. There are mentions in these log books of children
working at apple-picking, bird-watching, singling turnips,
stone-picking and other jobs, as well as many references to
unspecified field work. An entry in the log for Roxwell Church
School, in Essex, from 11 August 1880, pinpoints the urgency of
their seizing any chance to earn a few pence: 'Pretty good
school on Monday but many girls away in the afternoon for a
report was spread that some gleaning was to be had, however
proved to be incorrect.'[13]

Summer holidays were important for the work done during
them, and were often named accordingly: for instance in Kent
the break was known as the Hopping Vacation or Hopping
Holidays; elsewhere as the Harvest Holiday. The school log
book from Yalding in Kent has an illuminating entry (6 October
1873): 'Opened School today after the Hopping Holiday.
Attendance rather small children not quite ready to come.
Some are waiting to buy shoes.'[14] Harvest times were used to
accumulate money to pay off past bills (e.g., for the pig, or the
doctor), or to buy shoes and other necessities for the coming
winter and hard months; and everybody's work was needed.

Though in most agricultural regions there was a general
demand for children's and women's labour throughout the
year, there were obviously agricultural calendars peculiar to
various parts of the country which required specific kinds of
field labour at specific times – the common denominator being
that during the period of each particular harvest school
attendance would drop, so much sometimes that it was not
worth opening the school. The school log book for Roxwell
reports on 23 September 1867, 'Opened school, but obliged to
close it for another week – Harvest not finished therefore

children unable to attend',[15] and again some years later (19 September 1880), 'Attempted to open school but found it impossible to do so for the girls were out gleaning and hop picking'[16] (it eventually reopened on 27 September). The school could not escape the effects of the local agricultural cycle. Although the school calendar might be moderately flexible as regards the summer harvest, inevitably some of the other harvests and peaks in the demand for labour fell outside the vacation times. In Essex, for example, where market gardening formed the predominant mode of agricultural employment, attendance at the Roxwell school mentioned above, as at many other country schools, was regularly hit by the pea-picking harvest, which played a very important part in the economy of the agricultural labourer in this area, and fell during the summer term. The Roxwell log books during the months of July for 1866 and 1867, and June and July for 1868, 1869 and 1870, have many such entries as, 'Attendance small – children pea-picking';[17] '. . . Attendance rather low. Several children absent pea picking',[18] and 'Attendance very fair – pea picking'.[19] Entries in the months which followed pea-picking give some of the other forms of work that preoccupied such children, as follows: 23 July 1868, 'Attendance thin – children preparing for gleaning';[20] 20 August 1880, 'Very poor attendance towards the end of the week, several children being absent from 1st and 2nd classes engaged in picking up acorns'.[21] Other log books for Essex schools show the acorn harvest continuing well into the autumn; for instance Frating Church of England School has a reference on 11 October 1870, 'Several children away from school gathering acorns';[22] and Henny National School for 21 October 1870, 'There have been few children at School since the Acorns began to fall. Nearly all are busy picking up and selling these.'[23] Henny school log also cites (in 1875) some children being away from 1 to 5 November at 'bean dropping'.[24]

In Kent the hop gardens were the dominant source of agricultural work. Kent school log books show that from March until sometimes late October there was work being done in the hop gardens by women and children. So on 30 March 1868 the new head of the Adisham school in Kent wrote, 'The attendance less than last week among the elder children the work having commenced in the hop fields';[25] an entry from the Yalding log

book for 5 May 1871 states, 'Several of the children are engaged
in Hop, tying the forward Hops';[26] and in 1867 by the 13 May,
'all the elder children' in Chart Sutton school had 'left for work
in the hop gardens'.[27] Though most of the hop-picking actually
took place during the summer holidays, if the hops were late
in ripening or there was a heavy harvest it was not uncommon
for the return to school to be delayed until the harvest was
over and the children's labour no longer needed. At Adisham
in 1865 it was only on 2 October that 'School re-opened after
9 weeks Holiday', and even then there were 'only 17 present
owing to work not being finished in Hop-gardens'.[28] Besides
working in the hop fields, the children in Kent also worked
during term times in the orchards and market gardens at fruit-
picking or gathering, haymaking, gleaning, picking acorns,
etc. Whenever and wherever the agricultural calendar provided
children with a means of earning a few pence, the opportunity
was taken and school forgotten until the means was exhausted.

Outside the home, then, girls and boys were expected to
participate equally and directly in the economic existence of the
family unit; but within the confines of the home there were
forms of work exclusively performed by the female members,
which formed a further obstacle to their obtaining some form
of school education. Various log book entries from Essex and
Kent show explicitly that girls were expected to contribute,
indirectly, to the economic maintenance of the household by
acting as 'little mothers' to those children younger than themselves who did not go to school or who could not be left or
tended by the mother. Non-attendance at school by girls was
often given the explanation: 'their mothers want them',[29]
and 'home causes'.[30] In the Roxwell school log for 24 July 1876
there is the explicit entry, 'Eliza Joyce away every afternoon to
help her mother.'[31] The mother's two economic roles, as wage-
earner and as housewife, frequently conflicted, and when the
demands of outside work had to be put first, her female children
automatically took over the household duties, which involved
not only the housework and cooking but also the tending and
care of the younger members, as well as nursing the sick
members of the family. Thus, to allow the mother to go to work,
the elder female children frequently had to relinquish the
opportunity of going to school and stay at home. An entry for
8 August 1873 from the Troytown log, Kent, states: '. . . many

girls stay away a half day to mind the baby, go errands, etc.',[32] whilst a Canterbury school amplifies the explanation – 'to nurse the babies while the mothers are in the fields'.[33]

2   Farm work

The country girl's introduction to the fields would come early, probably before she could be useful, when she would simply be brought along by her mother. Soon she would be helping her mother, working by her side. As one of the Agricultural Employment Commissioners reported of the East Midlands: 'There is hardly any work which may be said to be peculiar to women, as distinguished from children.'[34] Independent work was a short step from assisting the mother.

Labour was often hired implicitly or explicitly on a family basis. In the Kent hop fields farmers expected the wives and children of their male labourers to help with tying the beans and with the hop harvest. In East Farleigh in 1867, at least 70 per cent of the able-bodied women were working with the hops in the harvest season.[35] The Newcastle Commission in 1861 noted an implicit understanding in hiring that the master should have a claim on the labourers' children when their work was needed.[36] In Dorset a man would be hired on the basis of the labour that his family could supply: a man with three sons stood a better chance of obtaining employment than a man with a smaller family. Families were advertised for: the Commissioners were shown a sample advertisement from the *Dorchester County Chronicle* – 'Wanted, a farm labourer with a working family.'[37] If for some reason the mother was unable to go to work, then she had to find a substitute; most often an elder daughter would be kept off school to take her place. (She might alternatively stay at home with younger children so that the mother could go out to work.) Wages in Dorset were notoriously low, not more than 8s. a week with a rent-free cottage, or 9s. a week with rent to pay. The *Morning Chronicle* of 6 March 1850 remarked that though the Kent labourer could not feed his family as cheaply as the Dorset one, '. . . his wages enable him to feed his family better than the Dorsetshire labourer does'.[38] (The Kent labourer's wage would be between 10s. and 12s. a week.) Even in counties like Devon, Somerset, Hereford, and Worcester, where the labour of children was not a condition of hiring, it would probably be provided when required, even at the expense of schooling,[39] for wages, employment, and often lodging were in the master's hands, and he was not to be lightly crossed. Moreover, as was correctly remarked at the time, 'The peasant's wages are *never* up to the mark that can allow of his sacrificing the earnings of his child to higher considerations';[40] where earnings were so low every little extra helped.

Even if no formal stipulation had been made for labour from all the family, at those times of year when a great deal of labour was needed, that is especially at harvest time, everybody would be roped in. There were many different harvests (corn, hay, peas, potatoes, hops, turnips, beans, peas, apples, and other fruit and vegetables), but the corn and hay harvests were common to most districts. Harvest time would be part of the life of the entire village and as the time drew near, the whole village would be mobilized, even those not regularly employed by the farmers: from the eldest to the youngest, all would find their way into the fields. All hands were needed so that the harvest be completed as quickly as possible, for the weather might break. Those who for most of the year worked away in gangs, during the harvest would return to join their families or friends: it was at times like this that the family as a solid working unit would earn together money to last them during the winter period. Harvest contracts were well adapted to this mode of work. David Morgan in his chapter on 'Harvesters' describes how individual families would be allocated areas, or acres, of crop to clear for which there would be one payment; the father usually did the reaping, and the mother and children the stooking and binding. Similarly, for picking in orchards, market gardens, and hop fields, families would be engaged as a group, the mother (or less often the father) would be paid by quantity, and the entire group would contribute to the earning of one family wage.

The more hands the better, even little ones, for the faster they finished one stint the sooner they could move on to the next, and the greater the eventual earnings. So children were indispensable, and it was accepted that schooling took second place. Commissioner Boyle in his report to the 4th Commission in 1870 described a custom that was prevalent in parts of Scotland: when it came near the time for harvest, the children would bring handfuls of the near ripening corn and place them on the teacher's desk as a reminder that holiday time was near.[41] Edith Mary Sargent, born in 1880 in Essex, recounts the work that she did whilst attending school half time and working the rest.[42]

> . . . as I was the 2nd eldest in our family I had to work half time and school half time, and during the harvest time my Brother and I worked in the fields with our Father most of the men worked in twos and my brother and I worked as one man with Father taking out the corn making the bens and tying them up and setting them into sheaves, then other times we had to stone pick that was to pick the stones from the stetches and make heaps of them and then they would be carted in a tumble marked with chalk and we had to pick a load for 1/6 and then we picked up acorns and sold them at 1/– a bushal and oh it did take a lot of them to make a bushal then we had to glean in the corn fields after the corn was carted and it was sent to the mill and made into flour to make us bread and then we went peapicking in the fields at 3 o'clock sometimes and then the cutting of beans and singling out of mangel . . .

After the harvest was over, gleaning would commence; its fruits – the bassings, gleanings or leasings – in the case of barley would be fed to pig or chickens if the family owned them. Corn gleaning, the gathering of ears of corn left by the reaper, was taken very seriously because if a family worked hard enough, they would be able to gather sufficient corn to supply them with bread during the winter months. The corn would be sent to the miller, who would grind it, keeping some as his payment; then the flour would be brought back and baking would commence. Gleaning was very much the work of the women and children, though others, it seems, would join in too: the Agricultural Employment Commissioners were told by a Lincolnshire doctor in 1867: 'One of the greatest sources of evil is gleaning. Young and old are congregated together in one field, and the greatest immorality results.'[45]

As well as working alongside their parents, children were also hired individually by the farmers, for such jobs as tenting (bird-scaring), the tending of cattle, sheep and pigs in the stubble, helping with the threshing machine and the feeding of cattle. Tenting was peculiarly the work of children. Hardy's Jude did it at the age of six and was paid 6*d*. a day scaring rooks from the farmer's land.[44]

> The boy stood under the rick . . . , and every few seconds used his clacker or rattle briskly. At each clack the rooks left off pecking, and rose and went away on their leisurely wings, burnished like tassets of mail, afterwards wheeling back and regarding him warily, and descending to feed at a more respectful distance.

Tenting was also done by girls. The Agricultural Employment Commissioners heard of a girl near Retford (Notts.) tenting in January, who had been at it nearly all the year.[45] It was a lonely, monotonous job, and involved standing out in all weathers. Mrs Field, an Essex woman brought up in the market garden district near Tiptree, not only helped her mother with gleaning, domestic work and errands, but also worked on her own as an independent child labourer.[46]

> I went out to work when I was 9, working for Mr Parrish – a seed grower. In winter we worked inside a shed cleaning out peas and beans and getting pips from marrows and cucumbers. In summer we collected carrot and parsnip seeds and everything you can think of – It was at Tiptree but I have forgotten the name of the road, it was on a hill just outside Tiptree. The very special thing we did was picking up Canary Creeper seeds from rows. It was the first that had been grown and very precious – Mr Parrish used to come behind us with a stick in case we dropped any – they were funny little black things – and we had to go back and pick them up. I earned 3/– a week and I gave it all to my Mother for my father was ill and could not work and he died when I was 21. – I used to pick water cress growing wild and had to go right into the pond to get it, I bunched it up and sold it and once I got enough to buy my father a tin of crab – he liked that better than anything as he couldn't eat much. We used to go to

Totham a long ride with Mr Parrish in a wagon, doing all sorts of jobs in the fields – mostly 'twitching' – we walked behind the ploughs and picked up every little bit of white root and burned it. We took all our food to the fields, cold tea to drink, and bread with something homemade or a bit of cheese.

I worked there until I was 14 when I went to service with Mr and Mrs Webb of Brentwood.

Fraser's report to the Agricultural Employment Commissioners (1867–9) on the counties of Norfolk, Essex, Sussex and Gloucestershire, contains the following cycle of children's work:[47]

January	Hop pole shaving and other coppice work in woodland countries.
February	Twitching, stone picking, bean and pea setting.
March	Potato setting, bird scaring, cleaning land for spring corn.
April	Bird scaring, weeding corn, setting potatoes.
May	Bird scaring, weeding corn, cleaning land for turnips, bark harvest, tending cows in the lanes, etc.
June	Hay making, turnip singling.
July	Turnip singling, pea picking, cutting thistles, scaring birds from ripening corn.
August	Corn harvest, gleaning.
September	Hop harvest, tending sheep or pigs on the stubbles.
October	Potato and fruit gathering, twitching, dibbling and dropping wheat.
November	Bird scaring from new sown wheat and beans, acorning.
December	Stone picking, spreading cow droppings; in Norfolk, scaring birds from corn stacks; in Essex, helping their fathers to make surface drains; in woodland districts, coppice work; topping and tailing turnips, and cleaning roots for cattle.

The part played by older girls in harvests was large, and sometimes they would be hired individually. A Yorkshire girl whom A. J. Munby talked with found employment in each successive harvest. In October 1852, when he saw her, she was gathering potatoes.[48]

> She & the others, she said, earn a shilling . . . a day,
> & work in the fields from 7 am till dusk: work at hay &
> harvest, at pea picking in June, at osier-peeling in May,
> at tater gathering in October, & then at turnip pulling, &
> so on. For these Brotherton girls are regular day labourers,
> & have no other occupation: & in the winter, alack! we
> have to stop at home idle . . . & do our own bits of
> household work & sewing . . .

The arrival of the machine in the 1860s and 1870s left women's and girls' work at harvest (stooking and binding) intact.[49] In the harvest described by Hardy in *Tess of the D'Urbervilles* a machine is doing the reaping, but the binding is still being done by hand, much of it by girls and women, among them Tess:[50]

> . . . Her binding proceeds with clock-like monotony. From
> the sheaf last finished she draws a handful of ears, patting
> their tips with her left palm to bring them even. Then
> stooping low she moves forward, gathering the corn with
> both hands against her knees, and pushing her left gloved
> hand under the bundle to meet the right on the other side,
> holding the corn in an embrace like that of a lover. She
> brings the ends of the bond together, and kneels on the
> sheaf while she ties it, beating back her skirt now and then
> when lifted by the breeze. A bit of her naked arm is visible
> between the buff leather of the gauntlet and the sleeve of
> her gown; and as the day wears on its feminine smoothness
> becomes scarified by the stubble, and bleeds . . . The
> movements of the other women were more or less similar
> to Tess's, the whole bevy of them drawing together like
> dancers in a quadrille at the completion of a sheaf by each,
> every one placing her sheaf on end against those of the
> rest, till a shock, or 'stitch' as it was here called, of ten or
> a dozen was formed.

It was reckoned that a woman's pay at common farm work was about half that of a man (in gangs it would be even less), and in some cases she would receive no rise until marriage.[51]

(Children of course received less again.) In the early sixties
rates could vary between 8*d*. and 1*s*. 8*d*.,⁵² according to local
circumstances and the nature of the work. Women were
generally preferred to men, because their wages came to less;
for some work special reasons were given – usually their
dexterity, as for binding hops, but sometimes their 'superior
industry and order'.⁵³

Like men, they often received part of their wages in kind:
sometimes fuel or produce, but most often drink for consumption
at work. This was particularly common at harvest time, when
warm weather would have its effect; but all agricultural work
was thirst provoking, and the labourer's flagon of beer or cider
brought necessary relief. In *Tess of the D'Urbervilles*, when Tess
and several others are working at reed-drawing, in bitter winter
weather, two of the women in the group – 'two Amazonian
sisters' as Hardy calls them – finish first: 'When two o'clock
arrived the professional reed-drawers tossed off their last half-
pint in their flagon, put down their hooks, tied their last
sheaves, and went away.'⁵⁴ Temperance reformers considered
that the custom of providing labourers with drink acted as
'an incitement to intemperance and to great detriment of their
families'; and approved the clause in the Agricultural Labourers
Bill of 1887 which prohibited 'every farmer or other employer of
labour paying to any farm labourer or servant in husbandry,
and not residing or boarding with his/her employer, wages or
portion of wages in beer, cider or other intoxicating liquor'.

A. J. Munby on his country excursions often provides very
minute detail and description of the work that such women,
individually and in gangs, would do throughout the agricultural
calendar. In October 1862 he talked with two women from a
group of field workers near Lower Rainham, in Kent. It consisted of a man, 'old and feeble', 'a respectable matron' and
'two young lasses of twenty, with blowzed healthy faces and
bony earth-stained hands'.⁵⁵

> They had all been pulling & trimming wurzel 'for t'beasts':
> they work from 7 am to 5 pm, & earn, at ordinary
> labour, such as this, 1/6 a day, and sometimes even two
> shillings: but at tatergathering, a lass can earn as much as
> 3/- a day. Each man afield has one or two such female
> assistants; he digs, & the girls grub up the loosened

potatoes, wipe the earth off with their hands, & put them into the sack . . . Most of the Lower Rainham lasses go out to field work; some regularly, . . . but more in the intervals of service. When a farmer wants hands, he looks out and says 'Oh there's Mary Jones out of place – she'll go.'

Some months later, walking from Dartford to Wilmington (again in Kent), he talks with some other potato pullers, who were earning rather less – '1/– a day and no drinkings' – for working from 7 a.m. till dusk, 'getting their dinner on the spot, under a shed of furze'.[56]

One was an elderly woman, the other a young one; & both, for health & strength & rustic costume, would have done credit to Yorkshire. The younger woman especially; for she stood five feet eight or nine, & had broad square shoulders & a masculine figure, & wore, besides her crumpled straw bonnet, a man's fustian coat, a rough shawl loosely wrapped about her neck, a short kirtle, & great ankle boots, heavy with the wet loam of the plough-lands; & carried on her arm a sacking skirt, yellow with earth; for she had worn it all day, kneeling in the furrows . . .

In Yorkshire many of the female agricultural workers were Irish, or of Irish descent, and they too earned a living by working in the potato fields. As late as 1902 when Rowntree made his study of poverty in York he mentions female Irish labourers earning in this manner. Munby saw them in 1862 and wrote of them as follows:[57]

I returned to York by Garrow Hill, and overtook a dozen Irishwomen returning from field work near Heslington. They had been tatergathering: wages 1/– a day for other labour, but 1/3 for this, because it's hard: we have to be on our knees in the furrows all day long sometimes; scarce ever a change to straighten one's back! After taters comes turnip-pulling; & then we are idle all winter & live on what we've earned in summer . . .

At the same time as noting the work that the women did, Munby acutely observed and appreciatively described their appearance. His appreciation is quite exceptional. Even

Hardy, though his knowledge and descriptions of country girls' life and work are so detailed and so graphic, seems to be slightly repelled by them.

One of the winter jobs – a cold and a solitary one – which Hardy's Tess and Marian slaved at whilst working as farm labourers, was swede trimming. 'At this occupation they could shelter themselves by a thatched hurdle if it rained; but if it was frosty even their thick leather gloves could not prevent the frozen masses they handled from biting their fingers.'[58] The root crops which they had grubbed from the fields had to be trimmed of surplus earth and fibres before being stored. Richard Jefferies described a woman doing this work:[59]

> She has a stool or log of wood to sit on, and arranges a couple of sacks or something of the kind, so as to form a screen and keep off the bitter winds which are then so common – colder than those of the winter proper. With the screen one side, the heap of roots the other, and the hedge on the third she is in some sense sheltered, and taking her food with her, may stay there the whole day long, quite alone in the solitude of the broad, open, arable fields . . .

Women who were hardened to field labour moved around the countryside performing such jobs as farmers required, like the 'Amazonian sisters' mentioned above, who 'did all kinds of men's work by preference, including well-sinking, hedging, ditching, and excavating, without any sense of fatigue'.[60] These were the 'noted reed-drawers', who outpaced Tess and Marian. Reed-pulling was an exacting but monotonous job, to which such labourers would be set when the weather became too bad for outdoor work; it was done in the wheat barn, whose shelter provided welcome relief from the weather, but 'reed-drawing is fearful hard work – worse than swede-hacking', said Marian.

> Putting on their gloves all set to work in a row in front of the press, an erection formed of two posts connected by a cross-beam, under which the sheaves to be drawn from were laid ears outward, the beam being pegged down by pins in the uprights, and lowered as the sheaves diminished.

All day they worked at it, gossiping at first, then later 'in a reverie, as they went on seizing the ears of corn, drawing out the straw, gathering it under their arms, and cutting off the ears

with their bill-hooks, nothing sounded in the barn but the swish
of the straw and the crunch of the hook'.[61] They were expected
to empty the barn, and thus worked sometimes from morning
light until it was too dark to see, bending and lifting and
wielding the hook till they were ready to drop. But exhaustion
must have been a familiar condition for the farm labourer:
though the forms of field work were diverse most of them involved terrific physical effort. Solitude was also familiar;
Munby often mentions women working on their own in huge
fields. One such, near York, he managed to talk with:[62]

> In one of the large ploughed fields there, I saw a woman
> all alone, diligently plying her hoe; cleaning out the hedge-
> bottom, one would say . . . I met her in the lane soon
> after, coming home, for it was now dusk. A nice looking
> young married woman she was, with light hair &
> sunburnt face; wearing a crumpled bonnet, a tattered
> cotton frock, & strong earthy boots; carrying her hoe, & a
> knife in her hand for cutting weeds. She had been working
> there by herself all day, since eight in the morning, except
> dinnertime: stubbing wickwood & hoeing. Put her
> children out to nurse meanwhile. Had worked afield all her
> life, woman & wench: hoeing, digging taters, harvesting.

A young woman Munby met between Woking Heath and
Pyrford, in Surrey, preferred to work with others: 'When a lot
of women get together it's the pleasantest, for then there's
company; but often we work alone – yesterday I was in this
field alone, hoeing, from eight till five, all day.' In those parts
men and women didn't work much together: 'the female
labourers will be on one side of the field, the male on the other'.
Although she thought it 'better for girls to go to service: what
is tenpence a day at fieldwork?', she found it healthy work; and
'there's many women, she said, and girls too, married and unmarried, that works afield about here: hoeing, & couching,
& reaping with the sickle: *she* can reap, & does'.[63] Reaping
seems to have been more often done by men, though Munby
reports more women reapers than usual in Sussex. Flora
Thompson refers to it as a dying practice. 'Formerly all the
able-bodied women not otherwise occupied had gone as a matter
of course; but, by the 'eighties, there were only three or four,
beside the regular field women, who could handle the sickle.'[64]

The living-in farm servant was much less free than the girls
I have been writing about, but she was probably better fed and
housed (one reason why the daughter of a labourer's household
was often sent into service at an early age). Indoors and in the
dairy she would work for the farmer's wife, but when extra
hands were needed outdoors with planting and harvesting, for
instance, she would be found working in the fields probably with
the ordinary field or gang worker. Whilst in this employment
she would also receive instruction in most of the fundamental
domestic tasks – ironing, washing, cooking, cleaning, etc. – as
well as in butter and cheese-making. Ruth Carey recalls
working as a 'general girl' in a farmhouse: she had to do all the
cleaning including scrubbing the endless 'pave stones', besides
doing dairy work such as the skimming of milk and the cheese-
and butter-making; you had to be able 'to dip your hand in
everything'.[65] Some girls, though not Ruth Carey, used such
situations as take-off pads for 'better positions' within the big
houses in the towns.

Another class of 'indoor' farm servant was the dairymaid.
Like the 'general girl' she was regarded as being definitely more
respectable than the common field labourer. She worked very
long hours, and got less money for her labour than her more
independent sisters; but the work she performed was less
physical in character and it did not involve so much mixing with
men (in regions where large dairy herds existed, however, it was
not uncommon to see girls and men working alongside each
other in milking gangs, a situation which was allegedly 'un-
favourable to morality').[66] Dairymaids were expected to
become skilled not only at milking but also in the arts of skimming milk and making butter and cheese. Their hours were
long, sometimes as long as 4 a.m. to 10 p.m.,[67] and if there was
a rush of work on – for instance during cheese-making – she
would not be able to down tools, even on a Sunday. On a
larger farm it would often happen that the farmer would hire
a milking gang for the duration of the milking season and then
lay off most of the workers when the cows were due to calve.
Those dairymaids that were kept on after the milking season
finished would generally reside with the farmer in his house.
Tess worked on such a farm, where there were about 100 cows
and each maid and man had to milk about eight or ten cows
twice per day.[68] The day would commence (as when I was a

child) very early in the morning: if there was no milking
parlour, the workers would walk to the field where the cows were
grazing and would squat down by the side of each cow with
cheek or forehead pressed into its warm side. When the bucket
was full, unless the milk was needed for making butter or
cheese, it would be poured into churns to be sent by wagon to the
dairy and then on to its destination, which at Tess's farm was
London.

In Northumberland there was a large class of female farm
workers – known as 'bondagers' – who lived in. They were
always unmarried and fairly young (Munby, who made some
inquiries about them in August 1863, suggests that ten and
thirty were the age limits).[69] Often the bondager was the servant
of the 'hind', himself the farmer's servant, but both would work.
On the larger farms around Wooler, Munby was told, there
might be six or eight hinds on a farm, each with two or three
bondagers; and they would work together in gangs, 'either by
themselves, or under a male overseer'. The bondager might be
hired by the hind at the statute fairs, 'yearly or half yearly',
and in this case she was fed and housed by him and paid at a
rate which Munby reports as 8d. a day or £12 a year. 'But
often she is his own daughter; and then he saves her wages. If
not she is the daughter of labouring parents living in some
neighbouring village.'[70] The bondager was strictly a 'servant in
husbandry'. Her work was chiefly out of doors, but if there was
nothing to do in the fields she might help with the heavier
household work, washing for example,[71]

> but she is not bound to such trivial tasks: she may lounge
> about like a lad & whistle or snooze, until she be ordered
> afield. Once afield, she is put to any thing, except
> ploughing and ditching. She takes up potatoes: she hoes
> turnips: she cleans the land of weed and stones: she
> harrows at times: she leads the team and drives the cart:
> she cleans out the byre and the pig stye, aided sometimes
> by a boy: she makes hay of course: she binds corn, and
> she reaps with the sickle.

The hiring of 'indoor' farm servants – men and women, boys
and girls – took place at hiring-fairs (they were also known as
'statues' and 'mops') such as the one described by Hardy in
Far From the Madding Crowd. This system of hirings – with its

general change-about of places every year or half year –
continued right down to the end of the century, though clergymen and moralists often condemned it as an evil. (Statute Day
was a general holiday-making occasion for the labouring
classes in the district where it was being held, and there were
stalls, merry-go-rounds and some heavy drinking after a bargain
had been struck.) It was also said to be demeaning for men,
and still worse for women and girls, to present themselves
for selection like beasts at a cattle market. But in fact the
process of selection took place on both sides, and a good deal of
bargaining went on. A. J. Munby had a glimpse of it when he
visited the 'Statties' at York and came upon 'a double row of
farm lasses' standing for hire on the pavement, underneath a
wall.[73]

Here and there a farmer or a farmer's wife was bargaining
with one of them. 'Esta getten hired, lass?', said a woman
to one girl. 'Naa.' 'Well, ye mun get hired here, or not at
all – what wage, de ye want?' The rest I did not hear, but
it ended with 'Well, ye mun cum te us a Munda.'

The indoor farm servant was favourably contrasted to the
field worker in point of respectability. She was thought to be
engaged in proper 'women's work' which would serve to
improve her as a prospective wife and mother, and also prepare
her for service in a 'big house' if she wanted to move on to
higher things. The farmer's wife, wrote Richard Jefferies,
'. . . is a kind of unpaid teacher, for ever shaping the rough
material which, so soon as it is worth higher wages than a
tenant-farmer can usually pay, is off . . .'[74] By contrast the
field labouring girl was held to be spoiled alike for domestic
service and for marriage, 'coarsened' by her work – and by the
mixed company she kept – to the point that womanliness was
destroyed. Field work, the Agricultural Employment Commissioners were repeatedly told, encouraged 'strong passions,
rough language, and general "loudness" . . .';[75] it corrupted
the girl's mind, perhaps irretrievably, and left her rough in
manner. 'Gentlefolk' would be unlikely to consider her for a
place: according to T. H. Harrison, a Norfolk headmaster who
appeared before the Agricultural Employment Commissioners
in 1867, every girl who worked as a half-timer had disqualified
herself: 'I could not recommend a girl for domestic service',

he told the Commissioners, 'who had been habituated to field work.'[76]

3   Gangs

The worst form of girl labour, from the point of view of bourgeois respectability, was the 'gang' system, which provoked a special commission of inquiry, and a great deal of outraged commentary, in the 1860s. It was most firmly established in the Fen districts of East Anglia and in the East Midlands. The farms in these parts tended to be large, but the labouring population was scattered and comparatively scarce because there were many 'closed' parishes, where cottages had been pulled down by their owners to avoid liability for poor rates, while their tenants moved away to 'open' parishes where they could find places to live. The labour to work the land then had to be brought from afar, often in the form of travelling gangs, who went from farm to farm to perform specific tasks.

A great deal of the field work in these districts fell to women and girls. In the Lincolnshire Wolds, for instance, the land was rough, and many hands were needed to clear it of gorse, thistle and stones: gangs of women and children were cheaper to employ at it than men. There was a great deal of work for them, too, in the Isle of Ely, as Dr Hunter reported in 1863:[77]

> It appears that the land in these districts is generally
> light, and that the recently reclaimed 'black lands' are
> very light indeed, and may be submitted to women's
> work to a far greater extent than anywhere else in the
> kingdom. The crops also for which these lands are best
> fitted, as for instance the great potato crop of the Upper
> Humber, are such as afford an amount of employment to
> women unknown elsewhere. The eradication of twitch is
> also a branch of women's work.

Some of the gangs in these parts were Irish, with whole families who came over for the summer harvests, but even more were recruited from the villages of surrounding districts. They were known by various names – 'jobbing', 'common', or 'travelling' gangs, according to the Children's Employment Commissioners reporting in 1867 on agricultural gangs. Local and seasonal circumstances affecting the availability on the one hand of work and on the other of labour, along with the nature of the work itself, influenced the composition of each gang; its size would range between ten and forty members – the average being around twenty. In charge was the gangmaster, who contracted with the farmer to do certain work, and his hirelings would consist of children and young people of both sexes, and some women.[78] The children might be as young as six, though probably with older brothers or sisters in the same gang. (At times when the demand for labour was high and the supply was short, some parents would insist that the younger ones be taken on along with the older.[79])

The gangmasters were given a bad character by the Children's Employment Commissioners. They were said to be mostly men who could find no other employment, whose character was such that no farmer would employ them full time. They were 'catchwork labourers', 'men of indolent and drinking habits . . . and in some cases . . . notorious depravity'.[80] Children were very much at the gangmaster's mercy and he worked them hard. He had his contract to fulfil; and often he would be paid on a piecework basis, so his interest was to extract as much work as possible from them. The children were paid so much per day, and the balance of pay left over from the contract with the farmer went to the gangmaster as his 'fee' or profits. Mrs Burrows, who was brought up in the Croyland district of the Fens in the 1850s, worked in such a gang when she was a little girl. In a memoir, written at the end of her life, she recalled:[81]

On the day that I was eight years of age, I left school and began to work fourteen hours a day in the fields, with forty to fifty children of whom, even at that early age, I was the eldest. We were followed all day long by an old man carrying a long whip in his hand which he did not forget to use. A great many of the children were only five years of age. You will think that I am exaggerating, but I am *not*; it is as true as the Gospel. Thirty-five years ago is the time I speak of, and the place, Croyland in Lincolnshire, nine miles from Peterborough. I could even now name several of the children who began at the age of five to work in the gangs, and also the name of the ganger. We always left the town, summer and winter, the moment the old Abbey clock struck six . . .

The work done by the gangs was very varied but invariably involved hard work, long hours and aching limbs. F. D. Longe in his report to the Children's Employment Commission outlines the type of work that women and children would do during the year whilst in such gangs.[82]

January	In this month children and women are employed in sorting potatoes in the Isle of Axholme, and in the fen districts of Lincolnshire and Cambridgeshire. During mild weather children are employed in gangs picking stones in many parishes. In all districts the number of women and children employed in this month is very small.
February	Very little work done, except as in January.
March	Towards the end of this month children and women begin to be employed in gangs and separately, (1) in picking 'twitch' (the roots of couch grass); (2) in spreading manure; (3) in hoeing; (4) in setting potatoes.
April	The number of children employed in the four kinds of work last mentioned is increased. Towards the end of this month weeding in the growing crops begins, and the gangs are considerably increased.
May/June	The greatest number of children are employed in gangs during these months at weeding, picking twitch in the fallows, etc. In districts where the common gang system does not prevail a great many children are employed in small farm gangs at the same kinds of work.
July	The employment of children in all districts at the above kinds of work is very much diminished during this month; gangs are still employed at weeding and singling turnips. In some districts a great many children and women are employed in getting up hay.

August/ September	During these months although few gangs are at work, the aggregate number of children and women employed in the fields in all districts is greater than in any other month. All who are not employed in harvest work, making bands in the wheat field, pulling flax, gathering woad, or in some other work are engaged in gleaning.
October	In districts where potatoes are grown in large quantities children and women are in the greatest demand in this month. They are also employed in gathering mangold wurtzel. Twitch picking and spreading manure still goes on.
November	Gathering potatoes, mangold wurtzel, turnips, and carrots still occupies a great number of children in many districts. Gangs are still employed at twitch picking. Stone picking begins in the highland districts but in most parishes the employment of children is reduced to a minimum towards the end of this month.
December	In the gang districts children and women continue to be employed at the same work as in November until stopped by the frost.

Some tasks, like weeding, stone picking and making bands for corn, would obviously be much easier than others, for instance the hoeing and pulling of roots such as turnips or mangolds. Sometimes a tool was used for the raising of such vegetables and for the topping and tailing of turnips, but these were not easily manipulated by the younger children. The pulling of flax which took place in September was considered by some too heavy for the young children (the flax was stooked like corn sheaves and then stacked, the seeds being beaten out later). Woad required to be weeded and pulled sometimes three times a year.[83]

Because of the distances from the villages to the place of work, it was not unusual for the children to have to walk many miles to work, and back again in the evening, as Mrs Burrows recalled:[84]

We had to walk a very long way to our work, never much
less than two miles each way, and very often five miles
each way. The large farms all lay a good distance from the
town, and it was on those farms that we worked. In the
winter, by the time we reached our work, it was light
enough to begin, and of course we worked until it was dark
and then we had our long walk home. I never remembered
to have reached home sooner than six and more often
seven, even in winter. In the summer, we did not leave the
fields in the evening until the clock had struck six, then of
course we must walk home, and this walk was no easy
task for us children who had worked hard all day on the
ploughed fields.

F. D. Longe, in evidence submitted to the Children's
Employment Commission, said of gangs in the Wolds,[85]

These gangs work in different parishes within a radius of
five or six miles from their homes, and they sometimes go
to a distance of nine miles . . . The Louth gangs are
regularly employed at Ruckland, Stennigate, Donnington,
and Withcall on land between five and seven miles distant
from Louth.

If the gangmaster had taken a particular piece of land by the
piece, job or 'great', it was possible that he would make
the gang complete the job before they could start on the
journey home, so that it could be near midnight before they got
back. They would have a couple of hours' sleep, wake up, eat a
scanty breakfast and return to the fields by 7 or 8 in the morning.
A mother in evidence to the 1867 Commission stated that she
had two daughters of eleven and fourteen and that on some
occasions they had eight miles to walk *to* and *from* work; this
had to be done every day. They worked from 8 till 5 and were
paid 7d. a day. At one time she had sent her six-year-old
daughter who was paid 4d. a day, but the child became ill after
three weeks and never went back.[86] Most workers had to supply
their own tools, and one girl of thirteen gave evidence that her
father had found all her tools for her – she had various sized
hoes, a muck fork, a carrot fork, and a twitch basket and rake – a
ganger's tool kit.[87] Sometimes, but very rarely in these districts,
a pony and cart might be provided to give them a lift home.

Because of distance the gang could stay overnight at the place where they were working, though this does not seem to have been a very common practice. Their lodging then would be a barn or a stable where they would be locked up for the night. Commissioner Longe reported such an instance: 'A day or two previous to my visit in November a gang had stopped a night at a farm in Ruckland. The gangmaster with his gang were locked up in a granary by the foreman of the farm, and let out the following morning.'[88] Sometimes they would stay away for weeks on end and someone would be sent home to fetch more food for the others. The long hours, plus the effects of walking to and from work carrying tools and food, plus the effects of a poor diet, must have had a debilitating effect. But the major source of complaint from the girls and younger women was about the weeding in high wet corn – their clothing held the damp, and it was often necessary to take off their petticoats, and wring them out and hang them up to dry. Rheumatism was a common result – one girl (crippled with rheumatism after joining a gang at eleven) remarked, 'We have had to take off our shoes and pour the water out, and then the man would say, "Now then, go in again."'[89]

In bad weather conditions were grim, and if the work had to be abandoned, there were no wages for the day. Mrs Burrows provides a very clear picture of such conditions.[90]

It was a most terrible day. The cold east wind (I suppose it was an east wind, for surely no wind ever blew colder), the sleet and snow which came every now and then in showers seemed almost to cut us to pieces. We were working upon a large farm that lay half-way between Croyland and Peterborough. Had the snow and sleet come continuously we should have been allowed to come home, but because it only came at intervals, of course we had to stay. I have been out in all sorts of weather but never remember a colder day. Well, the morning passed along somehow. The ganger did his best for us by letting us have a run in our turns, but that did not help us very much because we were all too numb with the cold to be able to run much. Dinner-time came, and we were preparing to sit down under a hedge and eat our cold dinner and drink our cold tea, when we saw the shepherd's wife coming towards

us, and she said to our ganger, 'Bring these children into
my house and let them eat their dinner there.' We went
into that very small two-roomed cottage, and when we
got into the largest room there was not standing room for
us all, but this woman's heart was large, even if her house
was small, and so she put her few chairs and table out into
the garden, and then we all sat down in a ring upon the
floor. She then placed in our midst a very large saucepan
of hot boiled potatoes, and bade up help ourselves. Truly,
although I have attended scores of grand parties and
banquets since that time, not one of them has seemed half
as good to me as that meal did.

A less formal sort of gang that existed in these parts was
called by the Commissioners the 'private' gang. It was similarly
constituted but the workers were found and hired directly by
the farmer, and superintended either by him or one of his
employees. The employment of such gangs was shorter term:
they would probably be hired for one job in particular and then
dismissed. In most areas both types of gang were found, but
on farms of 300 acres or more, it was more often 'public' gangs,
as farms of this size and nature '. . . afford such an amount of
work for this class of hands that the farmer is able to keep
10 or more children and a man acting as their superintendent in
regular employment during some months'.[91]
Full-time employment for girls and women in gangs was
not restricted to the Fens and East Anglia. The gang system
also existed around the Lancashire coast, where there were
cockling gangs, whose workers were paid by middlemen
('badgers') for the shellfish they collected. Children and women
were the main contingent of such gangs: they would go down
to the shore in parties of from ten to twenty whenever the tide
was out 'and pursue their occupation until the advancing tide
compels them to return'.[92] Children of only four or five would
venture out with others on to the sands in order to learn the
art. The chief places where cockling was carried on in the 1860s
were Fleetwood, Poulton-le-Sands, Hest Bank, Bolton-le-Sands,
Warton, Silverdale, Allethwaite, Flookborough, Bardsea, and
Baycliff – all on Morecambe Bay – and Sandscales and Souther-
gate in the estuary of the Duddon.[93]
Cockling involved the following proceedings:

The cockles lie about an inch under the sand, and their presence is detected by the appearance of a small hole; the cram, a small three pronged bent fork is then applied, and the shell fish is jerked by it into a basket held to receive it.[94]

They were usually sold by the quart and good cocklers were said to obtain 'as much as £4 a week by their own and their children's earnings'.[95] This work involved not only constant bending and exposure to the winds from the sea but also hours spent walking to and from the banks. Mrs Butler of Flookborough described how her three girls were[96]

generally absent from home 10 or 12 hours together; in spring tides they have to walk five miles to the banks, which, with a mile to the shore, makes 12 miles going and returning, besides cockling for five hours. They are a bit tired when they come home, and are quite ready for a meal; they have nothing when on the sands but a piece of bread, of which they eat a little now and then just to keep off hunger. It is a slavish life, but what are poor people to do? My girls went to the infant school until they were 8, but they have not been to any school since; they cannot read.

Like the children and women who worked in agricultural gangs, the cocklers had the reputation of being rough and their language obscene, to such a degree that 'respectable persons shrink from coming within hearing of their language or observation of their manners'.[97] The Rev. T. Rigg, incumbent of Flookborough, said:[98]

The children employed go upon the sands as young as 7 or 8, consequently they get no education whatever, rarely even going to the infant school. The occupation is continuous throughout the year. One of the principal cocklers of this place has seven children of from 8 to 17 years of age, not one of whom has received any education. The children and young persons engaged in this business are in a very demoralized condition; they never enter a place of worship, and their language when idling about the streets is disgusting. At 14 boys and girls become so independent that they often leave their parents and lodge with strangers, spending their earnings in drunkenness,

even at that early age. It is very desirable that some
restriction should be imposed by law on the age at which
children are allowed to cockle. I think none should be
allowed to go before 11 years of age. Taking the eight or
nine villages on the shores of Morecambe Bay there must be
several hundreds of children who, owing to this cockling
business, are growing up in a state of heathenism. Quite
as much necessity exists for putting this system under
regulation as in the agricultural gangs of which I have
read. Boys, girls, young men, and women are out for hours
together on the sands without the slightest control, and the
results to morality may be imagined.

Another kind of beach work was done by the 'bait girls'.
A. J. Munby came to know them at Filey, in Yorkshire,
and he has a description of them in his diary on 18 October
1868. In a previous year he had presented a bait girl called
Molly Nettleton with a rope of '24 fathoms' to use for reaching
the rocks below the cliff face where the bait was obtained; now
he looked for her but at first in vain:[99]

> Towards eleven o'clock, however, two bait girls appeared
> near the foot of the cliff, striding and stooping among the
> wet seaweed. Both were breeched up to the knee: and she,
> the tall one with the long legs, was evidently Molly. At that
> height [he reckoned 250 feet] one could not hear their
> voices; but I saw them clamber up to the base of the rock,
> and there, Molly seized the rope, tried it with her own
> weight, and began to mount. Hand over hand, sticking her
> toes into the crevices of the chalk wall, she went up, as
> easily as one might walk upstairs; and having thus climbed
> some 50 feet, she turned round, and with her back to the
> cliff, worked her way along a level ledge that just
> supported her heels, to an overhanging point. There,
> stooping forward as coolly as possible, she hauled up her
> full basket and her fellow's . . . When the baskets came up,
> she just loosened them, and hoisted them up, with one
> hand, upon a broader ledge above her head: then grasping
> the rope again, she climbed up to it, and sat down . . .

Variations on the gang system occurred in other parts of the
country. In Pershore in Worcestershire for instance women with

children were employed as follows. During the months of April
and May they would do first the weeding and then the tying
and thinning out of the vegetables. Then during the fruit
harvests they would be hired to pick currants, gooseberries,
raspberries, salad, vegetables and plums. They would go
around from one parish to another working in the gardens
and orchards at fruit- and vegetable-picking. (They were
particularly in demand for picking currants as men were
thought too clumsy.) For this type of work young children were
not hired independently, but went with an adult: each-woman
would take her own basket and into this she and her children
would put the fruit, and she would be paid for the work that
all had done. Likewise in Devon, Essex, Somerset and the
Home Counties, the same yearly ritual would be carried out
offering employment not only to regular female agricultural
workers, but to mothers who might not normally have worked,
or who could not work where their children would be excluded,
and also to straw-plaiters who wanted a break from the tedium
of plaiting.[100]

Pea-picking and bean-picking also gave rise to an enormous
demand for labour, much of which was supplied by women
and children, hired individually or as part of family groups.
Hundreds of workers were hired every season in Essex,
Worcestershire, Leicestershire and Somerset, where peas and
beans were major crops. A witness at Worksop, Nottinghamshire, told the Agricultural Employment Commissioners: 'I
employ sometimes as many as 400 to 500 women and children
in pea-pulling at once. They work in families, each separate.'[101]
Pea-pickers spent hours stooping or kneeling collecting the
pods into an apron and then tipping them into sacks; for this
they were paid by quantity – by the peck or the pot or the bag.
In the West Riding it was reported that girls could pick seven
pecks a day at 1d. a peck.[102] In Harvington, Worcestershire, the
peas were picked by women, children, and men from Evesham
and Alcester. 'They are brought into the parish in large carts
about 5 o'clock in the morning.'[103] Gangs were often hired
directly – whole families together – by the person who had
bought the unpicked peas, as a lot from the farmer.

In Biggleswade the growing of onions supplied women and
children with employment peeling them; one man at Sandy
'sometimes has 200 to 300'.[104] In Byfleet, in Surrey, the market

gardens supplied winter employment at washing carrots, an unpopular job as it caused a great deal of rheumatism.

London was fringed with market gardens where women worked. A. J. Munby often noted seeing them from trains. In July 1862, returning from Dartford, he saw gangs of[105]

> strong women . . . leaving work at the market gardens about New Cross & turnip fields in the Plumstead Marshes, as we passed, from 6 o'clock to 6.30. It was refreshing to see them rising from their knees in the furrows where they had crawled nearly the whole day, & trooping to the roads, wheeling empty barrows or striding along with their fustian jackets over their arms.

Or again, going to Greenwich on Whit Monday 1865,[106]

> . . . although this is a holiday I saw several large gangs of female labourers at work in the market gardens down the line; some going to and fro with large baskets on their heads, but most of them on their knees in the loam, moving on all fours across the field.

In Kent the hop gardens provided much work for women and girls at a variety of jobs throughout the year, but the most were employed during the tying of the hops, which took place in the weeks between late April and early June. Poling, the sticking of poles into the ground for the bine to climb, was regarded as men's work, though women and children assisted them to place the poles correctly. But tying the bines to the poles was considered women's work, because of the dexterity it required. According to the *Agricultural Gazette* of 1874,[107]

> Tying hops is very pleasant work for women when the weather is good: they earn from 1s. 6d. to 2s. per day at this work, which requires dexterity in fastening the rushes around the tender heads of the bines, not too tight to stop their progress upwards, nor too loose as to allow them to slip back again; and a good deal of judgement and discrimination in selecting the best and most promising bines to tie up, and in rejecting large, rank, coarse, bines which are usually more or less unfruitful.

Mrs L. Gilbert (who was first taken into a hop field in 1887 at the age of three) recalls in *Old Days in the Kent Hop Gardens*

how 'At hop-tying time we would get our rushes from the oast
and put them to soak all night in water and then take as many
as we thought we would need for the day to the farm in a
sack.' In the gardens 'the hops were marked out in cants. When
there were only two poles to a hill we tied four bines round each
pole clockwise, with the rushes in our "lap bags".'[108] Tying
work would last well into June, since each bine required further
tying as it grew up the pole, and had to be checked regularly to
see if it needed more binding. Women often took work by the
acre, or by some other unit of area; in 1850 a writer in the
Morning Chronicle reported that '9s. to 10s. an acre' was being
paid them in the area of Tonbridge, while around Maidstone
'the wages have been still higher – as much as 11s. and 12s. per
acre'. According to this writer, women with a little assistance
could tie from two to two and a half acres per week.[109] Day
work was also common. Here is an extract from the wage book
of a Kent farm for 21 June 1850:[110]

Mrs Hyde Laddertying 5 days		5–0
Edmeads 5 do		5–0
Kitchenham 5 do		5–0
T. Reader 5 do		5–0
Comber 3½ do		3–6
Ashby 3 do		3–0

These payments work out at one shilling a day: a considerably
lower rate than those given in the *Morning Chronicle* article.

It was reckoned in 1868 that during the harvesting of the
hops four pickers were needed for every one of the 41,000 acres
of hops grown in Kent.[111] Most of the pickers were women and
children. Some were the wives and children of labourers, the
rest either were local pickers hired 'through an agent in each
town'[112] or through a local subcontractor (often herself a
woman), or else 'immigrants' – Irish workers, or Londoners from
the East End. The *Morning Chronicle* maintained that as far as
Farnham and Maidstone were concerned, 'the entire population
which converges upon them about the beginning of September
is to a great extent, drawn from the surrounding towns and
parishes'.[113]

Picking the hops usually took three to five weeks, at the end
of August and in September, during which time whole families
would inhabit the fields, many of them making the hop garden

their home for the duration: there they would eat, sleep, work, and live. Since pay was by the bushel (or by the tally, which was an agreed number of bushels at an agreed rate, e.g., 1*s.* for five bushels), even the smallest contribution helped to fill the bin in which the family's hops were measured, and added to their earnings. It was a family affair: you might 'frequently find a mother assisted by a whole family, composed of five or six children, and varying from those who are bordering on manhood to the infant who is rolled in a shawl or a sack and laid upon the ground at its mother's feet'.[114]

In Kent, the hop harvest followed the corn harvest, so families had two 'field days' in which to earn the extra money 'to buy clothing and to pay their Christmas bills'.[115] Gloucestershire women around Crosshall were less fortunate: there the teazle harvest and the corn harvest were concurrent, so they could not work at both. In Somerset, in the Porlock district, it was reckoned that there were five harvests,[116]

> . . . which last from June to November, hay, whort, corn,
> acorn, apple. Women and children nearly all turn out for
> the whort harvest; whortleberries, for which they get
> 3*d.* a quart, are, as well as acorns, a great source of
> income in this parish.

Families would go out collecting acorns which they sold primarily to farmers for their pigs, or sometimes to the acorn buyer who came round the village. (In the same way, elderberry-flower vans used to come to our village, Ivinghoe Aston, when we children, and occasionally parents, could go out into the woods and pick bags of the flower which would be weighed and then so much paid out. For us it was a good way of collecting pocket money. Nineteenth-century children would be helping to earn their keep.)

Another form of seasonal gang work was withy or osier peeling. This involved cutting, stacking, and binding the willow rods, and then removing their bark, and was practised on Sedgemoor (in Somerset), along the banks of the Thames, in South Derbyshire and in Lincolnshire – wherever willows grew well. At Church Broughton in south Derbyshire, there were a tremendous number of willows grown for osier, and the peeling was done largely by women and children, as an employer described to the Agricultural Employment Commissioners:[117]

I have osier beds on the banks of the Dove, at Etwall and Eggington; the peeling season is from the end of April to the beginning or middle of June; in the peeling season I employ all the hands I can get, women and children, mothers bring their babies in cradles with them, whole families work together, the mother breaks the peel (draws the willow through a break), and the children peel. They do it by the bundle, some families will earn 4s. or 5s. a week.

In Lincolnshire gangs of 100 children (or sometimes even up to 250) were hired for this work; but more often the children were employed along with a parent, or other adult relative, and the work was paid jointly as piecework, so much per bundle.[118] The peel was used to tie the bundles, and also it was dried and used for kindling. The osiers were used for basket-weaving – another industry in which women's and children's labour was important.[119]

A frequent charge made against the gang system was that the herding together of younger children and older people of both sexes was '. . . very pernicious to their moral principles and conduct'; '. . . the interference to education', and the '. . . subjection of young children to an excessive amount of labour and other hardships' were also mentioned.[120] Bad discourse, bawdyism, swearing, etc., were said to be characteristic of the gangs; younger members were exposed to contamination by the older: 'young Irish women and English girls who have lost their characters'.[121] Certainly the gangs did not encourage the maintenance of 'modesty' and 'morality' as defined by Victorians. To start with, the girls' mode of dress, for most agricultural employments, could not meet 'ladylike' standards. Cockling was considered demoralizing because 'the women and girls turn up their dresses to their waists, and walk about with their legs bare'.[122] There was similar cause for complaint in field work. The rector of Ingoldthorpe complained that 'the dress of the women is to a certain extent almost of necessity immodest. When the crops are wet they tuck up their dresses between the legs, often leaving the legs much exposed.' Still worse,[123]

The long absence and distance from home often render it necessary that the women should attend to the calls of nature, and this they frequently do in the presence of lads, boys and men. Thus a girl or woman who is when she first joins these gangs modest and decent gradually loses her modesty.

Obviously whilst working in the Fens, and similar flat open countryside without bushes or hedges to shelter behind, it was still necessary to answer the calls of nature even at the price of abandoning what their betters called 'decency', and even if there resulted '. . . a loss of natural female delicacy which is, at least, some safeguard of morality'.[124] Gangs were also censured for the misconduct which allegedly took place whilst going to and from their place of employment. 'Injurious as work in the fields in the public gangs is to female delicacy and morality, more injury arises to both during the times of going to and returning from work.'[125] The Children's Employment Commission therefore recommended that there be segregated gangs and proper supervision of the workers to and from work.

The culture of the gangs shocked the vicars, church people and gentlefolk interviewed by the Children's Employment Commissioners; there were some who admitted such shrinking from the members of gangs that they would not 'venture to speak or scarcely to look at them, without the risk of being shocked'.[126] Dr H. J. Hunter in his report on rural housing was also shocked.[127]

These gangs will sometimes travel many miles from their own village, they are to be met morning and evening on the roads, dressed in short petticoats with suitable coats and boots, and sometimes trousers, looking wonderfully strong and healthy, but tainted with a customary immorality and heedless of the fatal results which their love of this busy and independent life is bringing on their unfortunate offspring who are pining at home.

What constituted immorality in his sense was the rugged look that these women would have had from working in the fields in all weathers. Pale skins, soft hands and flimsy clothes – these constituted morality, effectively underwriting the Victorian male's masterful vision of himself.

4 Rural industries

Where females did not actively (or regularly) participate in agricultural labour they did other work, for instance in village industries. Most of these industries were particular to their locality and related to local resources. They were many and various: there was basket-making, for example, where osiers were grown (in Sedgemoor and along the Trent and the Thames); net-braiding in the fishing villages on the southern and south-eastern coasts; in the hop countries pole-shaving, the mending and making of the poles, and the cutting up of rags for hop manure; bark-peeling in the counties of Hampshire, Berkshire and Worcestershire (but also in other woodland areas); lace-making in the south Midlands, Bedfordshire, Northamptonshire and Devon; straw-plaiting in Buckinghamshire, Bedfordshire, Hertfordshire and Essex; button-holing, bead work, knitting, slop work, cottage weaving in many parts of the country; turf-stacking in parts of Somersetshire; and so on in an endless list. Even when children had no major part to play in these processes, their help at odd moments or in preparation or finishing, or running errands was a contribution often of substantial value. As already mentioned, the willow provided much employment for women and children in its harvesting and its peeling. In the next stage, they would weave the rods into baskets of diverse types. In Old Brentford, for instance, in Essex on the Thames, they made punnets for the local market gardens;[128] baskets of all sizes for carrying fruit, vegetables and hops; and cradles and bassinettes. The women who went fruit-gathering in the summer would provide their own collecting baskets and these too would be made from possibly willow, or rushes. Jefferies, in *Hodge and His Masters*, describing the process of growing and harvesting and making up the willow into baskets, remarked that 'large quantities of willow, too, are worked up unpeeled into hampers of all kinds'.[129]

Children would also be employed in brick fields – they would run barefoot up and down the clay until it was like a paste and thus ready for brickmaking. 'Puggers' feet' were so sensitive after a time that they could feel even the smallest lump submerged in the clay. Brickmaking was often family work, with the men and women moulding the clay, and the children providing the clay paste.[130] Family work at brickmaking had not disappeared by the early years of the twentieth century: Mrs Quick, who was born in 1889, went to work in a brick field when she was fourteen.[131]

> I lived in a little village called Iver, Bucks. My first job was working in the Brickfields. I had to work from six in the morning, till six at night, we had half hour for breakfast, ½ hour for dinner and ½ hour for tea. My father was the moulder, and as he made the bricks I had to move them away and put them on a barrow, and when the barrow was full I had to sand them, and then a man would come and take it away, and then I would push another in and keep doing it all day, my poor back at the end of the day was dreadful but I stuck it for the time they were making them, I had nine shillings a week, I gave my mother 8/6 and had sixpence myself.

In the 1860s the Agricultural Employment Commissioners found children of six and seven thus employed at Fawlett in Somerset.[132]

Forests and woods provided numerous forms of employment at the woodland crafts – hurdle-making, chair-making (in beech country), brush-making, besom-making. The commissioners were told that around the village of Farnsfield in Nottingham there were fifteen families making their living from besom-making. In parts of Herefordshire there was to be a good deal of money earned by women and children in the stripping of bark from oak trees – 'rinding', as it was called sometimes. Men would cut down the trees and then the women and children would commence the stripping. The usual time of the year for this was around April and May, but whenever there was a 'fall of oak' women and children would be called in. After the stripping, the bark was collected and stacked (this again employed many children) before being sent off for use in tanning factories. In Martley in Worcestershire, women used to strip bark off poles and then dip them in creosote.[133] Marty South in *The Woodlanders*, who 'turned her hand to anything', worked at bark-peeling, helped with planting trees, and chopped and split hazel branches to make thatching spars, a skilled job which in her village was generally done by men.[134]

On the coast in the fishing villages net-braiding was an important form of work for girls and women. As a fisherman boatowner in Yarmouth told the *Morning Chronicle* in 1850, 'It costs me a hundred pounds a season for mending the nets of my boats . . . there's Mr Dogfish, he bites 'em to pieces, and soon wears 'em up.'[135] Sometimes the nets were made by the wives and daughters of the fishermen but[136]

> at other times girls and children are hired for the purpose. A girl if she works early and late, can work off about two skeins a day. In doing so her fingers fly as nimbly as do those of a lace worker over her cushion.

In the West Country the twine from which the nets were made was generally obtained from Bridport in Dorset. It was received in parcels containing twelve large skeins and there were seven parcels to make a pilchard or herring net. Even as far away as Yarmouth, fishermen obtained the twine for nets from Bridport; and there too it was the women and children who braided the nets into the required meshes, as well as mending them when they were ripped or torn.[137] In Cornwall and in East Anglia, according to these same *Morning Chronicle* articles, women were also employed in carrying the fish from the boats to the cellars, and in salting them, and splitting them for curing. In Lancashire very young children were employed[138]

> for the greater part of the day in picking shrimps. You may see in many houses mere infants seated at a table and thus employed for hours together. The shrimps are prepared for potting or tea parties, and children 4 years old can earn in this way 6*d*. or 9*d*. a day.

In the hop fields of Kent, Worcestershire, Herefordshire and Surrey, besides being involved in the tying and harvesting of the hops, women did jobs such as shaving poles for tying, chopping rags for manure, mending and making of hop pockets, mending of 'pokes' and bin cloths, and mending sacks. ('Pokes', which usually held 10 bushels, were used to convey the hops from the bins into which they were picked to the kilns, where they were dried; after drying they were pressed into bags called hop pockets.)[139] So, for example, records from the Peel Estate, in Kent, show[140]

August 8th, 1851
    Mrs Harris mending Pokes – 5 days   5s.   0d.
    Mrs Sears   ,,   ,,   ,,   5s.   0d.
    Mrs Bates   ,,   ,,   ,,   5s.   0d.

August 6th, 1852
    Mrs Harris 5 days mending bin cloths   5s.   0d.
    Mrs Bates   ,,   ,,   ,,   ,,   5s.   0d.
    Mrs Sears   ,,   ,,   ,,   ,,   5s.   0d.

In the Union of Hailsham in Sussex, young girls and boys were hired for pole-shaving during the winter months for which they were paid 5d. or 6d. per 100 poles.[141] Records from the Peel Estate also show this to be the work of women, helped by 'others' who are almost certainly girls.[142]

April 26th, 1850
    Mrs Wenham & ors. shaving 2000 12 ft poles   10s.
May 3rd 1850
    Mrs Wenham & ors. shaving 1187 12 ft poles   5s.   10½d.
                     500 14 ft poles   3s.   4d.
April 4th, 1851
    Mrs Wenham & ors. shaving poles   3s.   0d.
April 11th, 1851
    Kitty Tree shaving 500 14 ft poles   3s.   4d.

There was also the work of chopping up rags for manure. The ground for hops had to be prepared before February and manuring it formed a very important part of the procedure. The *Morning Chronicle* of 30 January 1850 describes the process:[143]

> For this purpose rags and sprats are used, and, in the absence of these, ordinary manure . . . When rags are used, they are generally woollen ones, which, being composed of animal matter, make a very good manure. Before being used they are chopped very small upon a block, in which state they are fit for use . . . The rags are also generally known as 'hospital rags', being in fact, the refuse of the metropolitan and other hospitals . . . When sprats are used, they are spread over the land to decompose upon it.

This work is shown in the Peel Estate records too:[144]

October 31st, 1851
  Mrs Comber & ors. cutting 7tons-0cwt-2qrt-8lbs at
                10/- per ton – £3. 10. 3½d.
January 16th, 1852
  Mrs Apps & ors. cutting rags – £3. 10. 0d.

Some rural industries were not directly connected with the
local agriculture. The Inspectors of Factories' report for the half
year ending 30 April 1874, lists as handicrafts to be found to a
large extent in villages: pillow-lace-making, lace-clipping,
chair-making, brickmaking, straw-plait-making, boot- and
shoe-making, winding for hosiery, seaming for hosiery:[145] to
this list could be added knitting and gloving and slop work.
Gloving was particularly important in Somersetshire though it
was practised elsewhere, for instance, in Oxfordshire. Women
and girls engaged in gloving did not work in the fields because
rough hands made gloving difficult. Some gloves – kid ones
usually – were made with the aid of a machine: it held the glove
in a vice, and had a 'row of little holes close together, through
which the needle passes, and which keeps the stitches regular'.[146]
Girls were 'learners' for twelve months – sometimes for the
first three they were not paid anything, after that they would
be given some form of wage but 'overlooked'. In the Yeovil
district they would commonly start work in the home of an
agent or overlooker; then at about the age of fourteen or
fifteen they would be allowed to work at home. The closeness
of the work, the shining of the brass machine, and the unchang-
ing position were not conducive to good health – bad eyesight
and stooping shoulders often resulted besides the illnesses
caused by sitting in a stuffy room for hours on end. In Somerset
the age for starting such work was about eight or nine, but
some commenced such employment earlier, like[147]

Emmeline Cox, Somerton, age 8. – began to make gloves
at 5. When began could make one pair a day, now can
make two. Gets a halfpenny a pair, small gloves . . . Get
tired gloving. Work from 7 in the morning till 8 at night.
Not with a machine.

The money paid for kid gloves was better than for other sorts
of gloves but 'a girl working hard all day and every day' could
not expect to earn more than 4s. a week.[148] Earnings depended

on the market, the ability of the glover, the type of material used and how much time was given to it. Sometimes the gloves were knitted as in the area of Blandford in Dorset and Ringwood in Hampshire. Ringwood gloves were in a particular style, and well known. At Stourpaine it was reported, 'There is a great deal of knitting and gloving done in the parish, which is a great hindrance to the school . . .'[149]

The Agricultural Employment Commissioners complained that the glovers' morality was very low and they were 'reckoned of rather easy virtue'.[150] The Rev. Mr Salmon of Martock remarked about the character of gloving girls:[151]

> They grow up in a state of deplorable ignorance, very few of them being able to write their own names. At an early age they become independent of their parents and submit to no control, even when it is exercised judiciously. The evil-disposed at once go out to lodge, if their parents will not allow them to keep late hours; their morality is very low, their ignorance excessive, and their language and behaviour often very rough and coarse. Sunday schools do a little for the best of them, but the roughest will not attend them, as they are ashamed of their utter ignorance, and impatient of any control.

Commissioner Boyle believed that the immorality of the gloving girls, in the gloving part of Somerset, was higher than anywhere else in the county. He comments:[152]

> In the purely agricultural districts girls go out to farm service, and few are at home after thirteen or fourteen years of age; in this district few go out to service; they like the independence of gloving, and either they stay at home and crowd the cottage or go out to lodge, and worse forms of immorality result. I was surprised at hearing from many competent witnesses that the women who work in the fields bear a higher character, as a rule, than either the glovers or the factory hands.

Cottage looms and sewing machines provided means of earning a few shillings at home, and also of course all kinds of sewing work. In Dorset, making buttons (i.e. 'thread buttons worked by hand on to a ring of brass wire') survived;[153] another possibility was the sewing of beads on to silk dresses.

In Hambridge in Somerset the Agricultural Employment Commissioners were told that some thirty to forty girls of eight to twelve were sitting all day doing button-holing, and thus derived no schooling.[154]

Slop work – the sewing together of pre-cut out materials (usually cheap material) – was done in some homes near the bigger towns but this did not become such a large industry until later in the nineteenth century.

Straw-plaiting was carried on in most rural counties, but the main centres were in Bedfordshire, Buckinghamshire and Hertfordshire, where the straw was of a superior quality and more pliable for plaiting. Grasses, rushes, and straw, were also sometimes used for plaiting and making bands; but information on straw-plaiting is easier to come by. In Hertfordshire, wrote Edwin Grey, 'The cottage industry of straw plaiting played a very important part in the village life.' There were many varieties of plait. Edwin Grey recorded that in his village, 'The proficient women plaiters made several beautiful varieties: plain, single-splint, pearl, bird's-eye, whipcord'[155] and so on. Sometimes an area would become known for a particular type or types of plait. Hitchin was known for its broad twist, Ivinghoe, where I once lived, for its narrow twist, for 'rustic', and for mixed coloured plait.[156]

In the plaiting districts straw-plaiting was a lifelong occupation. In order to be a good plaiter, it was considered that a child must start young and the ages of three or four were not considered too young. An article in the *Morning Chronicle* of 5 April 1850 quotes a young woman of already long experience:[157]

> I learned to plait at the straw school. I was sent there when I was three years old – that's sixteen years ago – and I used to get a penny a day, and the missus used to have the plait and find us with straw.

Edwin Grey also knew someone who had started young, and told him how

> she had her first plaiting lesson when only three years old; she was given three or four splints of straw and was taught how to twist them under and over, . . . to the words and tune of a little song 'under one and over two, pull it tight and that will do.'

By the age of four 'she had become so advanced in the art that she was able to earn 1*s*. 6*d*. per week by plaiting'.[158] At Houghton Regis in 1864, Assistant Commissioner J. E. White was shown Lizzie Ibbins there, 'who is between 2 and 3 years old, . . . clipping some plait made by her sister elsewhere'.[159]

Children in these districts, before the Education Act of 1870, were often sent to plaiting schools. Such schools would be an individual enterprise, set up by some commercially-minded or impoverished village 'dame' as a little source of income, perhaps to keep her off the parish. Apart from plaiting, the only instruction took the form of learning a hymn to alleviate the boredom of sitting for hours with nothing to occupy the mind but plenty to occupy the fingers; or there was the reading, or the learning to read of verses of the Testament. Edwin Grey recollects, 'I never knew (though there may have been) any of these plaiting schools where writing or arithmetic was taught, probably for the simple reason that these old ladies knew nothing of it themselves.'[160]

This view is held by many writing on plaiting schools of the time. A Miss Vaughan who had lived in Harpenden for thirty-three years maintained in 1893 that plaiting schools were really 'workshops' with a mere fifteen minutes a day being devoted to 'reading in the Testament'.[161] Parents, it was said, preferred to send their children to this type of school, because here they could earn money to help out the family finances. Often there were no other schools in the vicinity.[162]

On the opposite side of Dunstable I visited the villages of Silsworth, Stanbride, and Egginton; there is no school in any of these villages, but I visited seven straw plait schools and found 85 children under 13 years of age working in them. I saw at least 20 to 30 others in the lanes and at the doors of cottages.

Plait schools were very crowded. As many little bodies as possible would be crammed into the space of a single cottage room. 'They work in any numbers, from 5 or 10 to 50 of them, sitting on little benches or stools or anywhere . . .'[163] Mr White of the Children's Employment Commission found forty children and their teacher huddled together in a room measuring 11 feet 2 inches by 10 feet 8 inches by 7 feet 9 inches.[164] A detailed report by one of the Sub-Inspectors of Factories runs as follows. 'February 17th, [1868] – Leighton Buzzard, John Parratt, straw plaiter. Room in a cottage house. 34 children of from 3 to 16 years of age. Room hot and offensive . . .'[165] The children would often have to sit in stooped, cramped positions, both because of their numbers and because of the work itself.[166]

> A bundle of straw is placed under the left armpit from which three or four straws are taken, and placed in the mouth to be moistened by the saliva; the fingers being all the time engaged in plaiting, the head is bent forward each time a new straw is required, which recurs constantly . . . constant bending of the head and cramped position of the left arm, to say nothing of the injury done by the constant habit of holding dyed straws in the mouth.

According to a writer in *Once a Week*, in 1865, the children were so crowded into a room that it was impossible to light a fire 'so they have coal or wood in earthen or even tin pots, which they call "dicky pots" ', which they would take with them to their places of work.[167] Under these conditions it is not surprising that investigators often commented on the stuffy atmosphere; nor can confinement in the close crowded rooms all day have been conducive to good health. They would work from 8.30 or 9 in the morning until about 4 p.m.; then some children would return at 5 and work until 8.30 or 9 alongside others who had worked elsewhere and in the evening came to earn a little more.

The children in plait schools were set a task to complete – so many yards of straw. If the child had not finished her quota she would have to stay until it was done and so in the following recollection Edwin Grey claimed to have known 'workers whose fingers become quite sore and bleeding through working so hard to get the required yards of plait finished'.[168] There are reports too of children being threatened with the cane should they for a moment falter or lose interest in their work, for instance, in a Factory Inspector's Report in 1871[169] and in an article in *Good Words* in 1891.[170] 2d. or 3d. a week was paid to the mistress/master for the instruction, though sometimes the straw was bought by the mistress and the child would receive a penny for making it up, or the parent would supply the straw and would sell it when made up. The younger children would commence with the 'Dunstable twist' which was made with whole straws, less fragile than the split ones used for the finer kinds of work to which they would subsequently graduate. Splitting was done with a little instrument called the chine (or, in some places, 'cheen'), which could split the whole straw into much finer splints, to the number required for a particular plait. Five-straw, seven-straw, or even twenty-straw plaits were made. The *Morning Chronicle* commissioner in 1850 talked to a young woman doing a twenty-straw plait, for which she hoped to get 5s. 6d. a score.[171]

But plaiting also took place outside the schools: it could be done sitting on doorstep or wall, or strolling along, and it was perfectly compatible with conversation. Edwin Grey was told how one might 'come across a lassie and her lad sitting on a stile both plaiting'.[172] And the *Morning Chronicle* correspondent wrote of these districts 'that you can scarcely meet a child walking along the road that is not engaged in plaiting'.[173]

In some of the parochial schools, to encourage attendance, the teachers would allow plaiting to be done on several afternoons during the school hours, though instruction in it was not given. This was happening for instance at Henny National School in Essex:[174]

> November 23rd, 1863
>   Straw plaiting by Boys and Girls at 3.00
> November 25th, 1863
>   Straw plaiting at 3.00. Writing by those who have no
>   straw at 3.00.

Lace-making, a comparable cottage industry, was also learnt in schools. 'Mrs Howe, Turvey, has a lace school. 22 girls at work at present; has 32 when she's full; youngest girl 7, average age 11. They work from 7 a.m. till 12 noon, and from 1 p.m. until 5 p.m., or till they finish their task, sometimes 7 or 8 p.m.'[175] In Devon, Buckinghamshire, and Bedfordshire, it was generally 'pillow lace' that was made, as J. L. Green describes:[176]

> It is a process by which lace is made on a round cushion of about twelve inches to twenty four inches in diameter. This cushion is called a pillow, hence the term 'pillow' lace. On the pillow are a large number of pins, these being used to

form the pattern of the lace required to be made. The threads are twisted around the pins, and across one another in a dexterous manner. One end of each thread is fastened to the pillow, the other end being wound round the top of a bobbin.

The children were set to do so many score pins an hour. Hand manufacture of lace was carried on in a similar way to plaiting, though undermined increasingly by the machine-made lace of Nottingham. It was often much worn by fashionable ladies, and decorated their clothes, their handkerchiefs, neck ties, cap strings and such. Lace-making by hand was very skilled and very slow: one worker quoted in a *Morning Chronicle* article told how:

I've been making lace for a long while as wide as my finger nails, and it takes between sixty and seventy stitches to make six head-pins; the rest of it is point ground, but it's very thick and it takes me twelve hours a working very hard indeed to make a yard of it . . . I get 4*d*. a yard for it.

Working during daylight hours at the lace school, a child would earn 6*d*. a week, but 'you pays twopence ha'penny to the missus for larning of them'.[177]

Plaiting was a major home industry. The straw would be obtained in various ways: sometimes from retailers who before it was harvested would buy it direct from the farmer, thus ensuring careful cutting; or again the plaiters could obtain it straight from the farmer after it had been cut, but the straws then had to be cut to length and sometimes peeled; or they could be bought ready cut from the dealers who came round and bought the made-up plait; or from the local store, which might keep a stack of straw and buy the plait when it was made up. In Bowling Alley, a village in Edwin Grey's book, not far from St Albans, it was the custom for Jackie Saunders who ran the local store to buy the plait when it was made up, and in return straw and goods would be given though no actual money changed hands.[178] Mrs Gilbey of Weathersfield in Essex remembers when the plait was done in her home.[179]

As a child I remember how the straw plait was done in the home. my mother used to walk about three miles to a

farm, the Broad Farm, to buy a large bundle of straw.
that the farmer had picked out for making into plait then
mother would clip it into short lengths and tie it in small
bunches & put it in a box with some Brimstone & light it
& close the box. this was called stoving it, which would
make it White. then the straw would be split up with a
small Engine. there were different size engines to split the
straw the size it was wanted, then mother, and my Sister
& Brothers would start to make the Plait. this was done in
length at twenty yards. then put on a board to straighten
it out. there were a good many of these lengths made
during the week on Saturdays Mother & all the Neighbours
would come to Weathersfield where a man would buy it to
be made into Hats. but the Plait is a thing of the past now
it was quite an Essex Industry

Many of the women preferred to go into the plaiting markets
to buy and sell their plait because once they were there they
could look round the shops and have a greater variety of
products to buy. It was not an easy day out, and it might mean
walking a great many miles there and back in all weathers. But
before market day there was a lot that had to be done to the
straw. After, and sometimes before, it was plaited it would be
put through a little mangle to flatten it out and remove any
curls that might be in the plait.[180] If the mangle was not
available in the home of the labourer then it might be found in
the local plaiting mistress's home. After this had been done, the
plait was clipped of any jagged ends jutting out and made
smooth. It was then measured and put into the 'brimstone box'
to be steam bleached, after which it presented a much
brighter colour. For this stage of the proceedings a smouldering
coal from the fire would be placed on a saucer in the middle of
the box containing the plait, then a piece of brimstone put on it,
the box lid put on and the entire thing covered up and left for
some hours.[181] Later the bleached plait would be taken out
and looped into a bag, and the journey to the plaiting market
would take place next morning. The mother, sometimes
accompanied by the children, would start out for the market
very early in the morning in order to be there when the hand-
bell announced (at 8 o'clock in summer, 9 o'clock in winter)
the start of the market.[182]

In Luton the market day was Monday. On arriving at the
market the women would take their stand along the pavements
of the market street, unloose their bags, and sling the looped
plait over their arms. Then they would stand waiting for
buyers, with their arms held 'along the front of the body with
the linked plait hanging down from them (this was for easier
inspection by the buyers) . . .'[183]

The markets were alive with the carts of straw being brought
in and the bags and carts of plait being taken to the plait
warehouses for transporting to factories to be made up into
hats, bonnets, etc. – locally and in London. Haggling would
commence the moment the bell rang, different twists and
qualities fetched different prices, and there were also shifts
from week to week in prices. The woman had to stand out
for the best bargain. Then there was the straw to be bought
for the next week's plaiting and a round of the dealers to be
made, and perhaps – if she had made a good sale – household
goods to be bought at the stalls. Finally there was the long
journey home on foot. Often a village middlewoman did all
this, fetching the straw to the local cottagers and carrying
their finished product away to market; she might charge for
her services, or blossom out into a full sub-contractor.

Luton, as well as being a market town, was also a centre
for the manufacture of straw hats, and this attracted 'an
influx of female labour from the neighbouring villages'.[184]
Hitchin, another market centre, harboured many plaiters in
its back streets, as James Greenwood described in his book
On Tramp.[185]

Dozens and dozens of them, little girls and big girls,
buxom matrons and dames bent and grey, spick-and-span-
looking as the cotton print dresses and natty shoulder
shawl, and twinkling earrings, and smoothed hair could
make them; plaiting away, every one of them, as though
their very lives depended on it, with hanks and loops of the
manufactured outside festooning their neck, or worn
sash-wise across their shoulders and with a sheaf of raw
material pinned at their side. They moved amongst the
slipshod and tattered men and lads, laughing and larking,
but never for a moment staying the movement of their
nimble fingers.

Naturally whilst girls were employed in such work, they did not spend their time at school or preparing for wifely duties or for domestic service. Straw plaiting was condemned as a bad influence by both the Newcastle Commission of 1861, and the Agricultural Employment Commission of 1867–9:[186]

> The great want of chastity amongst the plait girls probably arises from the early age at which, when plait is good, the girls become independent of their parents, and often leave their homes, and from the fact that male and female plaiters go about the lanes together in summer engaged in work which has not even the wholesome corrective of more or less physical exhaustion.

(Even Munby had heard that 'The St. Alban's young women, who are all straw plaiters, have a very bad reputation'.[187]) Their financial independence was one factor responsible for this bad reputation: it was assumed to be incompatible with a decent subservience to men. And the fact that plaiting could be carried on while walking around, even away from the home, was supposed to make illicit escapades in the fields inevitable.

A rather different view emerges from the detailed account given by the *Morning Chronicle* correspondent. He argued that straw plait employment relieved

> to a great extent the pressure which would otherwise fall on the agricultural labourer . . . were it not for the assistance which he obtains from the earnings of his family at the straw plait, his condition would not be one jot better than the great majority of his brother labourers in other counties.

He also describes a use of such earnings which does not figure in the commissioners' reports. He found at one cottage a young woman working a twenty-straw plait while at the same time

> deeply interested in a conversation . . . with a stout robust-looking young countryman, who was sitting near her, and who appeared in his turn far more deeply absorbed in the contemplation of his companion than with the intricacies of the seven-straw plait upon which he was engaged . . .

Her mother and her three sisters all worked at plaiting too; her father got 8s. a week 'at work on the farm'. She herself had never 'had plait out of hand for a month together' in the sixteen years she had been plaiting.[188]

'Sometimes I don't make more than 3s.; sometimes as much as 6s. a week. I've got a savings-bank book, but I'm going to draw it out in the spring,' said she – a blush at the same time stealing over her features. 'So am I, too,' said the young man . . . 'We're both a goin' to draw out, and we're a goin' to be married on the plait money. Ain't we, Mary! When I leaves off work at night I sets on to the plait; I am not very first-rate at it, but still I can manage to do a little bit. Well, I've yarned a couple of shillings or so every week for ever so long, and I've put it all away, and a little too besides, so I thinks we may get on middlin' like. Do'ant you, sir and do'ant you too?' again addressing himself to his affianced one, and accompanying his question by a salute, which, if not given in the most gentle manner, was at all events given heartily, and, but for the presence of a stranger, would doubtless have been favourably received.

5 Moralities

In all societies there is a predominant morality – a value system – which decrees the do's and don'ts of that particular society and by which its members are judged. This is not to say that all classes have the same value system – they don't – but each creates its own to suit its personal situation, ideals, etc. The Victorian and present-day societies are not exceptions to this rule.

The Victorian middle class used their own ideals as a yardstick to measure the failings of their inferiors. Theirs was the epitome of a 'moral' existence; and anything different from it was thought to be immoral or a symptom of immoralities to come. The middle-class female was expected to be an ornament in the drawing-room, wholly withdrawn from physical toil and the

world of men. Her children were given different roles according
to their age and sex. Each room in the house had a definite and
limited role assigned to it – the dining-room, the drawing-room,
the study, the boys' bedroom, the girls' bedroom, the nursery
and so on.

This segregation was a luxury that the working masses, with
their crowded cottages, could not afford (and did not even consider as desirable). This did not stop them from being labelled
as immoral. According to the *Saturday Review* of 3 April 1858
the 'promiscuous herding of children in their immature years'
was 'not an infrequent prelude to a life of harlotry', 'the cottage
bedroom was the first stop to the Haymarket'.[189] 'They live
like pigs', a witness told the Children's Employment Commission, '. . . great boys and girls, mothers and fathers, all sleeping
in one room in many instances'; the alleged 'boldness and
shamefulness' of the girls, according to this authority, was not
equalled by some of the 'worst parts of London'.[190] F. D. Longe,
one of the commissioners, had a similar anxiety; he thought
that the 'want of decent sleeping room' and the 'teaching
of bad parents' had an even worse effect on the character
of the girls than the bawdy influence of field work and the
gangs.[191]

The immorality was in the eyes of the beholders. Living in
close quarters doesn't make people immoral, any more than
living in a country house or a vicarage kept their betters chaste.
My counterparts were denounced by people too ignorant of the
labouring classes – and too protected in the comfort of their
drawing-rooms or studies, to see that there was another world,
another culture than their own. Living so much on top of one
another – as did the labourer's family – meant that adults and
children were **used** to living together, and that the sight of a
naked ankle did not stir them to immediate and lascivious
desire.

The woman field worker was anathema to the middle class,
the complete opposite to what they expected in their own
women – helplessness. But wages paid to the farm labourer
were too low for him to be the sole provider for his family;
women and children had to sell their labour, too, in order to
survive. Women were forced out of the isolation of the home
into the society of the field; and thus out of domesticity into
something more gregarious. In the eyes of clergymen and

commissioners this was unwomanly, and their constant theme
was that field labour did irreparable damage to the female
character. Their work role was in conflict with the moral one
prescribed for them. They were too independent, too free.

It was a dominant fear that heavy physical work would make
girls unsuitable for their future roles of wife and mother; and
that the 'liberty' of the fields would disqualify them from
employment as domestic servants. The fact that they might be
injured or crippled at such work was not the issue. Women who
worked in the fields were accused of neglecting their homes, their
children, their husbands. 'Loss of evening comfort to the
husband' and 'loss of female refinement' are just two examples
of this abuse. Not only did fieldwork ' . . . almost unsex a
woman', making her rough, coarse, clumsy, masculine; but it
generated 'a further very pregnant social mischief by unfitting
or indisposing her for a woman's proper duties at home'.[192]
Their independence of their menfolk was another fear which
was made quite explicit.[193]

> That which seems most to lower the moral or decent tone
> of the peasant girls [wrote Dr Julian Hunter in 1864] is
> the sensation of independence of society which they
> aquire when they have remunerative labour in their
> hands either in the fields, or at home as strawplaiters,
> etc. All gregarious employment gives a slang character to
> the girls' appearance and habits, while dependence on the
> man for support is the spring of modest and pleasing
> deportment.

The work girl's clothing was also charged against her. If
it was coarse and tough, to protect her from the mud and
from the weather, it was said to be unwomanly – a degradation
of her sex. But things were still worse if her clothing were
flimsy and allowed her body to show through – an invitation to
promiscuity in the summer harvest fields. To show an ankle was
considered to be a sign of female moral depravity – thus the
country girl who pulled up her skirt and tucked it between her
legs when she was doing field work was depraved.

Another alleged inducement to the sexual promiscuity of the
country girl was the possibility of 'seeing sights among the
beasts'.[194] The implication was that seeing animals copulating
in the fields would induce them to emulate this pastime with

members of the other sex. I remember seeing pigs, cats, dogs, cows, sheep and horses copulating, and I can't deny that I was curious to know what the animals were doing and why, but I don't remember waylaying the first unsuspecting lad that crossed my path; neither do I remember having such a functional analysis of the situation as Flora Thompson's heroine Laura who[195]

> at about 12 years old stumbled into a rickyard where a bull was in the act of justifying its existence, the sight did not warp her nature . . . The bull to her was but a bull performing a necessary function if there was to be butter on the bread and milk for breakfast.

Many clergymen and writers of that time based their condemnation of the country girl on the amount of illegitimacy and cohabitation that occurred in the country. But once again they did not bother to look into the complete situation before making their value judgments. In many parts of England and Wales it was customary for a couple not to get wed until the woman had fallen pregnant – thus proving that she was capable of having children and providing the man with 'sons'. The *Morning Chronicle* of 18 January 1850 comments:[196]

> It really seems, in many places, to be taken as a matter of course that a young woman will be found with child before she is married. Many are married as soon as they become pregnant . . . Indeed, I have reason to believe that in an immense number of cases young people come to a distinct understanding with each other to cohabit illicitly, until the woman becomes pregnant, the man promising to 'make an honest woman of her' as soon as that takes place.
>   This they find more convenient than marrying at once, inasmuch, as the girl may be of service for herself, and the man elsewhere employed all the time. They meet occasionally, and are thus relieved at least of the responsibilities and the duties of housekeeping, living better on their separate earnings than they could do in a house of their own. This practice of cohabitation before marriage is almost universal. It is not only a characteristic of low rural life; it is also so with the miners and the fishermen.

When a girl found herself expecting an unplanned and 'illegitimate' baby then, as today, there were limits as to what could be done. She could either accept the situation and have the child, or she might try to abort, by taking such drugs as savine or turpentine. This might not directly remedy the situation, but it would have a debilitating effect on the unborn child, which when born would probably be in an even weaker condition than the mother's rundown state would have caused. There was not much choice after the child was born. If the girl was forced to work during the day – and bring up the child unsupported by the father – she had to find someone to mind it while she worked in the fields. She might leave it with her younger sister, mother, grandmother, the baby being taken to the fields to be fed at intervals. Or she would take the baby to a child-minder's house and leave it there whilst she was away at work, paying the child-minder out of her earnings. Many child-minders were inexperienced and this fact plus the often quite unhygienic and cramped conditions of the child-minder's 'nursery' would do the young child's health no good. But the mother had to go and support herself and to work in the knowledge that some dreadful accident might happen to the child while she was away.

In the 1860s there was a general movement of opinion among the respectable towards the need to educate the chlidren of the working classes; much interest was shown in the type of work that kept children out of school and it was for this reason that in the 1860s commissions were set up to investigate the condition and the employment of children in industry and agriculture in various regions of the country. The report on gangs by the Children's Employment Commissioners led to the passing of the Agricultural Gangs Act of 1867. This made it illegal for a child under the age of eight to work in agricultural gangs – amended by the Agricultural Children's Act of 1875 (taking effect from 1 January 1875) to read 'no child under 10 years should be employed in agricultural gangs'. These two Acts with the 1870 Education Act and its successors had the ultimate effect of removing girls from field labour, though it was difficult to enforce at first in the countryside because their work was an integral part of the village economy. It was not until mechanization had taken over the labour they performed, that compulsory education in the countryside became really effective. The people who had the power to enforce compulsory education locally also benefited from the results of women and girls' labour so it was not in their interest to be too diligent in this duty until they could find a cheap and efficient replacement.

By removing them from field labour and subjecting them to the influence of educational and religious institutions girls were placed under 'respectable' influences. Many went on to be female servants, and were found situations through the educational and Sunday school machinery. Some went to the local farmers; some went to big houses in the district and then perhaps moved on to the town houses of the rich. Servants were status symbols. The social position of a household was measured by the number of its servants. The servants were a constant proclamation of their employers' social standing; and they were completely at their mercy, having to work long hours for very little money and with their free time strictly supervised by the 'ladies' of the house. Escape from tutelage was difficult, except through marriage, because without a character reference from the mistress it was difficult to find another place. In such situations as these girls lived, they often fell prey to the appetites and lechery of the sexually repressed men of the household. It is not difficult for us to recall some story we have heard of how the under-housemaid was sent away in disgrace and the son of the house rebuked and sent back to university, etc. My great-grandfather, on my mother's side, was the product of such an occurrence: his mother, a kitchen maid, was sent home, while her seducer was packed off to America. Such servants were in a very precarious position alone in the big town, when it came to resisting the master or the mistress, because they knew they would need to have a character reference in order to get another job, and there was always another country girl willing to take up their place if, for whatever reason, they did not suit.

The inconsistency of Victorian middle-class attitudes towards female duties is illustrated by the notable absence of any commission inquiry into the working conditions and environment of their female servants. These servants carried out harsh and gruelling tasks, worked for long hours and were vulnerable to the whims and fancies of their employers; but such service was not thought degrading to the working-class female: far from it, it taught her to be feminine, a modest respectable girl.

Inquiry into this huge area of female employment – though it employed far more women than any other occupation – would have been viewed as an attack and questioning of the accepted and expected pattern of social and sexual differences (inequalities) that were inherent to that society and time, and upon which the entire social order was based.

Notes

1 Flora Thompson, *Lark Rise to Candleford*, London, 1954, p. 10.
2 Edwin Grey, *Cottage Life in a Hertfordshire Village*, St Albans, 1935, pp. 50–1.
3 P.P. 1868–9 (4202–1) XIII, *2nd Report of the Commissioners on the Employment of Children, Young Persons and Women in Agriculture* (abbreviated to *AEC* II), Appendix pt II (g), p. 245.
4 Thompson, op. cit., p. 11.
5 Ibid., loc. cit.
6 Ibid., pp. 11–12.
7 Thomas Hardy, *Jude the Obscure*, London, 1966 ed., pp. 70–2.
8 Thomas Hardy, *The Woodlanders*, London, 1965 ed., pp. 12–13.
9 Thomas Hardy, *Tess of the D'Urbervilles*, London, 1965 ed., pp. 322–3.
10 P.P. 1861 (2794–11) XXI–II, *Reports of the Assistant Commissioners appointed to Inquire into the state of Popular Education in England*, p. 86.
11 Ibid., p. 99.
12 R. R. Sellman, *Devon Village Schools in the Nineteenth Century*, Newton Abbot, 1967, p. 121.
13 Essex Record Office, E/ML 171, log book, Roxwell Church of England School, 11 August 1881.
14 Kent Record Office, C/ES 408/2, log book, Yalding National School, 6 October 1873.
15 Essex Record Office, E/ML 171, Roxwell School log book, 23 September 1867.
16 Ibid., loc. cit., 19 September 1880.
17 Ibid., loc. cit., 2 July 1866.
18 Ibid., loc. cit., 7 July 1870.
19 Ibid., loc. cit., 9–11 July 1866, 18–22 July 1867, 26, 30 June 1868, 8, 10, 15 July 1868, 29 June 1869, 27 July 1870, etc. And see 14 July 1880: 'Attendance thin, Measles and pea picking in the parish.'
20 Ibid., loc. cit., 23 July 1868.
21 Ibid., loc. cit., 20 August 1880.

22 Essex Record Office, E/ML/10/1, log book, Frating Church of England School, 11 October 1870.
23 Ibid., E/ML 155/1, log book, Henny National School, 21 October 1870.
24 Ibid., loc. cit., 1–5 November 1875.
25 Kent Record Office, C/ES 3/1/1, log book, Adisham Mixed School, 30 March 1868.
26 Ibid., C/ES 408/2, log book, Yalding National School, 5 May 1871.
27 Ibid., C/ES 83/1, log book, Chart Sutton Church of England School, 13 May 1867.
28 Ibid., C/ES 3/1/1, log book, Adisham Mixed School, 2 October 1865.
29 Essex Record Office, E/ML 171, log book, Roxwell Church of England School, 27 July 1874.
30 Kent Record Office, C/ES 362/2/1, log book, Swancombe Girls National School, 24 August 1874.
31 Essex Record Office, E/ML 171, log book, Roxwell Church of England School, 24 July 1876.
32 Kent Record Office, C/ES 304/3/1, log book, Troytown Board School (Girls' Dept.), Rochester, 8 August 1873.
33 Ibid., C/ES 54/9/1, log book, Canterbury Diocesan School, 1 August 1864.
34 P.P. 1867–8 (4068) XVII, *1st Report of the Commissioners on the Employment of Children, Young Persons and Women in Agriculture* (hereafter abbreviated to *AEC* I), Appendix pt I (c), p. 136.
35 *AEC* II, Appendix pt I (g), p. 81.
36 P.P. 1861 (2794–II) XXI–II, *Reports of the Assistant Commissioners Appointed to Inquire into the State of Popular Education in England*, p. 65.
37 *AEC* II, Appendix pt I (g), p. 78.
38 *Morning Chronicle*, 6 March 1850; Labour and the Poor: Rural Districts, letter XXXII.
39 P.P. 1861 (2794–II) XXI–II, *Reports of the Assistant Commissioners Appointed to Inquire into the State of Popular Education in England*, p. 65.
40 Ibid., p. 57.
41 P.P. 1870 (c. 221) XIII, *4th Report of the Commissioners on the Employment of Children, Young Persons and Women in Agriculture*, Appendix pt I (u), p. 284.
42 Essex Record Office, T/Z 25/17, Edith Mary Sargent, 'Essex Memories'.
43 *AEC* I, Appendix pt II (c), pp. 520–1.
44 Thomas Hardy, *Jude the Obscure*, London, 1966 ed., p. 19.
45 *AEC* I, Appendix pt I (c), p. 137.
46 Essex Record Office, T/Z 25/378, Mrs Field, 'My First Job'.
47 *AEC* I, Appendix pt I (a), p. 73.
48 Trinity College, Cambridge; A. J. Munby, MS. Diary, vol. 16, 7 October 1862, p. 123.

49 See David Morgan, 'The place of harvesters in nineteenth-century village life', in the present volume.
50 Thomas Hardy, *Tess of the D'Urbervilles*, London, 1965 ed., pp. 105–8.
51 P.P. 1867 (3796) XVI, Appendix (b), *6th Report Children's Employment Commission* (hereafter referred to as P.P. Agricultural Gangs), p. 163.
52 P.P. 1864 (3416) XXVII, Appendix 14 to the *6th Report of the Medical Officer of the Privy Council*, p. 460.
53 Ibid., p. 460.
54 Thomas Hardy, *Tess of the D'Urbervilles*, p. 239.
55 A. J. Munby, MS. Diary, vol. 16, 20 October 1862, p. 189.
56 Ibid., vol. 17, 3 January 1863, pp. 72–5.
57 Ibid., vol. 16, 20 October 1862, p. 79.
58 Thomas Hardy, *Tess of the D'Urbervilles*, p. 324.
59 Richard Jefferies, *Hodge and His Masters*, London, 1890 ed., pp. 132–3.
60 Thomas Hardy, *Tess of the D'Urbervilles*, p. 328.
61 Ibid., pp. 328–30.
62 A. J. Munby, MS. Diary, vol. 16, 3 October 1862, pp. 77–8.
63 Ibid., vol. 25, 21 May 1864, pp. 59–62.
64 Thompson, op. cit., pp. 257–8.
65 Ruth Carey, interview with the writer, July 1972.
66 *AEC* I, Appendix pt I (a), p. 70.
67 *AEC* II, Appendix pt I (g), p. 89.
68 Thomas Hardy, *Tess of the D'Urbervilles*, p. 127.
69 A. J. Munby, MS. Diary, vol. 21, 31 August 1863, pp. 232–42.
70 Ibid., loc. cit., pp. 235–6.
71 Ibid., loc. cit., pp. 236–7.
72 R. R. Sellman, *Devon Schools in the Nineteenth Century*, p. 137, for an example.
73 A. J. Munby, MS. Diary, vol. 16, 27 December 1862, p. 49.
74 Jefferies, op. cit., ch. 7.
75 *AEC* I, Appendix pt II (c), p. 543, para. 206.
76 Ibid., Appendix pt II (a), p. 375, para. 40.
77 P.P. 1864 (3416) XXVIII, Appendix 14 to the *6th Report of the Medical Officer of the Privy Council*, p. 460.
78 P.P. Agricultural Gangs, p. 71.
79 Ibid., p. 78.
80 Ibid., pp. 77–8.
81 Mrs Burrows, 'A Childhood in the Fens about 1850–60', in Margaret Llewellyn Davies (ed.), *Life as We have Known it*, London, 1931, p. 109.
82 P.P. Agricultural Gangs, Appendix A, p. 92.
83 *AEC* I, Appendix pt II (c), p. 543.
84 Mrs Burrows, op. cit., p. 110.
85 P.P. Agricultural Gangs, Appendix A, p. 96.
86 Ibid., Appendix (a), pp. 135–6.
87 Ibid., Appendices A and (a), pp. 98, 127.

88 Ibid., Appendix A, p. 96.
89 Ibid., Appendix B, p. 159.
90 Mrs Burrows, op. cit., pp. 110–11.
91 P.P. Agricultural Gangs, Appendix A, p. 92.
92 *AEC* II, Appendix pt I (L2), p. 229.
93 Ibid., Appendix pt I (L2), p. 230.
94 Ibid., Appendix pt I (L2), p. 229.
95 Ibid., Appendix pt II (L2), p. 791.
96 Ibid., Appendix pt II (L2), p. 789.
97 Ibid., Appendix pt I (L2), p. 230.
98 Ibid., Appendix pt II (L2), p. 789.
99 Derek Hudson, *Munby: Man of Two Worlds*, London, 1972, pp. 255–6.
100 *AEC* II, Appendix pt II (i), p. 497.
101 *AEC* I, Appendix pt II (c), p. 558.
102 Ibid., Appendix pt II (d), p. 630.
103 *AEC* II, Appendix pt I (I), p. 128.
104 *AEC* I, Appendix pt II (f), p. 745.
105 A. J. Munby, MS. Diary, vol. 14, 23 July 1862, p. 111.
106 A. J. Munby, MS. Diary, vol. 25, 16 May 1865, p. 46.
107 *Agricultural Gazette*, 10 May 1874, p. 635.
108 Mary Lewis (ed.), *Old Days in the Kent Hop Gardens*, West Kent Federation of Women's Institutes, 1962, pp. 27–8.
109 *Morning Chronicle*, 13 February 1850. Labour and the Poor: Rural Districts, letter xxxi.
110 Kent Record Office, V 106/A4, Peel Estate, loose farm wages accounts, 14 and 21 June 1850.
111 *AEC* II pt I (G), p. 82.
112 Ibid., Appendix pt I (G), p. 84.
113 *Morning Chronicle*, loc. cit.
114 *AEC*, Appendix pt I (I), p. 130.
115 *Morning Chronicle*, loc. cit.
116 *AEC* II, Appendix pt II (k), p. 678.
117 Ibid., Appendix pt II (j2), p. 657.
118 *AEC* I pt II (c), p. 544.
119 Jefferies, op. cit., vol. 2, pp. 88–9.
120 P.P. Agricultural Gangs, Appendix A, p. 93.
121 Ibid., Appendix A, p. 96.
122 *AEC* I Appendix pt II (c), p. 541.
123 P.P. Agricultural Gangs, Appendix (b), pp. 173–4.
124 Ibid., Appendix B, p. 167.
125 Ibid., p. 83.
126 P.P. Agricultural Gangs, p. 167.
127 P.P. 1864 (3416) xxviii, *6th Report of the Medical Officer of the Privy Council*, Apps. 13–14, p. 456.
128 J. L. Green, *The Rural Industries of England*, London, 1894, p. 76.
129 Jefferies, op. cit., vol. 2, pp. 87–91.
130 J. G. Jenkins, *Traditional Country Craftsmen*, London, 1965, p. 153.

131 Essex Record Office, T/Z 25/233, Mrs E. Quick, 'My first job'.
132 *AEC* II, Appendix pt I (K), p. 207.
133 *AEC* II, Appendix pt II (i), p. 500.
134 Thomas Hardy, *The Woodlanders*, p. 68.
135 *Morning Chronicle*, 1 February 1850, Supplement, Labour and the Poor: Rural Districts, letter XVIII.
136 Ibid., 8 January 1850, Supplement, The Fisheries and the Fishers of Cornwall, letter X.
137 Ibid., 29 January 1850, Supplement, The Herring Fisheries and Fishermen of Yarmouth, letter XVIII.
138 *AEC* II, Appendix pt II (*l*2), p. 791.
139 Mary Lewis (ed.), op. cit., p. 8.
140 Kent Record Office, U/106 A4, Peel Estate records, loose farm accounts.
141 *AEC* I, Appendix pt II (æ), p. 321.
142 Kent Record Office, loc. cit.
143 *Morning Chronicle*, 30 January 1850, Labour and the Poor: Rural Districts, letter XXX.
144 Kent Record Office, loc. cit.
145 P.P. 1874 (1086) XIII, *Reports of the Inspectors of Factories for the Half-year ended 30 April 1874*, p. 196.
146 *AEC* II, Appendix pt I (K), p. 205.
147 Ibid., Appendix pt II (k), p. 709.
148 Ibid., Appendix pt I (K), p. 206.
149 Ibid., Appendix pt II (g), p. 246.
150 Ibid., Appendix pt II (i), p. 495.
151 Ibid., Appendix pt I (K), p. 206.
152 Loc. cit.
153 Green, op. cit., p. 71.
154 *AEC* II, Appendix pt I (K), p. 207.
155 Grey, op. cit., pp. 68–9.
156 George Austin, *The Straw Trade*, 1871, p. 18.
157 *Morning Chronicle*, 5 April 1850, Labour and the Poor: Rural Districts, letter XXXIV.
158 Grey, op. cit., p. 70.
159 P.P. 1864 (3414) XXII, Appendix (d) to the *2nd Report of the Children's Employment Commission*, p. 281.
160 Grey, op. cit., p. 73.
161 Miss Vaughan, *Thirty Three Years at Harpenden*, 1893, p. 10.
162 P.P. 1874 (1086) XIII, *Reports of the Inspectors of Factories for the Half Year ending 30 April 1871*, p. 198.
163 P.P. 1871 (446) XIV, *Reports of the Inspectors of Factories for the Half Year ending 30 April 1871*. p. 679.
164 P.P. 1864 (3414) XXII, Appendix (d) to the *2nd Report of the Children's Employment Commission*, p. 281.
165 P.P. 1868–9 (4093–1) XIV, *Reports of the Inspectors of Factories for the Half Year ending 31st October 1868*, p. 459.
166 *AEC* I, Appendix pt II (f), p. 753.
167 *Once a Week*, vol. XII, December 1864 to June 1865, p. 466.

168 Grey, op. cit., p. 72.
169 P.P. 1871 (446) XIV, *Reports of the Inspectors of Factories for the Half Year ended 30th April 1871*, p. 679.
170 *Good Words*, 1891, p. 584.
171 *Morning Chronicle*, 5 April 1850, Labour and the Poor: Rural Districts, letter XXXIV.
172 Grey, op. cit., p. 70.
173 *Morning Chronicle*, loc. cit.
174 Essex Record Office E/ML 155/1, log book, Henny National School.
175 *AEC* I, Appendix pt II (f), p. 754.
176 Green, op. cit., pp. 177–8.
177 *Morning Chronicle*, 5 April 1850, Labour and the Poor: Rural Districts, letter XXXIV.
178 Grey, op. cit., p. 79.
179 Essex Record Office, T/Z 25/75. Old People's Essays, Mrs Gilbey.
180 *Good Words*, 1891, p. 598.
181 Grey, op. cit., pp. 86–7.
182 Frederick Davies, *History of Luton with its Hamlets*, p. 148.
183 Grey, op. cit., p. 88.
184 *Once a Week*, vol. 12, December 1864 to June 1865, p. 467.
185 James Greenwood, *On Tramp*, London, 1883, p. 28.
186 *AEC* I, Appendix pt I (F), p. 195.
187 A. J. Munby, MS. Diary, vol. 19, 10 May 1863, p. 75.
188 *Morning Chronicle*, 5 April 1850, Labour and the Poor: Rural Districts, letter XXXIV.
189 Cited in Duncan Crow, *The Victorian Woman*, London, 1971, p. 91.
190 P.P. Agricultural Gangs, Appendix (B), p. 167.
191 Ibid., Appendix (A), p. 94.
192 *AEC* I, pt I (A), p. 76.
193 P.P. 1865 (3484) XXVI, Appendix no. 6 to the *7th Report of the Medical Officer to the Privy Council*, p. 146.
194 *AEC* II, Appendix pt I (K), p. 197.
195 Thompson, op. cit., pp. 35–6.
196 *Morning Chronicle*, 18 January 1850, Supplement, Labour and the Poor: Rural Districts, letter XIII.

Part 4

'Quarry roughs': life and labour in Headington Quarry, 1860–1920. An essay in oral history

Raphael Samuel

1 'Quarry roughs'

Headington Quarry, a village now swallowed up by Oxford's suburban expansion, was seventy years ago still quite a primitive place. Its population had multiplied as a result of nineteenth-century development (from 264 at the time of the 1841 census to 1,437 in 1901), but the spirit of Victorian 'improvement' had passed it by. No railway stopped in the vicinity, despite a memorial from the Headington vestry in 1852, pleading the claims of the local brickworks:[1] industrial transport was left to the haggle-cart, the trolley, and the one-horse van. Quarry Fields Path was the only link between Quarry and its more respectable neighbour, Old Headington, some three-quarters of a mile away; it was no more than a gravelly path, with a stile at one end and a kissing-gate at the other.[2] In 1908 it was contemptuously described as 'practically a flood from one end to the other with two stepping-stones in thirty yards'[3] (the bad condition of the path may have been exacerbated by a dispute as to who was responsible for its upkeep[4]). The turnpike road from Oxford to London hardly half a mile away was difficult to reach. Pitts Road, the link today, was then a cart-track ('all ashes and mud and water'[5]), and the steep slope of Colman's Hill, the last stage of the journey, was too slippery for the brick-carts, at least when laden: 'It wasn't really a through road...only a track up there.'[6] Barracks Road, the link between Quarry and Cowley, was also rough.[7] It made its way across the Moors, a wide stretch of wasteland (known today as the Slade) which was a winter camping ground for gypsies. Its condition cannot have been improved by the marchings of the soldiers from Cowley Barracks, who used both the Moors and Shotover for their practice.[8]

Piped water did not reach the village until the eve of the Great War, despite the building of a waterworks on Headington Hill, some forty years earlier.[9] Water had to be drawn from the wells. (The sinking of garden wells was one of the chief domestic changes in nineteenth-century Quarry; in the middle years of the century many villagers were still having to draw their water from the 'Old Mauls', an abandoned claypit on the lower slopes of Shotover which had filled up with water.[10]) At Baker Vallis's, sixteen buckets of water were drawn every night to fill the boilers. This was a job Mr Vallis did as a boy; he recalls that it could be dangerous, especially in frosty weather. Reaching across the top of the well to pull in the full bucket, 'you couldn't help spilling a drop of water on the top . . . and in the bad weather it would freeze . . . you had to be pretty careful . . .'[11] (Even without ice there was a risk; in 1909 the twelve-year-old daughter of Razzell Bushnell was drowned while drawing water from a neighbour's well.)[12] Cottage laundries, a major village industry, also depended on garden wells; and 'pulling water' – a job often done by girls – is remembered as one of the most laborious of the washing-day tasks.[13]

It seems likely that the earliest dwellings were quarrymen's shacks, 'poor insubstantial hovels which could without difficulty be removed and set up elsewhere',[14] and some of those which Vallis remembers in the 1850s seem hardly to have been more substantial – 'thatched cottages with no upstairs'.[15] One-storey dwellings were still to be found about the Mason's Pit in the 1900s: 'Two rooms . . . that's about the limit they had at that time of day . . .' Crowy Kerry was brought up in a cottage like this: with a family of six children they were very crowded: 'The house weren't big enough for us to get beds . . . we used to lay in this bunk . . . sleep in this bunk with our legs out . . . there were only two rooms, you see . . . a little room at the back and one room in the front . . .'[16] In Sip Washington's family the cottage could not hold them all, and two of the children were put out to sleep in an outhouse. According to Will Webb this was quite a common state of affairs in the little group of alleys about the Mason's Pit: 'There was a lot of families, they either had a shed up the garden where two or three of the kids used to sleep or they had an old hovel.'[17]

Headington Quarry had its origins in a squatter's settlement on the waste, and seventy-five years ago it still bore something of the aspect of a temporary encampment. Stonepits, working or abandoned, remained in their original state and alongside them were old pit banks 'in some parts . . . nearly as high as these houses':[18] they remained undisturbed until the early 1920s, when they were sold off to Benfield and Loxley's, the Oxford builders, at five shillings a yard.[19] The village was studded with ownerless spots of land – 'nobody's land', 'useless land' – where the enterprising opportunist could put up a cottage, or extend a garden, more or less at will:[20]

They used to pinch the stuff about here – ground – years
ago, you know. I have heard my grandmother say, where
Franklin's* is, the Masseys, they went to Australia – mind
it's years and years ago, with a sailing ship, and she
always said that Franklin was a bit relation to 'em, and
they took the ground, you see, when they didn't come
back . . . That's how they used to do it years ago. I've
heard my granny talk about it . . . Spender* . . . when I
was a girl 'ee never had that because we used to have
Buckland's fairs . . . the coconut shies used to stand over
there . . . Well, as years come, old Spender took the ground
and walled it off.

Land was still easier to come by on the wasteland edge of the
village, where the brickfields ran into the Moors. An unusually
well-documented case can be found in the Charity Commissioners' archives. It records the successful establishment of two
squatting families, the Steels and the Parsons, on Peat Moor,
an allotment of about five acres of land made over to the
churchwardens of Headington under the Enclosure Act of 1802.
In 1869 the churchwardens complained that:[21]

Some forty or fifty years ago two small huts were erected
upon this land, and they were inhabited by some poor
people, and from time to time the buildings have increased
into two cottages and the occupants have enclosed a piece
of the ground as gardens, but for none of this do they pay
any rent.

The 'poor people' can be identified from a handbill issued in
1857, which showed that part of Peat Moor was rented out to
R. & H. Pether, and part used by the Oxford Surveyors of
Highways as a quarry, but no rent was paid for the rest,
although, as the handbill complains, it was lived on:[22]

Cottage and Garden occupied by Thomas Steele.
Yard and two Hovels occupied by Thomas Steele.
Cottage and Garden occupied by James Parsons.

Surreptitious encroachments like this might be checked, but
they were difficult to reverse once they had taken place: there
was still a family of Parsons at Peat Moor in Edwardian times,
'in that hollow below'.[23]

* Fictional name.

The local quarries were not fixed workings, restricted to a
single face of rock, but advanced in a series of scoops, yard by
yard, on to ever fresh terrain – like swidden ('slash and burn')
agriculture – so that the land surface of the village was in a
constant state of flux. This process was still going on in the
early 1900s, in the neighbourhood of the Pitts. 'They were
always digging bits and pieces out.' The brickfields, too, were
worked by fits and starts, with 'big runs of barrications'[24]
moving forward in sweeps, while the clay was being dug, and
then a shifting of activity somewhere else. The whole setting
was makeshift and extempore, and the villagers accommodated
themselves, as best they could, to the restless movement of the
diggings.[25]

> It used to be a pit right up close to the road, but then . . .
> on top of the ground used to be allotments . . . as they
> went . . . back – getting the gravel and stones and that
> out of the pit – the people who had allotments used to
> come down and have the ground that was down below.

Arkell's map, in *Oxford Stone*,[26] shows that the entire land
surface of the village had been quarried for stone at one time or
another during the five centuries when the Oxford colleges were
supplied with 'Hedington stone', and the rise of the brickmaking
industry, during the nineteenth century, produced a fresh
perimeter of disturbance on the village's eastern flank. All this
turned an originally flat terrain into a warren of sudden
declivities and ascents which even today, when the pit banks
have been levelled out and most of the hollows filled in, has
not lost its capacity to surprise the visitor, and which is
affectionately regarded by the villagers themselves – 'all 'oles
and alleys and 'ills, that's what Quarry is, all up and down'.[27]

It was in the crannies of these man-made irregularities that
the nineteenth-century cottages were to be found. Some were
built down at the bottom of the pits, as may be seen from
survivors today, with their submerged rooftops and windowless
backs. The tenements where cholera occurred in 1832, for
instance, were reported as being in a stonepit, 'four in number,
with two more about 500 yards off on the opposite side of the
pit'.[28] This was a problem raised in 1908, when the introduction
of a system of sewerage was under debate at the Headington
parish council. 'Headington Quarry is built in such an irregular

manner', local councillors were told, that it would be 'difficult' (and in parts 'impossible') to drain.[29] Sir William Markby, when the matter came up again, was not hopeful: 'He might say that the houses in Quarry were very difficult to get at . . . in that many . . . were down at the bottom of the pits. How they were going to get at them he did not know.'[30]

The pattern of settlement was highly individualistic. Cottages had been put up higgledy-piggledy, in ones and twos, wherever the diggings had chanced to come to a stop. Some, like Saccy Horwood's cottage, occupied a solitary mound or level, and were entered not from a road, but by their own little sideway. The census enumerators of 1861 were apparently baffled by the physiognomy of the village: they made no attempt to distinguish one part from another, but (in contrast to their procedure in Old Headington) lumped everything together under the single label 'Quarry'.[31] A list of the 'Aged and Chronic Sick Poor', drawn up by the churchwardens in the 1870s and preserved in the archives of Holy Trinity, may serve to illustrate the difficulty:[32]

Widow Trafford near the Church Gate
John Trafford (son) near the Church Gate
Mrs. Tolley (bed-ridden) opposite Six Bells
Old Parsons and wife – cottage on the 'Plain'
    near Pether's farm.
Old Morris Cottages opposite School Gate
Old Kerry
Ann Snow
Widow Bushnell in the hollow by Stiles the Bakers
Richard Webb under Tree.

Elderly villagers, recalling the cottage homes of the early 1900s, label them idiosyncratically. Old Mac Massey, the morris dancer, for example, is remembered as living 'down in the hole just at the top of the alley by them posties';[33] Mark Cox, the village fiddler, as 'in the alleyway . . . where you go through to Vallis's';[34] the site of Snuffer Webb's old cottage (he was a well-known poacher) as 'up the little cottage opposite the Six Bells down in the dip before the by-pass'.[35] One is a long way here from the terraced order of the model village, or the numbered symmetries of the by-law street.

There was no centre to Quarry, no ivied church or village

green, and it bore little resemblance to the Arcadia recently invoked by Ronald Blythe in his much-admired book on *Akenfield*:[36]

> A tall old church on the hillside . . . a pretty stream . . . a handsome square vicarage with a cedar of Lebanon shading it, a school with jars of tadpoles in the window, three shops with doorbells, a Tudor mansion, half a dozen farms, and a lot of quaint cottages . . .

No pretty streams coursed through the village, though the low-lying land was subject to flood (particularly in the neighbourhood of Quarry school[37]), and abandoned claypits, filling with water, provided the village horse-keepers with a liberal supply of ponds. Nor were there tadpoles to be seen in the school windows: the lower ones had been blocked up (at a cost of £10 10s.) in consequence of the 'terrible damage' inflicted on them by the village children.[38] The approach to the village was marked neither by meadowland nor leafy lanes, but by the smoking brick-kilns of Titup on one side, and stonepits and the district workhouse[39] on the other. The Vicarage, though handsome enough, was invisible to outsiders by reason of the trees which nevertheless barely separated it from the Clayhills, where the limepits are remembered as burning 'day and . . . night',[40] and the Vicarage Pit, on the other side of Quarry Road, where blasting with explosives went on when the rock was too hard to cut.

Pits provided the focal point around which village life arranged itself. The maypole was danced in an abandoned pit – 'it was just derelict ground . . . a pit that was run out'.[41] The travelling showmen set up their roundabouts in the pits – old Mother Dolloway in one generation, the Bucklands in the next.[42] The pit outside the 'Six Bells' ('the big pit') served Quarry in some sense as its village green. It was here that the morris men danced on Whit Tuesday, that the drum and fife band assembled on club days and Hospital Sunday; and that the annual sheep roast was held in November, the furnace being built up from the bottom of the pit 'and . . . protected from the wind by an oblong tent'.[43] In early Victorian times it had been an arena for village sports. 'I myself remember – seeing Cock Chasing in the pit at the Six Bells', writes Vallis in his memoir. 'Men could be seen running after these birds with their hands tied behind them trying to catch them with their mouth.'[44] Saccy's Pit (named after Saccy Horwood, a village totter who occupied a cottage at one end of it) is another well-remembered pit: it was still being used as a rubbish tip down to 1914.[45] The 'lino and carpet people' (an inter-war generation of travellers) used to camp there,[46] and earlier on it was one of the places where the showmen used to pull up their vans and where the Bucklands put on their pony roundabout.[47] The largest and most enduring of Quarry's pits – it is still substantially there today – was the Mason's Pit at the back of the 'Mason's Arms', which Vallis tells us in his memoir was the original nucleus of the village settlement.[48] It was for many years a favourite haunt of gypsies, 'the real old-fashioned gypsies',[49] as they are spoken of by old *habitués* of the Mason's, and in the early 1900s was the centre of a free-lance community of well-diggers, rabbit-catchers, horse-dealers and poachers, who lived in a cluster of little courts – Hunt's Row, School Place and Carr Matthew's Alley.

Pits provided Quarry children with their playgrounds, Saccy's Pit being preferred as a slide ('that was a nice steep one'), while the pit outside the 'Six Bells' was 'more . . . hide'n seek'[50] (a game also known in Quarry as 'high hirkey'[51]); Blondin's Pit, opposite the Vicarage, was also a popular slide; and so was Jack Phillips's Pit in Green Road.[52] The Mason's Pit is remembered as being full of children. 'There was a crowd of 'em . . . used to get in that pit . . . a proper playground . . . we used to slide down the bank . . . on tea-trays' (one of its uses in the early 1900s, according to an old villager, was as an ambush for Mr Bickley, the very unpopular headmaster of Quarry school[53]). Toys, like playgrounds, were improvised: pigs' bladders served as footballs, cart-ropes as makeshift swings, dustbin lids – or in earlier years, old pieces of tin – as toboggans.[54]

Quarry's moral reputation was as distinctive as its physical appearance was strange. It had a very bad name. Its poachers were well-known in the surrounding countryside; its 'roughs' – 'Headington Quarry roughs' as the newspapermen referred to them – made themselves felt at the neighbouring feasts and fairs, where the County Constabulary, in the early 1900s, drafted extra police to deal with them.[55] 'Quarry was a terrible place to us kids', recalls an eighty-year-old woman, who grew up a few miles away at Beckley.[56] An Oakleigh man, who as a boy once ventured to watch a cricket match at Quarry ('tough sort of cricket – not much style . . . plenty of barrels of beer'), remembers hesitating: 'If you didn't know somebody you were wise not to go – you might not get back – it was one of them sort of places.'[57] At Old Headington village opinion was no more favourable: 'a half-bred gypsy-poacher type . . . very clannish'. 'Put it like this', a Headington man explained:[58]

> They were chaps who got their living on the side – they were poachers, 'orse-dealers, cattle dealers – some may have been up straight and others may have been under-handed. If you'd been a stranger walking through there they'd have suspected you of nosing about; when they knew you it was all right – they was the best of blokes – but you didn't have to interfere with them . . . you had to mind your own business. They was that type. I think it was just suspicion.

Some of this may be folklore, but it is clear from Quarry villagers' own accounts that frightening things could happen to strangers:[59]

> We used to get some saucy buggers come out of different places . . . – when they throwed their old swank about they bloody got 'comidated – 'cos there was some handy blokes in this village at one time – there was an old horse trough up here . . . the old pub at the top here – the Chequers – this . . . bloke (he was a saucy bugger), well, they got hold of him one Saturday . . . and dragged him down – do you know, they bloody near drowned him – they got him and put him in that bloody horse trough . . . and he got out of that bloody horse trough and he got away, got through the village and he soon got away back towards Oxford bloody wet through.

The youth of Quarry played a big part in the village's reputation for roughness. When they ventured out of the village, they found themselves in trouble, whether for playing pitch and toss,[60] congregating near the churches and chapels on Sunday,[61] or creating disturbances – those who gathered at the top of Headington Hill (chiefly on Sunday afternoons) were complained of in 1879 as being 'more like Zulus than respectable English youths'.[62] Quarry children, too, 'the type that requires a firm hand in order to induce them to do their best',[63] were often in trouble with the authorities, and in the 1890s Quarry school seems to have been quite seriously disturbed. There were outbreaks of concerted window-smashing,[64] and a kind of subdued guerrilla warfare between Mr Bickley (an enthusiastic disciplinarian, appointed as headmaster in June 1894[65]) and a portion of the children (some parents seem to have sided with the children, and Mr Bickley was the victim of two assaults in his first year in office[66]). Children were prominent in the Quarry election disturbances of 1892, and when a riot against the Tories took place in the schoolhouse the effect on school discipline (according to the testimony of the vicar) was noticeable. As he wrote in the annual report:[67]

> During last year, the previous rule of refusing the use of the schoolroom for election meetings was reversed with disastrous results. On the first occasion of its use for such a purpose, a disgraceful riot took place, in which children were instigated to take a prominent part. The effects of this continued, and were shown afterwards in excitement during school hours, and rudeness and stone-throwing, from which the female teachers had to suffer in public. Similar bad behaviour was renewed on the attempt to supply Mr Mason's place in January, and in my last letter of August 13th, 1892 . . . the attention of the Department was drawn to the treatment of the school premises by the unintelligent part of the inhabitants.

Between the young men of Old Headington and those of Quarry there is said to have been something in the nature of a hereditary feud ('they didn't dare come any further than Quarry Fields'[68]). 'They were real tough, you didn't want to mix in too much with them,' an Old Headington man recalls.[69] Titup children were also frightened of them. 'They weren't a very peace-loving people,' Elsie Wright recalls. 'I know we used to be frightened to go to Quarry . . . to visit our Granny in Trinity Road, because of the children in Quarry.'[70] Telegram boys, if they were sent out from the Post Office in Old Headington, tried to give the village a wide berth: 'If they went to Quarry they used to be stoned by the local lads.'[71]

Quarry's dogs – 'long dogs' as they were locally known – seem to have been partly responsible for the impression which the village made upon outsiders. They had been a cause of anxiety as far back as the reign of Charles I, when a royal complaint was lodged in the Exchequer against the 'lewd and disorderly persons' who were said illegally to have settled in the neighbourhood of the Quarry, and who 'disturbed the king's game with their dogs'.[72] In the 1820s the Headington vestry was attempting to reduce the local population of dogs by stipulating that no one should have poor relief unless he got rid of his dogs.[73] Fifty years later, during the hydrophobia scare of 1877–8, the Bullingdon magistrates, in answer to a plea from the Chief Constable of Oxfordshire, launched a 'Crusade' against Headington's dogs with the aim of getting them put on leads.[74] But on the eve of the Great War Quarry's large population of dogs was still to be found wandering about the village, 'here, there and everywhere'.[75] In the 'Six Bells' they monopolized the stove and took up a good deal of the floor besides: 'there used to be more dogs in there than there was customers'.[76] Bull terriers, the poachers' dogs, were particularly fierce ('that's why they used to breed 'em – they reckoned they was *savager* than any other dog'[77]). Crowy Kerry's dog, 'never chained . . . up', roamed up and down Carr Matthew's Alley, 'a real terror' to more peaceful dogs, especially those on leads ('it was that sort of dog he went for . . .'[78]). Alan Edney, a resident of Old Headington, recalls the fright he got as a boy, when he took his own little dog for a walk, and inadvertently strayed into Quarry:[79]

> The thing that I can remember about Quarry as a boy,
> was very fierce dogs . . . mind you a lot of the Quarry
> chaps were poachers, and in those days, surrounded with
> the country . . . it was nice to get an easy, cheap dinner –
> you didn't go to the butcher's and buy it – you took the
> greyhounds out in the field . . . These chaps . . . they used
> to have these lurcher dogs . . . that was what I remember
> about Quarry, because I remember taking our little dog on
> a lead once, and I hadn't got very far before a jolly great
> mastiff thing came and shook it to bits – they didn't like
> intrusion . . . they didn't like people . . . nosing about. My
> dog was a terrier. It didn't kill it but it gave him a good
> shaking up. I can remember that never more I didn't take
> my dog to Quarry.

One set of strangers who seem to have been particularly
unwelcome were the County Police. For poachers and their
families they occupied the status of hereditary enemies,
'always a-waiting . . . always about',[80] and their dogs were
trained to keep a look-out for them in much the same way as
the household dogs of the bourgeoisie are taught to keep a
watch for burglars.[81] 'They used to cause all the trouble in
Quarry, the police,' an old lady told me, and went on to
describe the time when her father's dog seized one of them on
the prowl: '. . . They used to make the trouble in Quarry, the
police.'[82] Such views, it seems, were by no means confined to the
poachers, but widely shared. 'They hated a copper to come
through this village. They wouldn't interfere with 'im, but if
he come in there trying to cause a barney, 'ee never went home
right.'[83] Quarry, according to local tradition, was one of those
places where the police dared to venture 'only in pairs' – 'not
one policeman, two it used to take'.[84] One favourite story
concerns a policeman who was said to have been tipped (or
nearly tipped: the story has different versions) down a well.
Constable Hall, the officer involved, was a policeman who had a
local reputation for 'making trouble', and according to one
version of the story he had come to the village in search of a
barrel of beer which had been stolen from a brewery cart and
hidden down a well. Here is one account of the incident:[85]

> Did old Crowy tell you? as when they used to have to
> come in Quarry – now I be going back ninety years ago –
> what I heard Granny Webb tell me – that when the
> policeman come in the Quarry on 'orses they took'm off
> the horse and put him down a well. Did they tell you that?
> They took him off the horse and put him down Granny
> Webb's well . . . They let him down Granny Webb's well
> . . . that's in Quarry, right in the Quarry . . . that was
> ninety years ago, when they took him off the 'orse, and
> let him down the well, the policeman . . . Ah! there used
> to be some ructions in the village, our Mam used to say,
> and our Granny Webb . . . The policeman used to have to
> come in on horseback – no good 'em on feet, Granny Webb
> used to tell us.

Politically, as well as morally, the village stood out from its
neighbours. The *Oxford Times* in 1894 described it as 'a hotbed

of the most rampant, reasonless Radicalism'.[86] Conservative
meetings there were 'an unpleasant experience' ('the tactics
usually resorted to by the semi-savages from the Quarry . . . are
brute force and lung power'[87]), and at election times, when
class feeling ran high, it was said to be positively dangerous for
a known Conservative to enter the village. The story in Old
Headington (a place where Liberalism meant something
altogether more respectable) was that 'if anybody got cross
those fields that wasn't a Liberal they never ever were seen
again . . . if you were a Liberal you were all right, mate, but
outside that, your life wasn't worth tuppence'.[88] The story may
have been coloured by local prejudice but some confirmation is
provided by Mr Arnold Prosser's memories of election times in
old-time Quarry. His wife's father, who was engaged on the
estate of a well-known Tory squire, used to travel around on
horseback. 'During one election . . . he sported a huge blue
Tory rosette and all went well until he crossed into Quarry
territory. He was set upon, pulled off his horse, and badly
knocked about.'[89]

The political temper of the village was already exciting
comment in the election of 1885, to judge by a satirical handbill
issued by the Conservatives at the time, and preserved in the
Bodleian.[90] In the election of 1892 there was a series of disturbances. On polling day Quarry 'roughs . . . fully sustained
their reputation for rowdyism' and forced the Conservative
candidate, a wealthy brewer, to leave the village. (The riots
seem to have had their hard edge directed against the police:
the Tory candidate, though 'grossly insulted', was allowed to
get away unscathed. Not so, however, the County Police 'who
were assailed with showers of sharp flints'.[91]) In the 1909
election there was a famous disturbance when the Conservative
propaganda van was stormed. The van, which was campaigning
against the so-called 'People's Budget', encountered opposition
all over Oxfordshire. At Witney, there was 'disorder' and
'heckling';[92] at Littlemore (quite a Radical village in those
years)[93] there was 'what appeared to be a regularly organized
opposition amongst the youths of the village';[94] there was
trouble in Jericho and East Oxford.[95] But it was only when it
came to Quarry that the van came to grief,: it was attacked by
the crowd, tipped on its side and stoned (a celebratory postcard
recording the incident, is reproduced as Plate 13).[96]

Quarry radicalism was a defensive affair, a matter of preserving old-established rights and privileges intact. But it was marked by a predilection for spontaneous, unilateral action, and a reluctance to wait upon the tedious processes of representation and the law. It makes an early appearance in the Funeral Path disturbances which followed the Headington Enclosure Act of 1802, when Mr Lock, an Oxford banker, tried to fence in land which had been the traditional passageway for village burials. The villagers broke down the fences, and the vicar of Old Headington felt it prudent to take their side. 'The inhabitants of Quarry say that as they are to be deprived of their funeral path they will not come to Church at all, but intend to have a Methodist preacher come to them,' he warned the bishop.[97] The disturbances broke out in 1805, and feeling was still running high two years later, to judge by the case which came before Oxford assizes in June 1807:[98]

> Wm. Coppock, Benjamin Bushnell, Charles Edington, and several other persons were tried for a riot at Headington, in this county, and for forcibly entering a paddock of Joseph Lock, Esq., situate in that Parish, which has been inclosed under the authority of an act of Parliament passed in the 41st year of the present reign. All the defendent [sic] were found guilty, and Wm. Coppock, Benjamin Bushnell, Charles Edington, Henry Bushnell, Thomas Goodgame, Peter Goodgame, and Josephy Jacob were sentenced to be imprisoned in the Common gaol for six calendar months, at the expiration of which time to enter into recognizance with sufficient sureties to keep the peace.
>
> Bound over were John Adams, Ann Coppock, Rachel Goodgame, Elizabeth Bushnell, wife of Richard, and Elizabeth Bushnell, single woman.

A late example might be the resistance of Quarry Nomads, the local football team, when a reforming park-keeper tried to paint lines on to their football pitch.[99]

> I should say it would be about 1935, when they first started having a park-keeper . . . and his name was Parker . . . Quarry Nomads . . . were playing on the Rec. and we didn't want the bloody pitch marked out – we had

a linesman running where he thought the line was, and
that was fair enough. And we got up there one Saturday,
and the pitch is marked out, and . . . this man Parker
there wants five bob. Well he got five bob all right – he
got rolled in the bloody mud in the goal, mate, and he
never did come back again . . . We weren't going to pay to
play on our own ground . . . You staked it out, near
enough . . . a stick up here and a stick there – you never
had markings – football pitch – in those days.

The Quarry spirit of resistance can perhaps best be studied in
the long fight to prevent Richard Pether, a local farmer,
from enclosing the Open Magdalens, a stretch of open common
and wood on which Quarry, together with its neighbours,
claimed collective rights. Old Headington settled for a compromise, but in Quarry the fight was never called off. The fight
for the Open Magdalens began in the 1850s and continued for
some thirty years, taking the form of mass trespasses, large-scale
raids for wood, and the illegal grazing of cows.[100] (The story is
told in detail in a History Workshop pamphlet, *Headington
Quarry and the Fight for the Open Magdalens*.)

Quarry children were quite as assertive in defending common
rights as their parents, and took a leading part in the fight for
the Open Magdalens – particularly in the incendiary fires which
marked its later stages.[101] They treated the entire hinterland
of the village as their own, not only the commons, but also the
farmers' fields. 'Up Haines's' (Haines's field) was a favourite
spot for blackberrying, as well as for Sunday games of pitch
and toss ('with look-outs all over the show'[102]); Pether's fields
for mushrooming; Bannister's for buttercupping; Clayhills –
part farm, part waste, part limepits – was occupied by 'big
boys' as a camp.[103] They used the Vicarage gardens 'more or
less as a right of way', and the vicar's trees as swings.[104] They
laid siege to the local orchards. Alfred Quelch, a potato merchant, who owned one of them in the 1870s, complained that
he was 'continually losing apples and nuts' from it, though it
was protected by a wall.[105] Another orchard owner is recalled
as defending his ground 'like a citadel' with stone walls topped
by iron spikes.[106]

One of the later battlegrounds for Quarry children was
Quarry Rec. It had been given to the parish of Headington in

1877, in exchange for the disputed rights on the Magdalens,[107] and had been intended for the people of both Quarry and Old Headington. But the people of Quarry believed that it had been given to them alone ('can't ever remember New 'Eadington being mentioned in it'[108]): boys from Old Headington, when they ventured to play on it, were 'run . . . back home' by their Quarry rivals. Bert Blagrove, an Old Headington man, recalls the hazards of a game of football:[109]

> They used to come across – if you weren't pretty smart, your football would disappear pretty quick, They'd just take the ball away from you. P'raps about six or eight'd come running across, and if you kicked the ball where they were, that ball just disappeared quick – they pinched the ball and went back towards Quarry.

So inveterate were the hostilities that in 1908 a public appeal was launched in Old Headington for the endowment of a new and separate recreation ground, where their children might play alone.[110]

Quarry was a village which had grown up singularly free of gentlemen. For centuries it had enjoyed what was virtually an extra-parochial existence, a kind of anarchy, in which the villagers were responsible to nobody but themselves – ' . . . there was no lord of the manor – they used to do almost as they liked. There was laws, but they used to keep 'em when they thought they would, sort of thing.'[111] Until the disafforestation of Shotover in 1662, the very existence of a settlement was illegal, an encroachment upon what was then royal forest, and Quarry remained in the nineteenth century what was called an 'open village', that is, one where lands and cottages were distributed among a multiplicity of owners, rather than coming under the control of a resident proprietor or a great estate.

There were no such things as tied cottages in the village. A good deal of cottage property was owner-occupied – a legacy, in some cases, of earlier squattings – and it was still quite common in the 1900s for a man to put up his own home, partly because of the availability of indigenous materials (many Quarry cottages were built of rubble stone), partly because of the frequency of waste ('if ever there was a bit of ground . . . you could put up what you liked'[112]). Charlie Jones, the carrier, who had also worked as a carpenter, called in the aid of a

brother ('they built the house between them'[113]). Spot Wright
learnt hod-carrying helping Eddie Woodington, a bricklayer,
to build himself a house, next to Bessie Barrett's ('he done all
the bricklaying . . . Taylor . . . done the carpentering, old Bob
Taylor'); he also remembers helping his brother Hubby to
build a house when he got married.[114] The whole system of
cottage lettings, like that of building, seems to have been
organized in a comparatively informal way, with ownership
in ones and twos and threes, and tenancies taken up through
local and family networks rather than in the open market. The
landlord, even if he were not one of the family (one way in which
the more fortunate members of a family could help the badly
off was by renting them a house[115]), might be a neighbour (as
in the example given by Dr Hunter when he visited the village
in 1864[116]), or the relative of a friend.

The appearance, some time during the last quarter of the
nineteenth century, of a house which proclaimed itself the
'manor', by no means betokened the arrival of a landowning
presence. The title seems to have been a mere fancy on the part
of its owner, John Coppock, a farmer-brickmaster. The 'manor'
consisted of no more than two old cottages put together and
surrounded by a high wall.[117] The view from the upstairs
windows was hardly manorial. Tommy Trafford's coal heap
might well have been the first object to strike the observer's
eye in the 1900s – it stood barely ten yards away. Also nearby
was Piggy Baker's yard, where pigs were fattened to take to
market, and below that the 'Mason's Arms', the most plebeian
of the village pubs, with a fish-and-chip shop housed in a shed
at the back, a sweet shop in the middle, and a one-room
parlour in the front (if it were a summer day there might be a
game of Aunt Sally in the garden). Next door was Tommy
Webb, the carrier, with his sheds, his stable and his yard ('a
real old yard . . . where he used to bring his carts in'[118]). In the
middle distance, if it were a week-day, the Cuddesdon College
washing might be seen, hanging out to dry on Charlotte Webb's
clothes line; nearby was Nancy Hooper's laundry, the biggest
one in Quarry. Conspicuous in winter time would be the gypsy
wagons which drew up for the season in the Mason's Pit.

John Coppock Junior, though naming his residence so
grandly (the title 'Quarry Manor' first appears in a directory of
1899[119]), does not seem to have given himself airs: when he

went shooting his companions were Jack Phillips 'up the brickyard' and a man named Lee from Temple Street, Cowley, 'a plumber';[120] he spent a lot of his time looking after ducks. Mayo Appletree, who inherited the manor shortly before the 1914 war – 'Squire' Appletree as he was sportingly called in the local pub[121] – was a far from aristocratic man. He was a bricklayer by trade 'but he used to breed a lot of chickens' (in some accounts they were Aylesbury ducks[122]). His pedigree was uncertain – according to some he was a love child. He is said to have inherited the manor after marrying one of Coppock's daughters who then died.[123] He is variously remembered as 'a bit of a scallywag'[124] and 'a farmer-type man'.[125] He found his drinking companions in the bar of the 'Six Bells'.[126]

Colonel Miller, who 'moved about a good deal amongst the tenants and villagers'[127] in the neighbouring parishes of Forest Hill and Wheatley, found no such loyal dependants in Quarry, and his Shotover estate, which abutted on the village's northern edge, occasioned in Quarry a predatory rather than a deferential regard. Nor did Quarry fall within the orbit of the genteel establishments which had grown up on Headington Hill or by the London Road. No soup kitchens were opened in Quarry (they were a regular feature of the winter months on Old Headington[128]); there were no coal clubs or lying-in charities;[129] no sympathizing ladies made their appearance at the cottage door with words of comfort or exhortation, to bring the poor religion, to correct their spending habits, or to teach them how to cook. In times of distress Quarry villagers were left to fend for themselves.

Quarry seems also to have escaped the gentlemanly influence of the university. College washing made its way up Headington Hill and provided the village's women with their chief employment. But the villagers drew back from a more direct dependence on the colleges. Quarry's menfolk did not dance attendance, as college servants, upon the gentlemen of the university, nor serve as ostlers at the riding establishments or footmen at big hotels. If they went to work in Oxford it was as stonemasons, carpenters or builder's labourers. Nor were Quarry daughters sent out to service in north Oxford, with its clerical and academic households and masterful wives: they worked at home in the laundries. Proximity to Oxford, so far from promoting a spirit of deference, may indeed have reinforced the village's inward-looking tendencies by providing a stimulus for Quarry's chief indigenous industries – stone-quarrying, brickmaking, and laundry work – and a market for its totting.

The hold of the Church of England on the village was also conspicuously weak. It came to Quarry very late. For centuries the villagers seem to have lived almost outside the reach of organized religion. Bishop Wilberforce, preaching a sermon in 1847 on behalf of the proposed parish church, referred to Quarry as an 'abandoned' district, where 'evil' had found a 'ready home';[130] eighteen months later, when laying the foundation stone of the new church, he was no more complimentary, and 'spoke very earnestly' on the need for the Lord's coming to deliver the parish from unclean spirits 'that . . . infested it and . . . made it notorious'.[131] The building of Holy Trinity – it was consecrated in 1849 – did not immediately rectify this state of affairs. It was planned by strangers (the moving spirits were a small group of clerical dons led by Dr Plumptre of the university and Dr Cotton of Exeter), endowed by outside funds ('nothing was raised in Quarry because there was no money there'[132]), and it was for some years only able to maintain itself by subsidies from the Diocesan Society for the Augmenting of Small Benefices. As the annual report of that Society put it in 1865:[133]

> Of Headington Quarry it may be said, that the Church
> exists there in its efficiency through this Society. Had it
> not been for the endowment provided by this Society, the
> Church would soon have been closed.

'Indifference' and the 'prevalence of Dissent' were still being complained of in the 1860s, and 'years of neglect prior to the building of the church' blamed for the low level of church attendance.[134] Quarry was not at first a popular parish with its incumbents, and indeed the parishioners were scarcely of a kind to recommend themselves to the ambitious young clergyman, seeking a fashionable living, or to the tired scholar exchanging his college fellowship for a quiet country retreat . . . one of the Rev. Samuel Manguin's remembered parochial duties in the 1850s was that of attempting to separate the gypsies when fighting broke out amongst them in the Mason's Pit.[135] The Vicarage, moreover – the old Vicarage, replaced by the present building in 1865 – was supposed to be haunted,[136] and perhaps this may help to account for the remarkably high turnover amongst Quarry's early incumbents – there were no fewer than eight changes of vicar in the first eighteen years of the church's existence.[137]

The one religion to secure a real hold in the village was Methodism, a religion which had been made by the labouring folk themselves – an earnest minority amongst them. It preceded the Church of England in Quarry by nearly thirty years, and seems to have been originally planted by a family of Coppocks, framework-knitters and quarrymen, with a long tradition of Dissent in the family, who migrated from Nottinghamshire in the late eighteenth century.[138] Some of the early Methodist meetings are recorded as being held in a labourer's cottage,[139] and though a chapel was built in 1830, the congregation remained working-class. Robert Coppock, at whose cottage some of the early meetings were held, continued as a leading member of the congregation until his death in the 1860s; he is described in the Diocesan archives simply as 'labourer'; Vallis, who as a boy attended chapel with him, remarks that 'he used to attend this place of worship in his Smock Frock until he died'; 'he was rather rough in his appearance but his Heart was right and very loyal'.[140] A later example is Arthur Vallis, a bricklayer by trade ('he used to carry his dinner in a red handkerchief') and later on a timber merchant, who rebuilt Quarry chapel in 1930; he is said to have been a 'poor scholar as regards writing' ('he could hardly write his name'), but completely devoted to the chapel and the cause.[141]

The population of Quarry, right down to 1914, was overwhelmingly proletarian. There was not a single servant-keeping household in the village in 1841;[142] one appeared in 1851 (the recently endowed Vicarage);[143] in 1861 there were two;[144] in 1871 four (two of them, however, the households of working men).[145] At the end of the century, there was still nobody in the village, except for the vicar, who might have been recognized in polite society as a 'gentleman'. '. . . In a population of 1,300 there are only three tolerably large houses, of which one is nearly always un-let', wrote the vicar, in an appeal for Diocesan funds in 1897; 'the inhabitants are all working men; half of them being employed in brickyards, and most of the rest being bricklayers, masons, carpenters and labourers in the building trade.'[146]

In the mid-Victorian censuses (the only ones for which the manuscript returns have been released) by far the largest single group is that of 'labourer'. Although the category is in many ways a misleading one (for reasons which will be discussed in part 2 of this chapter), and – to make matters more difficult – seems to have been used in different ways at different times (in some cases statistical fluctuations from decade to decade owe more to the census enumerators than to changes in the village itself), it may at least serve to suggest a rough and plebeian bias (laundresses, stonemasons and agricultural labourers are the other largely represented groups):

Census occupations in Headington Quarry 1861[147]

Labourer	55	Brickmaker	5
Agric. lab.	16	Shopkeeper	4
Brickyard lab.	7	Carter	3
Quarryman's lab.	2	Shepherd	4
Mason's labourer	2	Farm boy	2
Mason	16	Hawker	8
Laundress	22	Servant	5
Quarryman	3	Nurse	2
Washerwoman	3	House propr.	2

Brick-burner, shepherd boy, teacher, clergyman, cordwainer, errand boy, pauper, gardener, lace-maker, coach-trimmer, farmer, whitesmith, gardener's labourer, porter, haggle-cart man, carpenter and wheelwright, charwoman – 1 each.

Census occupations in Headington Quarry 1871[148]

Labourer	81	Bricklayer	4
Bricklayer's lab.	4	Shepherd	3
Stonedigging lab.	10	Errand Boy	3
Agric. lab.	15	Printer's boy	4
Laundress	29	Farmer's boy	3
Brickmaker	16	Farmer	5
Field work (women)	3	Mason	21
Farm servant	2	Dealer	2
Publican	3	Servant	8
Baker	4	Gardener	3
Carter	3	Laundry servant	2

| Teacher | 2 | Hawker | 2 |
| Carpenter | 2 | Nurse | 2 |

Stone merchant, plasterer, plough boy, blacksmith, shirtmaker, brickmaker's labourer, clergyman, brick-burner, brick merchant, publican, grocer, cordwainer, dairy maid, lace-maker, dressmaker, washerwoman – 1 each.

By Edwardian times there was a greater diversity of occupation with more men employed as craftsmen in the building trade, and more traders, carriers and dealers. Certain men stood out in the village by reason of their respectability or prestige, such men as Baker Vallis, the Methodist ('if anyone was making a will they always had his signature on it'[149]), or Stephen Goodgame, the proprietor of a little coal and vegetable shop, who went to work in a bowler hat, and was also a church-warden.[150] He is described as being 'a sort of unofficial solicitor about here' ('a very clever man . . . one of the best longhand writers you could possibly see'[151]): one of his jobs was that of measuring up land for allocation among the village allotment-keepers. A certain amount of rudimentary social distinction hovered about the building artisans – bricklayers were held to be 'posh men in their way' ('you'd always see them on a Monday morning with their shoes shining'[152]); carpenters are said to have gone to work in Chipping Norton tweeds.[153] The Methodists formed 'a little kidney on their own',[154] and so, at the other end of the spectrum, did the poachers and the 'roughs'.

But distinctions like this, though real enough, do not seem to have undermined the village's fundamentally plebeian character.[155] Winter was one great leveller: if it was a bad one all classes of Quarry labour were liable to be thrown out of work, building artisans, such as bricklayers and stonemasons, no less than the labourers. Kinship was another. So many of the villagers were related to each other – 'like the children of Israel, almost'[156] – that it was difficult for the better off to hold themselves aloof, or to set themselves up as a class apart. Marriage seems to have worked in the same direction; instead of reinforcing the lines of class it often cut across them, as in the case of the marriage of John Coppock's daughter to Mayo Appletree. Intermarriage also drew the villagers closer to the gypsies, and helped to stabilize their settlement in the Mason's Pit and on the Slade.[157]

Popular culture also helped to keep the forces of 'improvement' at bay. It was comparatively little touched by outside influences. There were four pubs in the village, but no temperance hall like the 'British Workman' in Old Headington,[158] nor any of the other later Victorian additions to life on the other side of Quarry Fields – Band of Hope,[159] night school,[160] reading room,[161] Juvenile Temperance Cadets.[162] Village feasts had no wealthy patrons or ladies' committee to dignify their proceedings or regulate their joys: Teddy Butcher presided over the November sheep roast (he was the village pig-killer in the 1900s) backed up by Sip Washington, the dancer, with a fool's bladder on a stick; and at Whitsun it was the morris men who took the lead, not the Friendly Societies, even though it was the day of their anniversary.[163]

Culturally the village seventy-five years ago was still to a marked extent self-contained – 'a little school on its own'. High days and holidays were spent for the most part in and about the village itself rather than in the streets of Oxford, or on excursions. Whit Tuesday was the chief holiday of the year, and Quarry sheep roast in November figures much more frequently in old people's memories than St Giles's Fair – the great holiday event of the year in Oxford city. Shows at Whitsun and in November were provided by the Bucklands, a well-known family of travellers, who treated Quarry as their winter base and then in the spring took their pony roundabout on the circuit of the local feasts and fairs. It is perhaps this self-sufficiency which explains – or helps to explain – Quarry's survival as a morris-dancing village, certainly the feature for which it is best known, for it was here, in 1899, that the English morris was rediscovered by Cecil Sharp. When Quarry people went dancing it was to the tunes of a local fiddler or accordionist – many of them, it seems, learnt from the local gypsies who 'had lots of old tunes'[164] (the leading fiddler of the 1870s, Sampson Smith, was a local gypsy, and he also danced in the local morris side[165]). Quarry was a very musical village, but the music was its own: there were no brass bands.

Whereas in many working-class communities there was a gravitational pull towards respectability in the later nineteenth century, in Quarry the 'roughs' were able to hold their own.

The police kept a wary distance from the village, and disputes were settled among the villagers themselves: '. . . there was no fetching the police, no messing about – they'd have you in the pit . . . or outside the Chequers'.[166] Physical strength was admired, and fights, so far from being something to be ashamed of, were eagerly followed – a 'real good punch up', according to older villagers, could go on for as long as two hours.[167]

2   Work

The industrial evolution of the community, from its early days until the coming of the motor-car factories in the 1920s, was largely within the class of heavy outdoor labour. 'No trade or manufactory carried on', runs an early nineteenth-century note. 'The Poor are all employed in Husbandry and at the Quarry Pits.'[1] Quarrying was the mother industry of the village, and it can be traced back at least as far as 1448–9, when 'Headington stone' first makes its appearance in a college building account.[2] The village was still known under the expressive title of 'Hedington Quarries' in the 1860s.[3] By this time its great days as a source of college stonework were over, but stone continued to be dug for a variety of useful, if less dignified, purposes – 'planking stones' for laying cesspits; 'binders' and 'breezers' for garden-walling; cobbles ('that was the small stone'[4]) for roadmaking, 'footings' and foundations. The Ordnance Survey 1:25000 map, published in 1881 and based on surveys made in 1878 and 1880, shows three separate pits being worked in and about the village, and two others nearby at Titup. Three pits were still at work in the 1900s: the Corporation Pit off London Road (later taken over by Magdalen College); the Vicarage Pit, worked by George Taylor as an appendage to his brickworks; and Jack Phillips's Pit, also an auxiliary to a brickworks. There was also at least one working pit at Cowley[5] (Greening's Pit, later known às Gale's, where a gang from Quarry was employed), and another at Holton. The last pit in Quarry – the Magdalen Pit off London Road – was still being worked in 1949.[6]

In the nineteenth century, brickmaking came to rival quarrying as the major industry in Quarry, and laundry work established itself as the major occupation for women. The brickmaking settled at the outer perimeter of the village, where the Coral Rag gave way to a vein of blue Kimmeridge clay.[7] The O.S. 1:25000 map shows two brick-and-tile works at Titup, a detached hamlet of the parish,[8] and three more on the lower edge of Shotover, up what came to be known as Brick-Kiln Lane (then it was only a track for the brick-carts, '. . . all mud an' water'[9]). Quarry provided many of the bricks for Oxford's Victorian suburbs, just as it had provided much of the stone for the colleges.

A third phase in the history of Quarry labour came with the development of the building industry, which in the later nineteenth century overtook quarrying and brickmaking as the chief local source of livelihood and jobs. One reason for this was the progress of 'improvement' – particularly in sewerage, water supply and drainage – which affected the country as well as the town. Another was the spread of Oxford and the rise of the new suburbs and out-townships, such as Summertown (a tiny cluster of cottages in 1832),[10] New Headington (an 'immense outgrowth' of Old Headington, on the eastern side of the London Road)[11] and New Marston.[12] (In the new suburbs the whole paraphernalia and substructure of urban life had to be built up more or less from scratch: in the early 1900s, for instance, there was a great deal of work for local labourers on Headington drains and sewers.)[13] Big contract jobs, such as the building of Headington Water Works ('the monster new reservoir')[14] in 1876–7, or of Cowley Barracks, also had their effect (Radley College and Wolvercote Paper Mill are two of the best-remembered contract jobs of the early 1900s).[15]

As an industrial community Quarry was comparatively free of the disciplines associated with steam power and the machine. No mechanical inventions lightened the burden of human labour; no repetitive processes dictated its rhythm and pace. Quarrying itself was still governed by an ancient hand technology. The stone was dislodged with a 'puggle' – 'a flat spear-headed piece of steel at the end of a long pole';[16] it was raked out with a long shovel (locally known as a 'shrid'); it was split up into its respective shapes and sizes with beetles and wedges – long metal chisels with very sharp points.[17] The larger falls of rock were dealt with by the sledge-hammer:

> sometimes they would go . . . perhaps ten or twelve feet
> under the rock, ready for blasting, they'd get a *'uge* piece
> come down, big as those two houses, put together, then . . .
> split them up into what they required, large, small, thick,
> thin, long.

Splitting the stone was tough work, combining bodily toil,
with a kind of rudimentary stonemasoning skill: 'you'd see
'em swinging these 'bout forty pounds hammers over, just like
a machine – bang, bang, bang – it marvelled me how they managed to split the stuff up as they did.'[18]

Brickmaking, like quarrying, was hard, rough work. In winter
the clay had to be dug from the cold, sometimes half-frozen
hillsides – 'all solid blue clay . . . just one mass of blue clay';[19]
in summer – when the making season was on – there was a
fearsome rush of work. 'Some of them never went home, they
used to sleep up there on the hacks. 'Cos they got so much a
thousand.'[20] Tempering the clay – 'making it soft and pliable . . .
before it got onto the table'[21] – was done by treading it under-
foot ('you know how these foreigners tread currants'),[22] and
gangrene is said to have sometimes resulted (one brickmaker,
who had been a morris dancer in his youth, had a leg off, the
result, it was said, of treading down clay).[23] The clay was
scooped out of the heap by the brickmaker's bare hands, and
the moulding, too, was done by hand ('no machines, not like
they make 'em today').[24] All accounts agree that the brickmakers worked tremendously hard, especially in summer:
'Start at peek o' light in the mornin' and they used to stop till
dark at night – worked very hard in them days – waren't a lot
of money about – Oh, very 'ard, very 'ard.'[25]

Employment in the building trade – the chief alternative to
the brickyards and quarries – perpetuated the bias towards
rough, open-air work. Quarry men were not plasterers and
painters or staircase hands, but bricklayers, stonemasons,
scaffolders and outside labourers. Most of the stonemasons and
bricklayers served an apprenticeship and ranked as artisans;
they were credited with a superior status to quarrymen and
brickmakers, but they worked in the same tradition – out of
doors, within the limits (and with the freedom) of a hand technology, at work which called for physical strength, endurance,

and an understanding of brick and stone. The stone-sawyer in the mason's yard worked under cover, but his work (all done with a hand-saw) was hardly less demanding than that of his cousin in the stonepit, though physically more monotonous. As for the builder's labourers, they were still very often diggers – 'the shovel and the pick and the wheelbarrow, that was their work, wasn't it?'[26]

Well-digging – 'quite a business round here one time'[27] – was one class of builder's work which had close affinities to quarrying. It was 'peck-and-shovel' work, though the pick was a smaller one than was used in a quarry – what they called 'kibbles'.[28] If the ground was clay the work could proceed steadily, but if rock was encountered steel wedges and gunpowder had to be used just as in a quarry: '. . . it would take a long time . . . five or six weeks if you came across rock – there was a lot around here . . . used to blow it'.[29] Well-digging involved an arduous form of bricklaying ('they used to be shaped . . . proper well bricks')[30], and the timber work was a complicated matter of wedging and shoring up in a narrow, confined space.

Most Quarry men were classed in the census as 'labourers'. But the term is a misleading one and gives little idea of their actual work, or of the variety of skills which made up their livelihood. In Quarry the distinction between artisan and labourer was by no means hard and fast. It did not exist at all in brickmaking and quarrying, and in the building industry it was qualified by the irregular conditions of employment: both artisans and labourers were employed as jobbing men and in winter they shared a common experience of being thrown out of work. The man with the permanent situation was an exception rather than the rule.

Occupational statuses in the local building trade were comparatively fluid, with men moving up and down in the class of work they performed according to the openings available. Apprenticeship was by no means the only title to advancement. Bricklaying, for instance, was quite often picked up on the job.[31] The builder's labourer 'carrying the monkey' often had enough all-round experience to take up jobs on his own. Sip Washington, for instance, who worked sometimes as a well-digger, sometimes as a builder's labourer, would turn his hand to 'nearly anything':[32]

Course he was only a labourer, he was, but some people be
handier than others. He was a handy chap, old Sip . . .
he'd do bricklaying or anything . . . one bit was at his
son's place . . . he built a greenhouse down there for him.[32]

Moggie Coppock was another builder's labourer who would
'turn his hand to anything': 'he'd do a bit of jobbing building
and that . . . rough walling . . . any garden wanted repairing. He built three sties and a feeding place for old Joe
Narroway . . . done the bricklaying well too, good as any bricklayer . . .'[33] At the other end of the scale, craft status was no
guarantee to the tradesman of employment in a particular class
of work. Jack Gurl, for instance, 'a bricklayer mostly' ('if he could
get it'), turned to well-digging and quarrying jobs when work
on new buildings was slack; he also did work on the sewers.[34]

The nobblers – an important and very characteristic element
in the local building trade – were usually men who had started
out in life as labourers. The nobbler was a kind of rough stonemason whose work stood mid-way in the hierarchy of skills
between those of the stonepit and those of the mason's yard. It
was a native village skill – as Quarry's surviving cottages testify
– and closely associated with the stone-digging. The job had the
status of a craft – 'an art in itself', 'same as bricklaying'[35] – but
it was open to all comers. Some men learnt enough while
working in the pits to set themselves up as nobblers – the case,
it seems, with Jackie Snow, one of the best-remembered of
them – others by helping out on a job. 'They used to pick it up
theirselves a lot in those days, they used to work as labourers
. . . and then they would [watch] what they were doing and
pick it up like that.'[36] In later years the nobbler seems to have
been confined to lesser jobs, such as building pig-troughs and
dry-stone-walling. Their standing may have been higher
earlier (one village nobbler of the 1870s is credited with the
stone archway at Cowley Barracks)[37] and they may well have
done most of the local cottage-building before the shift from
stone to brick.

The labourer in Quarry was often a man with his own, distinct,
'specialities'. They were not of a kind that would class him as a
'tradesman', but they were none the less real. Well-digging, for
instance, was in its own way a specialist job, with a definite
following among a limited number of men – 'round about a

dozen altogether', according to Bert Coppock.[38] In the 1900s it is possible to identify four distinct schools of well-diggers in Quarry (or 'sects', as they were once described to me). One was led by Mucky Gurl, the stone-digger, who turned to well-digging at times when there was no call for stone; another was led by Jack Gurl, a bricklayer, who contracted to provide wells for some of the new houses in Kennington; a third was led by Sip Washington and Mac Massey, the morris dancers; and a fourth – still often employed at it in the 1920s, and said to have been composed of men with a particularly strong taste for drink (well-digging was thirsty work) – led by Scabs Gurl.

The stone-digger, though classed as a labourer, was usually a man of parts – he had to be since work in the quarries was often available only for short periods at a time. His quarrying skills – the legacy of centuries of stone-digging – equipped him for employment in a range of kindred occupations: clay-digging on the brickfields, well-sinking for the householder, land-draining for the local farmers, trenching to prepare the way for water mains and sewers. Another alternative was to set up as a nobbler on his own, either alongside his job or instead of it: 'People that had anything to do with the stonepits, if they wanted a job in their spare time, they'd know how to knock a stone wall up, the labourers and people at the pit.'[39]

Brickmakers, too, had their own skills. 'They had to be really *choice* with their pick of clay to keep up the standard of the bricks.'[40] A man's work had his own individual stamp on it, as distinctive in its own way as the cooper's blockmark or the mason's sign. Unlike the quarrymen's, however, the brickmakers' skills were not easily transferable, and perhaps this is why the brickmakers were the most settled element in the village labour force (another reason was that, for a nucleus of men at least, there was work all the year round).

The typical Quarry labourer of the later nineteenth century was an all-round man within a certain class of work – a skilled and free-lance navvy. His reputation for physical strength enabled him to make a livelihood without binding himself to any single employer, or restricting himself to one exclusive trade: '. . . They'd always get a job, Quarrymen, because they was always good workers.'[41] Shifting easily and frequently from job to job he was likely to have picked up a variety of accomplishments and skills. Bobby Cooper, who went on working

right up to the time of his death as a very old man in August
1914, is a good example – a big man and a strong man ('about
six foot three or six foot four', according to a grandson's
recollections). He would do 'anything . . . in the 'eavy line.' He
worked sometimes as a stone-digger in Jack Phillips's Pit, which
was only a few yards away from his cottage; he went well-digging
with the Washingtons; he did trenching and foundation work
for Morris, a local builder in Old Headington to whom he was
related by marriage; he went haymaking at Bayswater Farm 'if
it was a rushed job'. 'He'd do anything', his grandson recalls.[42]

> He was anybody's man . . . slinging a sledge, or a pick . . .
> that would be easy meat . . . he had big, hard horny hands.
> There used to be a man living . . . somewhere down the
> old village [Old Headington] . . . named Morris. He was a
> builder, and very often he used to tramp over the village
> and say to Gramp 'I've got a few days do' – load of
> trenching or drainpipes or something . . . to get fixed . . .
> He used to go down to Bayswater Farm, the other side
> of the main London Road, where the old mill was . . . as
> a spare man if it was a rushed job . . . Then there was
> besides that a bit of work down the pit . . . he used to go
> down the pit certain times . . . George Coppock used to
> call him in occasionally, to do . . . trenching . . . He was
> here, there and everywhere. I couldn't pin him down, but
> I know he did a lot for this man that lived in the old
> village, because they were buddies more or less, 'cos
> apparently this man's wife and Grampy's wife, I think they
> were two of the Jacobs' family.

Labour in Quarry, like landholding, was dissociated from
any notion of deference. There were no big farmers to act as
village employers, no harvest homes where the master's health
was drunk in return for his hospitality and his beer (the case
at Watson Taylor's, for instance, in Old Headington).[43] Nor
was there a class of industrial capitalists to take their place.
Even on the brickyards, the nearest approximation in the
village to a conventional capitalist industry, the master was far
from enjoying a unilateral control. Each of the makers had his
own working precinct, 'his little cubby place', as one old brickmaker described it, with two thatched hurdles 'to keep the sun
off your head'.[44] He worked at his own table, from his own pile

of clay, and the bricks were regarded as his own until they reached the kiln. ('Should a sudden storm arise during the night, it meant losing your home, going to the yard, and cover up the bricks or risk them being ruined.')[45] Hours, too, were the maker's own, though this was a doubtful liberty when he had to work such very long hours to make up a living wage.

During the making season, which lasted from April to October, the brickmaker was free to use members of his family to help augment his earnings. There are still men alive who went up to work with their fathers as boys, but women's work in the brickyards is almost beyond memory. 'Old Mam Wharton' is the best remembered – 'as good as a man – in fact she was . . . stronger than a lot of the men', according to Putt Phillips, who was brought up on a brickyard.[46] Crowy Kerry also remembers her:[47]

> She used to come up all day and sand the mould and help her husband . . . She was a tough old gal . . . stout, got some go in her. Coorse, they done very well, the two on 'em, at that time of day.

Braddy Webb's wife, who used to push the barrow to the kiln, is the only other woman brickmaker who is remembered by name, but it seems likely that in Quarry, as in other brick-making villages, women's work was at one time common.[48]

The maker was master of his working environment, but at the mercy of the master when it came to pay. At such rates as the remembered 5s. to 6s. a thousand bricks – which was even lower before the strike of 1893[49] – close supervision was unnecessary: the master had only to go round 'occasionally'[50] to see if everything was all right.

A good deal of stone-digging seems to have been undertaken by independent companies of men, recruiting themselves for the job. At Taylor's Pit the employer, an active Methodist, was very much in control with a regular group of men at work – 'four . . . five, perhaps, when they had an extra big fall' – with Chass Cooper, a Bible-carrying ex-sergeant, as their foreman.[51] Jack Phillips, on the other hand, seems to have had no regular workforce at his pit, and for the rest stone-digging in the 1900s was dominated by the Gurls, a large extended family with many brothers who worked together on a variety of pits 'more or less . . . like a clan'.[52] At the Corporation Pit (locally known as

the 'parish pit' and later on taken over by Magdalen College)
their hegemony was complete: it was said 'you didn't need a
Union card to get into the pit, you needed a name – Gurl'.[53]
The same system seems to have prevailed at Forest Hill, on the
other side of Shotover, where the Holton stonepits were worked
by Thomas Slaymaker and his three brothers.[54]

The local stonepits did not provide permanent employment
but were worked by fits and starts, often for quite short
periods at a time. The labour force was far from settled. At
Gale's Pit, Cowley, where the Gurls worked for a time – 'two
pits in the same field' – there was a continual ebb and flow. Tom
'Mucky' Gurl contracted for the work 'at so much a yard',
and formed the nucleus of a group together with one of his
brothers. These did the 'hard grafting'. The remainder of the
group was made up by relatives who came down 'occasionally',
'at odd times', 'if they wanted a job for a day or two'. Bert
Gurl, who worked with his father on the job, recalls it:[55]

> My eldest brother he went down there at odd times, he
> weren't employed there, he only used to go down to give
> Dad a hand . . . and my two cousins, they come there for
> some time, Harry and Iver . . . Uncle Steve he'd come
> down . . . for half a day . . . They allus looked to Dad for
> a job.

(Centuries earlier, in the Merton College building accounts for
1448–9, one has a similar picture. The quarry was worked for a
period of seven months and sixteen different men were employed
on it. None of them lasted the length of the job. Two worked
for fifteen weeks, one for fourteen, two for nine, two for seven,
three for four, one for three, one for two and four for one week,
the average length of employment being six weeks out of a
possible twenty-seven.)[56]

Well-digging was organized rather like Mucky Gurl's quarrying, with one man contracting for a job, recruiting friends or
relatives to make up the gang, and finding tools, timber and
plant. It was unpredictable work – everything depended on
whether or not rock was encountered – and taking it on '(nearly
all piece work' and paid for at the rate of so many shillings to
the foot) was something of a gamble: 'You'd got to take that
with good and bad, you see, you might have a decent digging
all the way down – you might come across . . . rock . . . it was a

risk all the time.'[57] Sometimes the money was good, and sometimes it was bad, but in all cases direction was in the hands of
the diggers themselves, with no one giving orders. When
explosives were used the well-diggers adjourned to the pub:
'Because of the fumes they used to come up then. Go to the
pub. They spent a lot of time in the pub, in those days.'[58]

There were usually four men in a well-digging gang, 'couple
down, two up top',[59] but the composition of the workforce was
unstable, even though the jobs themselves were short-lived
(four to six weeks on average). Some men would stay for the
duration of a job, others for 'some time', while yet others would
put in an appearance only for a day or two, when extra hands
were needed. On one well-remembered job of the early 1900s
(a well dug at Kennington for Lady Argyle of Liverpool, where
the well-diggers had to drill through some forty feet of rock),
'a smart few' came.[60] There were 'generally about four' on the
job, Spot Wright recalls,[61] but there was a great deal of coming
and going. Jack Gurl, who contracted for the job, and Spot
Wright, who was employed by him, were the only ones who
lasted for the duration of the job (eight months according to
Wright, because of the special difficulties with the rock).
Crowy Kerry was there 'a good while', but then went off with
one of the others and took a job on his own.[62] Mucky Gurl the
stone-digger (who also took on well-digging jobs) and his
brother Steve both came down 'to give a hand' ('they was good
chaps in . . . a bit of rock . . . it was mostly to help us get the
rock out'): they 'didn't stop too long'. Dimmy and Dusty
Wright (Spot's brothers), Scabs Gurl and one of the Parsons
family all turned up at one time or another, but 'jacked up and
went' when they found the job too difficult.[63] Kenny Hedges,
who in later years was to be one of the village's leading well-
diggers ('the first time he ever went up a ladder was down a
well'[64]), was also there, and nearly involved in disaster when
winding a man down to the bottom.[65]

The drainers, too, worked in this way, hiring themselves out
to the farmers for short periods at a time. Often the work was
undertaken as an autumn job by men who spent the summer
months 'on the building'. 'They'd get there, a couple, or three
on 'em . . . They'd . . . say to the old farmer they'd do it for
so-and-so, and if that was a wet day they'd go in the pub and
have a good booze-up.'[66]

Rabbit-catching, another autumn employment, like well-digging and draining, was often undertaken by a small company of men, or sometimes by an individual working alone. The price for the job (which was subject to on-the-spot bargaining) varied according to whether it was woodland or hedgerow which had to be cleared: payment was sometimes in rabbits (which the catchers could sell off), sometimes by the yard, often both. In the 1900s the Kerry family, who were famous poachers, had almost as strong a hold on these jobs as the Gurls had on quarrying. Here is an account of them at Joey Rose's farm by one who was a shepherd boy at the time:[67]

Tiddle Kerry – Crowy's father – Gaffer, Crowy, all that family . . . was up there, ferreting for him. I had to take them half a gallon of beer every dinner time from the house – for their dinners and . . . Tiddle said to me one day, 'Tommy boy', he said, 'you've been a very good boy to bring the beer', he said, 'and pretty punctual bringing it', he said, 'and when us four is finished', he said, 'I'll see you have a rabbit for your trouble'. And of course a rabbit in them days was a rabbit . . . They went all round the hedges, ferreting . . . with the ferrets and nets – they used to net all the holes, you see – put the ferrets in and net the holes . . . They got this last fifty, sixty yards of hedge to do afore they finished, and I hadn't had no rabbit. As I went up that day with the beer I happened to go up under a little scrubby oak and there was six rabbits laying down there. Dead. I thought, 'Right, I must have one of them when I goes back.' So I goes down the bank, and out in the road, and goes up the gate, and gets over the gate, and rattles the chain . . . rattles the chain so they hear me getting over . . . Come off back I rattles the gate again, comes down, gets through the hedge, a-fetching this rabbit out. They misses him. They come down the farm that night to know if I'd had one on 'em. I said, 'No, I ain't received no rabbits. I come over the gate and went back over the gate', I said, 'you must have heerd the chain rattle each time.' 'So we did . . . Well there's one gone away.' That's the only way I got my rabbit off of them – go and take one myself.

When farm work was available it was likely to be given out –
and bargained for – by the job: 'take it on for so much, to do
the lot'.[68] In the corn harvest, women helped, chiefly at binding,
and families might take employment together. Mowing was
undertaken by men only, and sometimes it seems, as an 'extra',
brickmakers would take on mowing jobs before starting work
in the morning[69]). Mucky Gurl, the stone-digger, took on
harvest work 'when he couldn't get nothing else' ('he wouldn't
leave off in the pits to go on them jobs'). He took some of his
family with him and drove a hard bargain when the harvest
contract was made:[70]

In the summer time, this time of year, they'd go
harvesting, fagging and that. Mother used to go out along
with us. I can remember making the bands for 'em, when
I was a toddler. He went all over the place at it – that's
cutting the corn, shocking it up – so much a acre they used
to take it on. Piece-work. I can remember going band-
making . . . with him, and Uncle Harry, and Uncle Punch
I think it was, Uncle George . . . down the Ridings, in
that . . . big field. They was cutting some wheat there for
White's, at Wood Farm, and 'ee come round and asked
Dad how much he'd shock the oats up for, what the binder
had been a-cutting. And Dad looked round it. He said
'So many acres, Tom, that's what there is . . . Eighteen
bob', he said. 'No, fifteen', the old man said. 'Eighteen bob,
or I don't touch it.' 'All right', he said, 'have it your way
then.' 'All right', the old man said. First thing he said to
me – soon as this White was gone – 'Go and start laying
them sheaves in, boy', he said. 'Two in one tray and two in
th'other.' I started going up and down the field out there
. . . Him and uncles and that they shocked up their . . .
lot . . . in couple o' hours. Finished with it. Course, my
help was a lot to 'em, you see, they hadn't got to walk all
over the place, pick these sheaves up . . .

The working man in the building trade was often – by
necessity – his own master. Employment with the Oxford
building firms was intermittent and uncertain, but locally –
in and about Quarry and the neighbouring suburbs and
villages – there were endless and varied individual or sub-

contracted jobs which a 'handy' man, who had a working
knowledge of the different branches of the trade, might turn to.
Formal training was not necessary in order to put up or repair a
stretch of garden wall, to lay a cesspit, mend a roof, or build a
pig-sty, all common jobs in Quarry; nor was any more elaborate
equipment needed than a saw, a hammer and chisel, or a
waller's trowel. Often it was easier to get work by jobbing
around for it yourself than by trying to get employment with a
firm. Will Gurl took on cottage-building jobs. He was a bricklayer and had the reputation of being a 'good tradesman', but
sometimes he worked as a stonemason, and sometimes as a
nobbler; and when there was no work at any of these he went
quarrying with his brother Tom, or well-digging. When he took
on a house he seems to have expected no more from it than from
his other jobs – just a living wage:[71]

> . . . According to as I've heard Uncle and that say, he
> used to take on building houses on his own. I can tell you
> one house he built, and how much he had for it – Brook's
> house up London Road – where Evans's taxis be now . . .
> Uncle Harry was the labourer to him. Charlie Packford
> and his wife paid for it (the one that actually found the
> money to pay for the building, and the material and that
> was George Taylor . . . Mrs Packford's father) . . . They
> did the outside but not the carpentering or painting – they
> had to find somebody to do that theirselves – but I've seen
> the bills, what they paid for the bricklaying . . . and that
> included the garden wall – right round the garden, and
> that's a squarish piece of ground – outside lavatories and
> two piggeries. He built it for *twenty one pound ten*. That's
> what Uncle Harry told me . . . Mrs Packford showed me
> [the bills] 'cos I lived with Mrs Packford when I first got
> married – they was my wife's uncle and aunt . . . Twenty
> one pound ten he got. There was a big cellar and all there,
> you know, he had to dig that . . . The first price he put in
> for that house was £12, and old . . . Taylor . . . said,
> 'You can't live on that money, Will', he said, 'so you go
> back home and make a proper account of what you can do
> it for, and a living', he said. 'Don't matter what the price
> the others puts in', he says, 'you'll have the job, 'cos',
> he said, 'I'm finding the money to pay 'ee . . .'

Nobbling – Quarry's one indigenous craft – was usually undertaken by a man on his own, though nobblers also sometimes worked for master builders. The nobbler did not work from a yard, like the mason, but sorted the stones out on the job itself, 'straight from the rock-pit' (if he was walling) or at the quarry (if he were making kerbstones).[72] His working equipment was primitive: a walling-axe, with which he nicked the stones into shape, a quantity of lime and water 'mixed up to a good todge',[73] and a dexterous pair of hands, which enabled him to fit the irregular assembly of stones together as quickly as a bricklayer would lay his course. Setting up as a nobbler seems to have been for most men a phase rather than a lifetime's vocation, though one village nobbler – Jackie Snow – is said to have made a lot of money at it, and earned a village reputation in the 1902s as 'Lord Nuffield the Second' on the strength of a donation to the Wingfield Hospital.[74] Gerry Jones, on the other hand, 'a very good stone waller', moved in and out of self-employment: 'Gerry . . . worked on his own, mainly: not all the time . . . occasionally he was on for a firm.'[75] Bobby Trafford, 'another old nobbler', sometimes worked on his own ('the stone was brought straight from the pits . . . he never had no yard nor anything . . . he used to give them a price for the job'[76]); sometimes he worked for the council in the Corporation Pit, making kerbstones.[77] Blondin Bushnell, who put the wall up round Coppock's orchard, spent more time working for the builders ('generally for Benfield and Loxley')[78] or as a stone-digger in the Vicarage Pit.[79] Cribbie Coppock worked for Sims and Company, the Oxford builders, but he also had his own yard in Quarry, where he made gravestones, and took on walling jobs after hours. ('Anybody wanted a job they'd go to him.')[80]

The man with the horse and cart was another of Quarry's plebeian independents. It is difficult to fix their number, or to trace them further back than living memory. The 1861 census records only one: John Jones, 'Haggle Cartman'; the 1871 census none at all. The directories do not begin to list carriers until the 1890s, and even then confine themselves to very few names. Kelly's 1906 *Directory* lists only three carriers in the village – Tommy Webb, Charles Kerry and Charlie Jones.[81] There is no mention of Piggy Baker, the chief horse-dealer in the village, who took the cottagers' pigs to town, and whose mare

was in frequent requisition on the allotment grounds for ploughing and on the farmers' fields at harvest.[82] Ben Wright,
the sand-dealer, does not appear, nor does his cousin Joseph,
though both of them made their living by keeping horses and
hiring themselves out for individual jobs.[83] Nor does Harry
Horwood, who did haulage work for the local builders, nor
George Boulter, the best-remembered of the haggle-cart men.
Apart from Tommy Webb, none of the laundry-carriers are
mentioned, not Stunt Kerry, who, with his donkeys or his
pony '. . . went . . . a-taking this washin' about, back'ards and
for'ards';[84] nor William Goodall, the landlord of the 'Mason's
Arms' ('twice a week he used to go with the laundry . . . fetch it
on the Monday and deliver it back on the Friday'[85]); nor Jim
Hedges ('his old pony used to be out every day nearly, taking
the washing and that'[86]), nor Tom Hooper, whose wife had the
biggest laundry in Quarry, and who carried the laundry 'back
and for'ards to Oxford' on an old white pony.[87]

The laundry-carriers are remembered as an easy-going class
of men who relied in large part on their wives' laundry earnings,
though they took on other kinds of work spasmodically. Their
loads were comparatively light, and save on Monday, when
they brought the washing up from town, and on Friday or
Saturday when they returned it, they seem often to have had
time on their hands. (The more energetic did coke-selling on the
middle days of the week or combined carrying and dealing.[88])
Jim Hedges, squire of the Quarry morris-men, was one of them.
His wife took in laundry – 'in the sheds at the back' – with five
or six women and girls working for her, including her two
daughters;[89] his only regular work seems to have been that of
taking the laundry hampers to and from Oxford and Abingdon,
with his 'old gingery 'orse'.[90] In the summer he went 'all over
the place with the mowing'[91] and he also took part in harvest
work – 'he used to cut the corn with the old-fashioned scythe'.[92]
But for the most part he is remembered by one who grew up in
his household as doing 'nothing' very much, only 'roam about',
'see to his horse' and show-off his onions at the pub:[93]

Uncle Jim . . . he used to grow great big onions, and take
'em up the pub and sell 'em – he used to string 'em up
on a stick – great long ones. He had allotments, his
garden wasn't big enough to grow onions, he always used

to grow onions – I can see them onions now. He used to pull them off so far and then tie 'em up the stick, you see – they comes round selling 'em like 'ee used to do years ago.

Like many morris dancers he was a hard drinker, but very musical when in his cups:[94]

he used to get drunk but he wasn't one as 'ud quarrel with anybody; he'd get drunk and 'ee'd very likely have a jig, because he was one of the Morris dancers, 'ee used to whistle the tune and a man used to come with the fiddle and pick the tune up on this fiddle and that was how the Morris dancers started. I used to do it meself, 'ee used to whistle it: 'Come on Luce', he said, 'whistle this one' and I used to do it.

Tommy Webb is also remembered as 'an easy-going sort of person',[95] though in his case carrying was a full-time occupation. Both he and his family had the reputation for keeping very irregular hours – 'proper night birds', 'buggers for mornings'. It was said to be almost impossible to wake him up even when there was an urgent call: 'About 1 o'clock before he saw day-light.'[96] Will Webb, one of his sons, remembers arriving in Oxford at eleven o'clock at night to collect the Roebuck washing, and returning to Quarry well past midnight.[97] But he was generous with both his horses and his time – helping in removals (on one occasion he is said to have travelled as far as Banbury to help in a moonlight flit[98]), and lending his horses to those who had 'messages' in Oxford (such as a visit to Grainge's, the pawnbroker's, in St Ebbe's).[99] He helped the poachers bring in their hauls when they deposited them for safety on the allotments.[100] He carried on a sideline in coke, but not, it seems, in a very commercial way; 'if he thought they was a poor family he told them to forget it. That was silly, he couldn't afford to do that.'[101]

The haggle-cart men worked much harder. Instead of light deliveries they were engaged on heavy haulage jobs, carrying bricks, scaffolding and timber for the building firms, manure for the allotments, coals for the hospitals and the workhouse on the London Road. Sometimes they hired themselves out for work in the quarries. Their carts were heavily built, and drawn by a cart-horse rather than the laundry-carrier's fast trotting 'vanner'. Journeys (sometimes made on foot, leading the horse from in front) were slow: it took an hour to get from Quarry to the railway station at Oxford, and a journey to and from Thame took a day.[102] At the end of the journey there might be a great deal of loading or unloading still to do. Georgie Boulter, one of the best-remembered of the haggle-cart men, was a 'terrible powerful strong man' who had been a 'navvy bummer' in London (a sort of ganger); when he settled in Quarry he became a Methodist lay preacher, and after starting with one horse, which he drove himself, added another, for which he hired a boy. Bill Trafford, who worked for him as his first job on leaving school, remembers the work as laborious:[103]

Coal was the biggest item . . . Fetch a load from Oxford – I used to have to go twice a day . . . and it's an hour's walk from here to Oxford Station and an hour back – so long to unload – so long to load . . . they were big heavy cart-horses, you see . . . I used to like to go to the Warneford – they had a chute there, you could tip it down the chute, in other places you had to carry it or wheel it.

Laundry work, 'the greatest industry in Quarry, apart from brick-making . . . and stone-quarrying',[104] was a major occupation. It seems to have been well-established in the village at the time of the 1861 census, which records a large number of Quarry women under the heading of 'laundress' or 'washerwoman'. By the end of the century 'nothing else but lines of washing' was to be seen in Quarry on a Monday. The village acquired the same relationship to Oxford as had Kensal New Town ('Soapsuds Island') in London to the fashionable districts of Bayswater and Belgravia: it was a chief recipient for the weekly 'washings' of the rich. Quarry's laundries were cottage laundries and more or less domestic in character. A shed was put up at the back, where the scrubbing and ironing was done: the clothing was hung out to dry in the long cottage gardens ('used to plant a willow tree for posts'[105]) – or sometimes on nails in the kitchen.[106]

Like Quarry's other trades it was all hard physical work. There was water to be drawn continually from the wells, washing to be done piece by individual piece ('all hand done . . . all scrubbing';[107] 'it had to be like the driven snow when it was sent back');[108] there was the hanging out of it, the ironing, the folding and the packing in big wickerwork baskets. Here is one woman's memory of the work:[109]

> Course we used to do laundry work here, you know my grandmother . . . I can remember the horse and cart they used to take the washing to Oxford in, and the horse used to be kep' out there in an old shed, I can remember that, I was only a girl, but I can remember it. There was backways you see, to the washhouses . . . My mother kep' 'leven of us, we had to *work* – I've been up at laundry work at four o'clock a Saturday morning and I haven't finished till six o'clock at night, and hard work never hurt me. I'm sixty six nearly, so it didn't hurt me did it? The women in Quarry . . . they were the hardest working people as ever you come across. 'Cos it was all laundry work, all laundry work here, well they'd got to do it to exist, because the men, some of the men didn't bother. Only way they could bring up the family. Well we used to have second hand clothes, but we always had a good pair of shoes on our feet, *always*, always we did. My mother, my grandmother, worked hard, so did I work hard. Very hard I worked. But I don't think it hurt me. I don't mind work. I go out now of mornings, two hours. I don't mind work – well you couldn't live on the pension could you? . . . They used to work . . . the women used to work damned hard. They'd have a child one day – I've heard my mother say she'd had her child, and she's been up three hours afterwards polishing shirts. Jolly hard they used to work, the women did. If you come across any old Quarry people they'll tell you how the women worked. They *had* to . . . To live. They didn't go to service, they used to . . . go into the laundry . . . I know I had to go and 'elp do it . . . And after I was married I helped my mother.

The most successful laundrywomen were those who had regular contracts with the Oxford colleges, the city churches, and the big hotels – the 'gentry and college washing', as it is sometimes referred to. Emily Gurden, the second wife of Mac Massey, whose cottage laundry stood 'in the dip', below Green Road, took in laundry from the 'Roebuck', the 'Golden Cross', 'and all these big places in Oxford';[110] Mrs Tolley had the surplices and altar cloths of St Mary's, the city church

('2*d* for an altar cloth . . . 6*d* for a surplice')[111]. The Balliol
washing went to Mrs Narroway, the wife of a local builder.[112]
The washing from the Anglican seminary at Cuddesdon Palace
went to Charlotte Webb, who also took in washing from the
university lodging houses;[113] that of Sir Paul Vinogradov, the
medieval historian, to Mrs Horwood in Elms Road. In addition
to such established connections, numbers of cottagers at one
time or another took in individual 'washings', of the kind
advertised for in the newspapers:[114]

> LAUNDRY WORK wanted by good laundress (widow with
> three young children to support): recommended by Mrs
> Hayes 5 Rawlinson Road – Address, Mrs Morris, Old Road,
> Headington Quarry.

Laundry work was far from being a mere supplement to the
man's earnings; in winter time it had often to serve in their
stead. And in the family where the husband drank – or where
he was disabled – or was never able to get much work – or
where he 'didn't bother' – it might be the household's chief
support. This is the reason which some villagers give for the
enormous amount of laundry work undertaken in the village:
the wife's drudgery at the washtub – and that of her daughters –
paid for the husband's freedom:[115]

> Nearly all the women in Quarry used to take in laundry
> work 'cos half of their husbands didn't take any money
> home . . . they used to sup that in beer while they was at
> work . . . women had to do laundry work to keep the
> family going.

In some households laundry work was the only means of
support. Four of the eleven laundrywomen recorded in the 1861
census were widows, and in later years, as laundry work
developed into a major village industry, it seems to have
become the usual means of giving a widow independent support
– relatives and friends helping a woman to set up on her own
if she lost her husband. Harry Kimber's grandmother is one
example: 'She was left at 33 with six children, she had to
bring them all up without any help whatsoever, she did all
that by the washtub.'[116] Sarah Horwood had already set up a
small laundry when her husband (a haggle-cart man) died.

She developed it on a larger scale, and built up a good Oxford connection,[117]

> some titled people and heads of colleges, a few undergrads
> . . . like the Earl of Rosse . . . There was a Sir Vinogradov
> – he was a Russian and his wife was Norwegian . . . Sir
> David Ross . . . he used to live in Norham Gardens . . .
> we were always recommended.

Charlotte Webb's husband, Dick, died at the age of thirty-seven. She was left with a large family of children to bring up. Her laundry work provided the chief living of the household, supplemented, as the children grew up, by the rabbiting money which her boys raised from poaching, and by the breeding of Aylesbury ducks in the yard. Here is the account of Waggle Ward, a grandson, now in his seventies, who spent his early years in the household:[118]

> Granny Webb brought th' whole family up, when Grampy
> Webb died – that was our Mam's Dad – he died there
> when he killed hisself up in the brickyard a-making bricks
> – they used to want to just beat one another – it was the
> talk of Headington Quarry that Grampy Webb killed
> hisself at work, he did – and I've heard our Mam say
> plenty of times how ha'ard they was brought up . . . and
> Granny Webb then took washin' in . . . Our Mam . . .
> worked for Granny Webb, and they had one or two women
> in the Quarry, workin' for 'em, and Aunt Sarah – that was
> Uncle Dusty's brother's wife . . . They used to talk about
> how Granny Webb brought that big fam'ly up. Our Mam –
> Sarah – Sarah Webb – what we called Boxer Webb, old
> Boxer Webb, Tommy Webb, Charlotte – that was the girl,
> named after Granny Webb – Aunt Luker, Aunt Liza –
> there was a gang o' them waren't there? – and Emmy. Now
> shall I count them on my fingers to 'ee? Yes there was
> Flimpy, that was him. Let me get them on this hand. That
> was Snuffer, Flimpy and Buster. That was the three
> brothers, then Uncle Dick, Boxer, Flimpy, Buster, and
> Dick Webb. That was four brothers. Then there was our
> Mam, Aunt Luker, Aunt Liza, and Aunt Charlotte – four
> sisters – that was eight on 'em, eight on 'em she brought up
> arter he died in the brickyard.

The delivery was done by the older boys:[119]

Me and our Flimp – Flimpy, that was my uncle – used to
drive old Peter to take this washing back every Friday . . .
all round Oxford, up Banbury Road, up Woodstock Road,
all them houses . . . Granny Webb worked for . . . Used to
have this old Peter, used to have to borrow him off of
Uncle Tom – old Tom Webb, lived opposite the school –
you know, you've heerd talk of him – we used to generally
take it at night time . . . if it was summer time we'd start
about four, then . . . take our time . . . We used to deliver
round Oxford . . . on a Friday. Allus took the washin'
back on a Friday, yes and I think it was Cudd'sdon
College on a Thursday . . . Granny Webb was very
good at gettin' them up – doing them white, you know
– what the choir 'ud wear – surplices, they was very
particular on them – that was one big hamper from
Cudd'sdon, they used to have to be done *white*, and Granny
Webb was a good washer – she 'ud do 'em – one or two
people 'ad 'em, they didn't do 'em so well as Granny Webb
did, see . . . It was white clean washing – Oh there was two
big hampers like this, look, much as we could lift up in this
old cart . . . that 'ud be on a Thursday, and then we used
to have to take them round the Banbury Road on a Friday.

Widows in Victorian England are very often to be found
in conditions of near destitution, and in some of the poverty
surveys of the time 'widow' and 'pauper' seem almost inter-
changeable terms. In Quarry, however, laundry work provided
an independent alternative to going into the workhouse or
dependence upon parish relief.

3   Secondary incomes

The standard of life in Quarry is difficult to measure. Wages in
the building industry, for instance – the chief employment of
Quarry labour – were, by the standards of rural Oxfordshire,
high. Snow, the stonemason whose diary for 1882–4 has
survived, was earning 30s. or 35s. a week at a time when the

average farm labourer was fortunate to be earning much above
15s. a week. But employment was uncertain, and could vary
from day to day, depending on the state of the weather, and
the progress, or otherwise, of the job in hand. It was the same
in brickmaking. 'If it rained for two or three days you had
no money, you had nothing, you had to lose it.'[1] Hard work
and idleness, as so often was the case in outdoor labour, were
apt to follow close on one another's heels.

There were two economies in Quarry rather than one, two
sharply contrasted standards of life. In summer the means of
subsistence were comparatively plentiful, especially for those –
a majority of Quarry villagers – with substantial gardens or
allotments. There was a second season of plenty in mid-autumn
with the September windfalls, the potato-lifting on the allotments, and the killing of the cottager's pig. Jobs too were
comparatively easy to come by: in the building trade there was
so much work at the colleges during the long vacation that
stonemasons travelled into Oxford from as far afield as
Cheltenham;[2] at haymaking and harvest all hands were needed
whenever there was a rush of work (not only in Quarry itself:
in 1882 three local harvestmen were involved in a manslaughter
case while working at Noke).[3] Very long hours were worked in
summer, and there was a good deal of 'moonlighting' – i.e.,
taking on second jobs. Mowing was often undertaken as an
extra: 'They used to do it at nights, to get an extra bob or two.'[4]
So was some of the harvesting. 'Lots of them used to, when
they'd finished up the brickyards . . . harvesting . . . Oh, all
round Shotover.'[5] Steve Gurl, who worked at Taylor's brickyard, used to join his brother in the stonepits when he had an
'early mornin'' day.[6]

> They'd be up at 1 o'clock in the mornin' on that job. If
> they started at 1 o'clock (that was what they called
> 'drawing the kilns', taking the bricks and that out) they
> was finished at ten. That was a day's work. Twice a week
> they had that 'early mornin'', then next day they'd be
> on five o'clock in the mornin' and they'd work to about
> two o'clock in the afternoon – 'set the kilns' they called
> it . . . When he had done his stint he could go home.

Beer money was comparatively easy to come by in summer.
It was a recognized component of the wage in mowing, hay-

making and harvesting (at Noke, in 1882, the harvest company
in Hundred-acre Field had drunk fourteen gallons of beer in the
space of a single day, without, it seems, betraying any signs of
being the worse for wear).[7] Cottage-building, it seems, was also
encouraged in this way: 'a lot of it was done at night after they'd
knocked off . . . half of them, they didn't get any money at
all . . . there was plenty of beer on the job, and that's all they
went for'.[8] The morris-dancers enjoyed their harvest at Whit
week, when they performed in Oxford and the nearby villages,
as well as on club day in Quarry itself. Thomas Plowman
recalls their annual appearance in Oxford, eight in number, with
the 'fool' of the side collecting the by standers' contributions in
a tin.[9] Drink was closely associated with the morris, and free
beer one of the privileges which the dancers earned: Merry
Kimber's father had originally forbidden him to join the village
side 'because he was afraid of the drink'.[10]

The brickmakers, too, were plentifully supplied with drink.
Most of it they had to supply for themselves, but at Jack
Phillips's yard it seems the employer sometimes helped out,[11]
and there was also, from time to time, a 'Monday beanfeast'
when Davies, a coal merchant in St Clements, sent up a
'niner' of beer: Crowy Kerry remembers it:[12]

Davies . . . he used to serve . . . the brickyard . . . serve
'em in coal, you see – well, every so often . . . he used to
give . . . a niner of beer . . . He'd bring that up a Monday
mornin'. Well, they used to go up under an old tree . . .
and they'd have a day there, have that barrel of beer and
food, and then at night, if they was run out, then we used
to have to go down the Six Bells . . . They'd stop all day,
they'd have a sing-song and all that – and there was a lot
more as come to join in, y'know that's what made me like
beer so much, 'cos I had it when I was young, see. There
was an old oak tree, you know . . . 'bout a couple o'
hundred yards away from where they worked, used to have
this old tree, and sat there – prop'r enjoyment – Ah! they
used to have some good times at that time of day – though
there was not much money about . . . A 'niner' the man
used to send up – nine gallons barrel – and they used to
stand it on an old box there and tap it. About every two
or three months – something like that – he used to give it

them. Oh, he was a good man, Mr Davies in St Clements, Davies the coal merchant – he was a beautiful man – he ain't like they be today, they be very '*ard* today, a lot of them. All Monday . . . that's when they had the do, that was a Monday's beanfeast. Ah! they'd sing and stop there . . . I can remember that plain and yet it's a terrible long time ago, terrible long time ago, must be over sixty years. All day, they used to stop all day, till dark at night – or sometimes they'd pack all up and . . . go down to the Six Bells and . . . and then wind up . . . with a good sing-song . . . We boys, we boys used to have to go down the Six Bells, we used to have a strap – there was a handle to these big jars – two gallon jars – there was two handles – and we used to have a strap put through one handle, through t'other, and put it over our shoulders – and that's how we went on. But we allus got down an old ditch and drawed the cork and had a good drink, us boys did . . . They used to give us plenty of beer, you see – we was only young then, perhaps nine or ten year old . . . that was their favourite time, might have been twice a year, might be three times, summat like that.

Things changed with the onset of winter, and when the weather turned frosty, every branch of outdoor labour was hit. In a bad winter – and winters are remembered as being ''arder and worse' seventy years ago than they are today, 'longer and and colder'[13] – the distress could be severe: '27 away with various forms of cold', runs an entry in the school log book for 23 January 1914. 'I am afraid there are some who are but poorly fed – the pinch of poverty is being felt during this hard weather; eight degrees of frost last night.'[14] In the building trade, according to the memory of those who worked in it during the 1900s, men could be out of work for as much as fifteen weeks at a time. 'Trade is awfull here', wrote Merry Kimber, the bricklayer, in January 1908. 'We are walking about in hundreds and it don't seem as if its going to get any better for a time.'[15] Two years earlier, in the bad winter of 1905–6, he had a similar complaint. '. . . I have only earned a few shillings this last month with so much rain and now frost and snow and the town is very bad off for trade. My Christmas don't seem as if its going to be very bright.'[16] It was distress like this which first

brought Quarry morris (most of them men in the building
trade)[17] to the notice of Cecil Sharp. He was staying with a
friend at Sandfield Cottage, Old Headington, in December 1899,
when a 'strange procession' appeared in front of the door, 'eight
men dressed in white . . . with pads of small latten bells strapped
to their shins, carrying coloured sticks . . .' The men apologized
for being out at Christmas ('they knew that Whitsun was the
proper time'), but work was slack 'and they thought there would
be no harm in earning an honest penny'.[18]
Crowy Kerry, who worked in the building trade during the
summer, turned to rabbit-catching in the autumn, when the
trade turned seasonally slack. Here is his account of how he
started up:[19]

. . . Stokes . . . he was the man put me on my feet. Came
to me one Sunday morning and he said, 'Mr Kerry', he
says, I said 'Morning, Sir', he said, 'Well, will you come
and kill my rabbits', he said, 'I've been told you're a good
rabbit catcher.' 'Well', I said, 'I'm half tidy, sir', I said,
'Could you come now?' he said – I shall never forget it –
I'm going back some years now – 'Well, yes', I says. I
went and put me things on and he took me round the
farm and when I got to an old bank . . . it was *alive* . . . I
said, 'Well, sir, it's like this . . .' I says, 'This is no good to
me', I says . . . 'The rabbits will have to be trapped',
I says ('cos you could set the steel traps at that time of
day) . . . 'Well', I said, 'I'm at work for Kingham's now',
I said, 'But I expect I can get away for a bit', I said,
'They knows me – they knows this game I was at.
Anyway,' I said, '. . . There's one thing, Mr Stokes, I ain't
got sufficient traps to get a living', I said, 'I've only got
a few', I said, 'I ain't got the money', I said, 'to spend on
the traps.' I shall never forget the man as long as I live.
He said, 'Well, how much money do you want, Kerry?'
he says, 'Well', I says, 'I shall want a fiver, sir', I says,
'to send away 'cos steel traps be dear.' I shall never forget
it. He got his wallet out and he give me five pounds – well,
there wasn't a lot of five pound notes about at that time.
Well he give me five pound, 'Now that'll be for catching
the rabbits, Kerry', he says, 'I'll give you that: I wants
them rabbits killed down.' Well I sent away for five

pounds worth of traps – I don't know how many but I had
a tidy lot – I went on to his place – Oh God blimey,
rabbits wasn't in it – and then . . . other farmers and all
that – that he knowed – he told them all what I was
doing and that. The other farmers come after me then.
Norman from Denton (he left a wife and six daughters,
he was a beautiful man, he was) he comes after me . . .
his farm was adjoining Stokes's. Come after me one morning
up there, know if I'd come to him. I said, 'Well, yes, I'll
come over and see if it'll do any good' – 'cos it was
trapping country – all big sandy old holes. Well, then, I
had another farmer . . . Trinder, t'other side. I had his
farm; and then there was another farmer . . . t'other
side – I had his farm, just up the bloody hill . . . he wasn't
a big farmer, but he had a lot of big old earths there . . .

Brickmaking was very much a seasonal trade though it
seems that in Quarry a nucleus of men retained their employment all the year round. But the contrast between winter and
summer earnings was steep. During summer, the making
season, work was paid on piece-rates – so many shillings a
thousand bricks – and the man who was prepared to rough it, in
the long white nights, could make good money. Earnings could
be swollen by bringing in the children (and in some remembered
cases, the wife) to help on the 'lighter' kinds of work, such as
tempering the clay, sanding the moulds, and wheeling the
bricks from the table to the kiln. In October the making season
came to an end, and with it piece-rates and over-hours. Those
who stayed on were employed at clay-digging, and paid at low
and uncertain rates: 'It was day work in the winter-time – and
then if it rained you couldn't have nothing.' In winter the
brickmakers were able to get by only by going into debt, and
then attempting to recoup when summer – and the making
season – returned. 'Oh it was hard work, jolly hard work,'
Dutchy Wharton told me, recalling the time when he worked
with his father in the brickyard:[20]

I know my old father, and a lot more, the brickmakers,
they used to sub in the winter . . . you couldn't live on ten
shillings a week, and they never earned that sometimes.
If it was a poor week – so they would get a bit of grub,
they'd sub about five bob.

Quarry villagers of the nineteenth century did not depend
upon cash incomes alone: to do so would have been foolhardy
when employment was so uncertain and the all-the-year-round
occupation the exception rather than the rule. As cottagers they
produced a good part of subsistence for themselves. Meat came
to the family table from the pig salted down in the trough, the
rabbit snared in the hedgerows or the wood, even, in bad times,
from blackbirds – 'warent such things as joints about . . . in
them days'.[21] Vegetables, so far as possible, were home-grown;
fuel – for those who used wood, and who were ready to fetch
it from Shotover, Open Brasenose, or the Magdalen – was free.
In winter especially, all kinds of supplementary resources came
into play. Here is how Mrs Gaitha Kerry put it, a Beckley
woman who married a Quarry bricklayer in 1905:[22]

Oh, you couldn't work in the winter [on bricklaying]
because of the frost. I don't know what we did do.
Nothing much, we had to save our money, we'd do the
best . . . We never did get much money, we've never had
a lot of money . . . if we'd have had half, a quarter, or
been able to do like they do today it would have been a
wonderful life. [How did you get by?] Well, you see,
they had their own gardens, you never bought vegetables,
never such a thing, and you kept a chicken – chickens –
or a pig, you made everything yourself, you see, you had
your fruit, you made your jam, your pickles and
everything, and I suppose really that's how we did get by.
Because there was no 'unemployment', nothing of that,
no dole money or anything of that. Everybody had a garden;
and everybody had an allotment. We never bought
potatoes or anything of that, you hadn't the money to buy
them . . . Why, you couldn't buy those sort of things, on
the bit of money you had in those days, if you had a family.

The pig was a major standby in the harsh winter months
and in Quarry, as in other Oxfordshire villages, it played an
important part in the cottage economy – the means by which
a household, when pushed to it, could live off its own
resources:[23]

. . . you get a couple of foot of snow, or a period of hard
frost, there was no work going *anywhere*, neither brickyards,

stonepits, *nowhere* . . . in a hard frost period – which they
used to get years ago – went on five or six weeks
sometimes – then it was a very thin time. That's when . . .
pigs and things came in very useful, that was the mainstay.
There was always something to eat then. Even if it was
dry bread with it, it was all there to eat.

Pig-keeping reflected the seasonal cycle of plenty and want:
piglets were bought in the summer ('any time between May and
September'),[24] fatted while the season of plenty lasted and then
killed before Christmas, in time to provide a winter supply of
meat (if there were a second pig it might be killed in the spring).
Pig-killing, it seems, never occurred in summer: 'The old saying
was "pork wasn't good unless there was 'R' in the month" –
September, October, November, December, January, right
through to March, April, after that they didn't used to reckon.'[25]
  Quarry had an unusually large population of pigs. Whereas
in many villages the labourer's family fatted one pig – going
into debt with the miller to do so – in Quarry it seems to have
been quite common (even in a poor household)[26] to fat two –
one for 'indoors' to hang on the wall, the other to pay off debts,
and perhaps to provide money for extras[27] (one man is remembered as building his house on the strength of pig money). A
lot of pigs were kept on the allotments, but in the 1900s many
were still to be found 'up against the house almost'[28] and
seldom at what the sanitary authorities decreed to be a safe
and seemly distance. An attempt by the Headington Rural
District Council in 1896 to force the village pig-keepers to move
their sties at least fifty feet from the dwelling-place was
successfully opposed on grounds of the 'great hardship . . .
entailed on the poorer parishioners'.[29]
  There was also a good deal of cottage poultry. 'They used to
feed 'em mostly with grains and toppings . . . Butler's – he was
the cheapest man in Oxford in them days for it and Webb used
to bring the grains round, Saturday nights.'[30] 'Leasings' – the
left-over corn at harvest – was another source of feed. 'If you'd
got a few fowl you'd thrash it out for yourself with a stick.'[31]
Chickens were the most common form of poultry, but the
Kerrys kept Aylesbury ducks, which they sold to the Oxford
dealers. Richard 'Pinnel' Kerry, who made a notable contribution to late-nineteenth-century Quarry life (he is said to have

had twenty-two children by his two marriages, and is variously described as a 'poulterer', 'cricketer' and 'dealer')[32] bred Aylesbury ducks on a large scale: together with poachers' rabbits (which he dressed for local sale) they seem to have been his chief source of livelihood. Tiddle Kerry, one of his sons, kept fifteen or twenty ducks. 'I used to drive them ducks', Crowy Kerry recalls, 'up through Quarry, down the Green Road, to an old pond, the end of Kiln Lane – this end of Kiln Lane – I used to have to stop 'bout half an hour with 'em – swim on this pond – and then I used to drive them back home.'[33] Tod Kerry, another descendant, was a 'proper old duck man', and the pond at the bottom of Kiln Lane seems to have entered into his inheritance.[34] Charlotte Webb, his sister, also fatted ducks: '. . . There used to be a race . . . who 'ud get them off the quickest . . . young ducks . . . for Christmas . . . In the market Richards's was the best buyer.'[35]

Quarry's long cottage gardens were another important resource. They had been carved out of the waste, more or less at will ('up went the fence, that was theirs').[36] Straggling and irregular, they were large enough to accommodate a promiscuous variety of activities. Pigs were often kept there, laundry laid out to dry, horses (in one or two well-remembered cases)[37] stabled; henhouses built. Tommy Webb's garden, behind the 'Mason's Arms', 'used to be an orchard . . . used to be a laundry too . . . currant trees, apple trees . . . a monstrous walnut tree. Vegetables. And we used to have a lot of pigs up there.'[38] William Green, a builder's labourer and navvy, is remembered by his son as having 'something of everything' in his garden, a quite extensive stretch of land in the neighbourhood of Pitts Road.[39]

We had . . . fruit trees all down the centre . . . vegetables – potatoes and so on . . . we had the well half way down the garden – where we got the water – pig sties half way down . . . hen houses . . . something of everything . . . We never bought vegetables.

Mark Cox, the fiddler in the morris side which performed at Oxford Corn Exchange in 1897, had a very large garden at the back of his home ('Industry Cottage'), and cultivated roses. 'It was a very large family and we had very little money', one of his daughters told me. She remembers taking a bunch of roses to sell in Oxford market 'now and then'; and sometimes some snipe, which he had shot with his gun (they fetched 8*d*. or 9*d*. each). Sometimes he went out clay-digging on the brick-fields, and in the spring of the year he would 'do a bit of mowing'. 'There was nothing really regular but we had little bits and dabs.'[40]

In addition to the cottage garden – 'the big gardens at the back' – many villagers could boast of an allotment. Quarry was unusually well-endowed with allotments, and they seem to have been established at an earlier date than those of many other villages. Frederick King, valuer to the parish of Heading-ton in 1857–8, complained of there being no fewer than thirty-seven 'Garden Allotments' on the Slade, 'the Rents upon which are . . . paid irregularly';[41] and an auction notice, dated 1876, preserved in the Bodleian, records the existence of another group of allotments – for 'Sober and Industrious Labourers of good Character' – at the bottom of what is now Windmill Road.[42] The amount of land available was further increased under the Allotments Extension Act of 1882 when 'upon application by a number of inhabitants of Headington Quarry', the Poor's Land on Shotover, which the churchwardens had been leasing out to John Coppock at a yearly rental of £7–8, was divided up amongst the villagers.[43] Finally there was the partition of Quarry Farm in 1908, some of which went to allotments.[44] By the 1900s, the allotments were the chief focus of the villagers' gardening activity.

Apart from gardens and allotments there was also what older villagers somewhat vaguely refer to as 'ground' – one- and two-acre individual holdings on the village's wasteland edge. Tod Kerry had a big pond with some land around it where he bred Aylesbury ducks and kept a kennel; it was variously known as 'the Lake', 'Shelley's Pond' (or 'Shelley's Pool'), and in later years he referred to it affectionately as his 'Dardanelles'.[45] Bloomer Cooper, a carpenter, 'used to have a smallholding up of Shotover – type of smallholding – kept animals up there'.[46] Dick Webb, the brickmaker, who died as a young man of thirty-seven, 'owned a piece of land along the Moors . . . acre of ground along there'.[47] Mucky Gurl, the stone-digger, had 'a lot of ground up here'. He ploughed it with horses (hired from Piggy Baker), and grew barley to feed his pigs ('he used to have the little rick an' all'[48]):[49]

Grampy used to go along there every night, with a big
bath full of pig dung, and then come back with a big
bath full of cabbages or whatever was about – potatoes –
never came back empty-handed – and that's where he got
his name, they used to call him 'Mucky' . . .

Gardening in Quarry was a major activity. Men are remembered as going on to the allotments straight from work, and
having a go at them until it was dark: 'They didn't come home,
you see . . . we had to take their tea up there.'[50] Charles Snow
the stonemason (according to family tradition) was up at four
on a summer morning, worked at his garden till five, and then
set off for Oxford.[51] Some entries in his diary for January 1884
show that it was a continual preoccupation:[52]

2.1.84   Wednesday. Very dull. planted row Rasberries
             canes cross Garden
12.1.84   Saturday slight frost but a very Beautiful day
             Shifted apple tree and goosberries put Well lid on
15.1.84   Very fine day done the flower bed up and shifted
             plum tree
22.1.84   very rough day planted Rhubarb by Rasberries.
             Ducks laid first eg.
29.1.84   very damp day made Mallet planted Gooseberries
             cuttings.

Fred Tolley's father, who had an allotment on Peat Moors
('it was only 12 pole, but it seemed a hell of a lot when you
started diggin' it') went out there 'every spare minute he had . . .
straight from work at night'. Potato-pulling is the time which
Fred remembers best. 'The old man used to march us up there.
I can hear him now, when we were picking up 'taters. "Take
'em up, don't tread the buggers in." '[53] Potato-pulling was
treated like a harvest; the whole family was roped in, and the
mother and the boys spent more time on it than the old man
himself:[54]

We used to have a couple of days off school, when we got
the 'taters up. We used to . . . borrow the old man's pony
and cart, to get them home (he used to have a little farm
place, his old man) . . . We used to go up, mother and us
boys, and dig up all day and when the old chap come
home from work, he come straight up and load them up

and away we come. Once we dug up the wrong plot –
someone else's potatoes – and the old man come up at
night: he swore, but he took them round to the fellow . . .
it ended all right . . .

Mucky Gurl, another strong character ('he was ever so strict'), is
also remembered for the way in which he could mobilize the
family when there was anything to be done on his ground:
'All the boys had to help, mind you, even though they went
to work. When they come home their work wasn't done, and
his wife used to go up there.' 'When I was a boy I used to go
and take cabbages all over the place for him,' one of his grand-
sons recalls, '. . . he wouldn't give you money . . . but he'd give
you a cake or a slice of bread and jam.'[55]

Livelihood in Quarry was built up in quite complicated ways.
Charlotte Webb, for instance, with her large family of boys to
bring up, relied not only on her laundry work, but also on the
Aylesbury ducks which she bred in the yard, and sold to the
Oxford dealers, on the pigs that were fatted there, and on
the rabbits which her boys (expert poachers) brought in for
the hotpot or for sale. The household did not break up on her
husband's death. No one went on the parish, despite the
absence of a male breadwinner, and though a widow she was
able not only to bring up her own boys, but also to provide
meals for Pedgell Webb, after his wife died in 1902, and to
give a winter home to another cousin, Nobby Webb, an itinerant organ-grinder, when he returned from his season's travels.[56]
This kind of double-banking was common. Publicans in
Quarry, for instance, usually had second and third strings to
their bows. Natty Rivers who was at the 'Mason's Arms' in
the 1860s and 1870s – he is remembered as a very old man in a
little cottage near the bottom of the Mason's Pit[57] – was a
'labourer' as well as a 'beer retailer' according to the census of
1861;[58] Stephen Goodgame at the 'Chequers' was also a
quarryman; George Coppock at the 'Six Bells' a farmer – and
later on a brick merchant – while his namesake at the 'Crown
and Thistle' was, like Stephen Goodgame, put down in the
1861 census as 'quarryman and publican'.[59] William Goodall,
the well-remembered landlord of the 'Mason's Arms' in the
1900s, went round well-digging, contracted for walnut-bashing

jobs ('no trouble to sell 'em, twelve a penny'[60]), did some
carrying work for the local laundrywomen, and in the 'Mason's
Arms' itself carried on a supplementary trade in fish and chips,
pickled salmon, potted meat and sweets.[61] Carpenters, according
to one of them, often did 'little odd jobs' on the side. Jack
Taylor of Titup, as well as working in the building trade, used
to make coffins at the bottom of his garden 'just for friends'.[62]
Bob Coppock's father 'used to do little odd jobs for people
. . . they nearly all had a workshop in them days'. Mostly it was
windows and window frames ('somebody had a window blown
out or anything of that'), or else ironing-boards and wash-trays
('a lot of laundry work done in Quarry'). He also helped out
with the woodwork 'if a chap was a-building a house for
himself . . . there was a lot of that done at one time'. Another
remembered job was that of fitting up the 'Six Bells'.[63] Charles
Snow the stonemason was another man who turned to jobbing
carpentry, especially, it seems, in weeks when he was unemployed. He also spent a lot of time improving his garden, both
of them activities which brought him in a few shillings even if
they did not make up for the loss of his wage. Here are some
more entries from his diary:[64]

Tues Jan 1 Dull raw cold day
       fetched tools from Institute
       Bot well Rope 3/4
Friday 4 Jan very Dull and Damp sharped Saws
1–5 Jan week bot stool top from sawyer . . . made stool
Tuesday 8 Jan . . . made . . . stool
Saturday 12 Jan . . . put well lid on
18 January Friday made Trough very fine day Pea soup
for Dinner
12–19 January 1/2 Bus lime & 2/4 in pipes Stone for
trough 4d
19 Jan Sat fine day made Ducks Pen

Trading and dealing provided a number of villagers with
a secondary income. There was no separate class of shop-
keepers in Quarry until a very late date (even today the village
is singularly deficient in shops), but there was a good deal of
'penny capitalism'. Numbers of working men dabbled a bit in
trade, if only as a sideline. Edmund Vallis, for instance, before
he set off to work in Oxford as a 'banker' mason, would bake

a few dozen loaves and leave his sons to carry them round in a basket.[65] (The business he founded is now Quarry's only baker's.) Charles Coppock, a foreman carpenter, set up 'a bit of a place' selling meal 'in his spare time'.[66]

> The millers used to deliver the stuff and the people used to go round and get the meal for the pigs and all that sort of thing . . . corn for the fowl – they nearly all kept fowl and pigs, you see – that was his spare time job.

He is remembered as 'a sort of middleman' and 'a bit of a merchant'.[67] Harry Coleman, one of the three village blacksmiths, 'used to have a bacon shop . . . used to make his own 'og puddings'.[68] Moggie Coppock, a builder's labourer, was also a Sunday morning barber: ''Ee used to have a wash house place the side of his house, and 'ee used to . . . cut their hair for about twopence a time.'[69] His hours were strictly limited, he would never start before ten in the morning, or miss opening time at the pub: '. . . If the workhouse bell went for twelve o'clock and he'd half cut your hair, 'ee wouldn't finish it – straight up the pub – 'ee'd leave you with half an haircut, 'ee wouldn't cut it after . . . twelve o'clock . . .'[70] Alf Kerry, a scaffolder with Sims and Company, Oxford, bred pigeons which he sold in the village at a shilling or two each ('a pigeon like that 'ud make a hundred pounds today').[71] Tommy Trafford, a small-scale farmer, also had a little coal business ('his daughter used to serve the coal – Maud').[72] Bill Trafford, his grandson, remembers wheeling a barrow round the village 'on a Saturday or in an evening'.[73]

The man with a horse and cart was often a trader, in a small, informal way. His journeyings to and from Oxford put various opportunities in his way. College dripping (a favourite relish in other Oxfordshire villages as well as in Quarry[74]) was one. 'It wasn't exactly a business', one old man recalled:[75]

> A lot of them . . . used to get it, these chaps, when they used to take the washin' down, . . . the College washing . . . they used to get it from . . . the . . . buttery . . . That was a big item in the diet at that time of day, College dripping . . . They'd sell it to anybody. Not very dear . . . 'bout sixpence a pound I suppose. Say I knew the carrier and he was coming to our place, they'd say, 'Ask him,

Charlie, for a pound of dripping' . . . He used to bring it on
the off-chance, it wasn't exactly a business, they knew
when he was deliverin' . . . and . . . they'd probably waylay
him on his way home.

Another trade which grew up in a similar way was that in
coke:[76]

They all used to do it, that's how our Dad first started the
coal. See, they used to fetch the washing up, Oxford,
which used to carry 'em over Friday Saturday Monday –
and the rest of the week they were looking for work.
Well everybody with a horse – they all had 'orses up here –
you could say I suppose, 25 per cent of the people in the
village were self-employed – they were looking for a way
and means of making a living – and I think they all used
to . . . sell . . . the old bushels of coke . . . I can remember
our old man, he used to do that, and he gradually went
into coal from there . . .

Charlie Jones (who traded in college dripping too) was one
carrier who fetched up coke: he set up a coke yard next door to
his home. Another was Tommy Webb, who also brought up
brewery grains for the village pig-keepers ('it used to be five-
pence a bushel in them days'),[77] and had another, more
occasional, sideline, selling off his horses' surplus hay ("bout
tanner a truss').[78] Stunt Kerry sold coke out of his donkey-cart
for a penny and twopence a bushel ('. . . used to fetch that coke
. . . from the gasworks down in Oxford – in Gas Street . . . St
Thomas's, he used to fetch it with a donkey').[79] His business
prospered. Starting with one donkey – 'old Peter' – he later on
had two. In 1913, when a maintenance order was made against
him on behalf of a girl at Barton, his coke round was valued by
the police as worth from £2 to £3 a week (Kerry himself said
his average earnings were 10s. a week).[80]

Some trading was more occasional than this, as when the
poachers had a surplus of rabbits to dispose of, or an allotment-
holder had some prize onions – or seed potatoes – to spare. All
kinds of little transactions went on as private deals, sometimes
in the home, sometimes on the allotments, sometimes in the
pub. Those who kept chickens were liable to find themselves,
whether they chose it or not, treated as retail outlets for eggs:[81]

If you'd got a lot of fowl, anybody 'ud come to your house, and ask if you'd got half a dozen eggs, they used to get rid of the surplus like that, they didn't do it as business, but . . . anybody want half a dozen eggs they'd come to you for 'em.

When a pig was killed the surplus pieces might be sold to neighbours:[82]

. . . you didn't have to be told – you'd hear the pig squealing and . . . go in the direction of the sound. And then your mothers . . . they'd go and sort of put an order in . . . have, say, spare ribs and brisket . . . sixpence a pound you'd get, a spare rib.

Garden surpluses gave rise to a certain amount of more or less impromptu trade. Tod Kerry used the 'Six Bells' to dispose of his, and swapped them for beer: '. . . he'd just take a bit of green stuff of a mornin' there, for anybody give him a pint of beer . . . or a bunch of flowers . . . they'd give him a pint, but he 'udn't sell nothing'.[83] Charles Snow, on the other hand, sold his surpluses for money and registered sales in his diary. In the week of 3–9 February 1884 entries show a total income of of £2 1s. 3d.: £1 13s. 5d. came in wages, 3s. 6d. from mallets 'sold . . . to F. Collett', and the remainder from potatoes, shallots, and peas: other weeks have entries such as 'flowers, 1s. 4d.', 'Flowers, 1s. 5d.'.[84] Between gardeners themselves a good deal of swapping went on, especially on the allotments:[85]

These old chaps never reckoned to buy seed potatoes – they used to swap with someone else . . . make a change . . . he'd save some seed out of his and I'd save seed, and then we'd change them over. Perhaps he had a bit of ground that was heavy, and you had some ground that was light . . .

A good deal of trading went on in piglets which, at six or eight weeks old, could fetch (in the 1900s) from 15s. to £1 apiece, depending on the state of the market.[86] It was cheaper than fatting a pig "cos they didn't use to keep a sow so well as they kept a fat pig' (sows were fed on 'rough stuff', fat pigs on barley meal).[87] Even so it was a risky business: 'One time they'd be dear, 'nother time they'd be cheap. If you were lucky you were

alright, but if you were unlucky, well, you lost money on it.'[88]
All kinds of men tried their hand at it, nevertheless. One of them
was Merry Kimber, 'the proud owner of eleven young pigs' (as
he wrote to Cecil Sharp in 1910, after his pig had successfully
farrowed), who relied on his piglets to 'square him up' at the
end of the season.[89] In October 1913 he met with disaster, and a
letter he wrote at the time shows the strain of speculating on a
tight income:[90]

> I have had the misfortune to lose my sow and eleven
> small pigs, I tried my best, so did the vetinary [sic]
> surgeons but it was no good, you see she has a slight cold
> and this caused her to farry a month before time. Its all
> gone and buried – as you know bacon is well up in price so
> is pigs these eleven & sow would have been worth £14
> now I have lost all my whole summers work throwed
> away, its fairly knocked me up . . .

Fatting a pig for sale was much more general than attempting
to breed them, but all the same there was a risk:[91]

> sometimes the meal would go up in price and the price of
> meat would go down, and by the time you'd get your pig
> fat the price of meal was up – you'd lose money on them
> then. Then another time it 'ud be the reverse. You had
> to take a chance.

Some pig-keepers, like Merry Kimber, took a chance on fatting
more than two. Vic Morris's father kept eight:[92]

> . . . that's how he bought this house. He used to have
> eight pigs, two sties, four in each, and he wouldn't touch
> a penny of his money – or mother's – to rear them up, and
> that's how he bought this house, he borrowed the money
> off the Oddfellows, paid them back out of his pigs.

Charlie Packford bought his house on London Road in the same
way. 'He used to keep pigs in them sties and fat 'em, and the
money from them pigs used to pay the father off for the
house.'[93] In later years pigs were sold off to Bessie Barrett, a
pork butcher who set up shop in the village about 1914. She
'arranged' with the locals as to when the pig should be killed.[94]
Other pigs went to the butchers in Oxford, the middleman being
Piggy Baker, who also dealt in piglets. Fatting pigs for sale was

even more risky as a speculation than breeding them, though Quarry Pig Club, set up in 1903, tried to minimize the possibility of loss.[95]

Making a living was a family affair rather than a matter for the man of the house alone. The wife's laundry work might count for as much as the husband's earnings – more so if he were in and out of work; and housekeeping itself depended on her own efforts rather than the amount of his allowance. The children's clothes, for instance, depended upon her skills with the needle and thread: 'You done your own sewing – you didn't have new things like you do today.'[96] Pig-keeping was the joint responsibility of the husband and the wife – one great source of feed being the allotments ('the old cabbages they used to bring down for the pigs, anything off the allotment'),[97] while the other was cottage waste. (The pig served as both a dustbin and a sewer: one argument advanced in defence of cottage pig-keeping, when the question was debated before the Headington parish council in 1896, was that if the sanitary authority did away with pigs they would be creating another nuisance in their stead, 'because the district was not like a town where all the rubbish was fetched away in the cart'.[98]) Children too played a part, 'hunting for pig-nuts' (acorns) on Shotover[99] and foraging up and down the village – and the neighbouring fields – for waste.

When the pig was killed, the woman of the house was involved in a whole series of manufacturing activities. 'Flere', the pig's jacket, was melted for lard ('we used to prefer it to butter');[100] blood, gathered at the killing, was made into black puddings ('nearly everybody, when they had a pig killed, they used to make black puddings');[101] chitterlings, the pig's innards, went into faggots ('boiled and fried 'em, didn't you?'),[102] trotters into jelly for soup. The pig's head was preserved as brawn ('still see it now with the whiskers sticking in'):[103] hams and bacon were taken off the body and treated with saltpetre ('they used to chuck it in these brine baths').[104] When the salting was finished the pig was hung up on a wooden rack 'right across the room', for pieces to be cut off as they were needed. 'That was a better picture than a oil painting because . . . you could take it down and have your piece off of it . . . And then you could have 'am for Christmas, home pickled my mother used to have her own recipe.'[105] Once there, the bacon was freely available for the early morning breakfast, the luncheon basin (kept hanging on the wall, then tied up in a handkerchief and taken to work), or the evening hot-pot. One popular dish made out of it was bacon 'clanger' (a roly-poly of bacon chopped up with sage and onion, and rolled in a suet crust).[106] Another was 'shackles', the Quarry stew:[107]

> Coorse, that home-cured bacon, when you went and got
> that . . . in a pot – and there was cabbage and that
> cooked with it – you had some *food*, yes, you had some
> good food at that time of day – that's what made 'ee
> live so long – now today they don't want nothing of that,
> do they? people don't want . . . a piece of fat home-cured
> bacon – I've got a son who told me 'ee wouldn't have no
> fat – just what would do them good – a bit of fat bacon, at
> that time of day they were glad to . . .

Pickling vegetables was another species of manufacturing activity which, in the autumn, took up a lot of the woman's time. In the household where Charlie Jones and Elsie Wright grew up, everything was put to the pickle. 'As far as our mother made it, it was mixed pickle wasn't it? – piccalilli and pickled onions, pickled shallots . . .' 'They make a better pickle than onion.' 'And of course mixed pickle got all the vegetables in – marrow, onions, cauliflower, beans . . . September . . . that was the season, you see . . .' 'Your shallots ripening, and your cauliflower with a head in it . . .'[108] Fruits were also extensively preserved. 'There was no bottling in those days, you didn't hear of bottling fruit . . . it used to be made into jam, that's how you preserved the fruit . . . That keeps all right.'[109] Jams were made in enormous quantities, and in a greater variety than today. They are remembered with affection by those who grew up with them in childhood. Ida Bache recalls that her mother made a cupboard full of jams 'for the winter': '. . . Gooseberry jam . . . blackberry and apple . . .'[110] 'A hundred pound of jam it had to be, of a year, that was the quota.' Elsie Wright recalls:[111]

> Every fruit that came along . . . Fig and rhubarb (the
> dried figs helped to make the rhubarb set, you see),
> blackberry and apple; gooseberries; plum and apple;
> damson jam . . . I remember her making carrot jam, one

year, didn't she? Crab-apple jelly; . . . gooseberry and
strawberry. There was a jam they used to call 'mixed
fruit' with all different kinds of fruit which were at that
part of the season . . . Blackberry jam . . . blackberry and
apple . . . marrow jam . . . jam roly polies and jam
tarts . . .

Eggs too were preserved 'enough to last all winter . . . when
chickens didn't lay'. 'We always panned eggs in the winter',
Mrs Stowe recalls, 'You had some preserve, and you put the
egg in and they'd keep.'[112]

A few women were able to stretch their household production
to bring in a little money. Those who sold eggs, for instance, or
who had a speciality in cooking or homemade sweets,[113]
like Nancy Kimber, who made 'a bob or two' with her black
puddings: 'She had a reputation for 'em . . . she used to make
good ones . . . If they knowed she was making some, they used
to go there for it.'[114] Emma Webb's toffee, sold by her husband
Pedgell on Quarry Rec., as well as out of their tiny cottage in
School Place, is still affectionately remembered: '"Rumple-
stiltskin" they used to call it – it was nice – and "Calley
Bunker" – course they had to be ha'porths and penn'orths.'[115]

No two families made their livelihood in precisely the same
way. In some households the woman's earnings were a supplementary resource, in some they were the major standby. As for
the man, his earnings – often through no fault of his own – were
liable to be fickle: a great deal depended on the state of the
labour market (and a great deal, too, on how he spent his
money). Often he turned to two or three different occupations
in the course of the year, with corresponding changes in the
rate of remuneration.

Shoe money – always a problem in the poorer family – was
raised in a variety of ways. In some households it came from
extra earnings; in some from the profits on the pig. Nobber
Coppock's daughters (he was partly crippled and helped out by
his better-off relatives) raised their shoe money themselves.[116]

We each had our money box and that was called the shoe
box. We went out cleaning knives and forks or scrubbing
floors, and that was threepence, you see, that had to go in
the shoe box. That was towards the shoes. I used to go to
my grandmother's.

Plate 1   Westmorland farm labourer with scythe, circa 1890. This is rather an unusual scythe because it has a swivel-end—usually they were fixed. It is long bladed and too long to be used in the corn harvest (the man is obviously cutting meadow hay). The mowing machine was beginning to replace the scythe from the 1860s, but the introduction was uneven: often the headlands continued to be cut by the scythe even when the machine was used for the rest of the field. Perhaps that is what is happening in this picture: it would take two or three days to cut a whole field by hand.

Plate 2 Women harvesters in Norfolk. This is more than a striking picture of women working in a wheat field, late in the nineteenth century, for it also illustrates the first three operations in the corn harvest and points to the precise division of labour. A mowing machine drawn by two horses and operated by one man (centre background) has displaced hand-cutting, thus dispensing with the labour of several men using either hook or scythe. The women's work is to make bands (into the strands of wheat in hands of the centre two in the group of women) and then gather and tie the loose corn into sheaves (the binder would have cut out this operation). The men are following behind, picking up and forming the sheaves in shocks. In the left and right background the men can be seen among those already set up. The sheaves in the centre of the field have still to be dealt with while the machine has part of the crop still to cut. Although it is probable that some of the women were the wives of some of the men they were not as such working with them, but formed a separate team and were paid probably a rate per acre for this work, to be divided equally between the eight of them. Similarly it is probable the men worked as a team for shocking the corn at so much an acre, again to be divided equally. As regards the mowing machine operator, he was probably the carter and although paid at normal rates received in addition possibly 6d. per acre for cutting the corn.

Plate 3 *above*   Fagging wheat in Herefordshire. A huge field. It was usually reckoned that an acre of wheat was a day's work with fagging hooks such as these men are using. The two fagging hooks visible in the picture are not identical, the one on the left looks heavier and more open in the blade. Fagging sticks, such as the ones that can be seen in this picture, were cherished, though they could easily be replaced by cutting a fresh one out of the hedgerow. Those shown here look quite worn, and may have been used in several previous harvests.

Plate 4 *below*   Two men and a woman. This looks like a field of oats, which was a lighter crop to cut than wheat. The unusual feature is the use of both the scythe—a cradle scythe, to keep the cut tidy—and the fagging hook, which the man on the right is holding. Normally a crop was cut with the one or the other. In this case perhaps parts of the crop had been flattened by the wind or the rain, and were therefore difficult or impossible to cut with the wider sweep of the scythe. Note that the man on the right is carrying a fagging stick in his left hand. This was always used with the fagging hook to hold the crop up while the cut was made. It is not clear what work the woman is doing—perhaps she has been tying the sheaves which was often women's work.

Plate 5   The harvest field just before stooking. The two men have been
scything the corn and the woman has been raking. Note the shorter
blades than in the Westmorland picture—more suitable for the heavier
wheat crop than for hay. The two scythes are different from each other
and were probably, like most hand-tools, individually owned. The long
hand rake is an old one and has been reduced to three and a half teeth.
The woman has probably already tied the sheaves and the two men will
shock them.

Plate 6 Fagging wheat, circa 1900. Six men and three young boys.
The men are cutting with fagging hook and sticks, the boys have been
tying the sheaves. The shocking of the sheaves in the background was a
heavy job—especially with wheat—and would be done by the men rather
than the boys. Shocking was a job done towards the end of the day after
a long stint of cutting. No crop except barley would be left to lie
over night in the fields unstooked.

Plate 7 Washing day. A much more out-of-doors job than today and heavier work, though shared. In this photograph you can see different stages: the lad in the foreground drawing water from the stream; beside him, on a crude tripod of stones a cauldron of clothes being stirred cautiously by a girl. In tubs behind more washing is being done, the home-made wash board at hand. On the left two women are trampling out the most stubborn dirt (as kids we used to enjoy trampling the blankets clean, but indoors, and in a bath).

Plate 8 Out-door kitchen, circa 1860. Kitchens, if separate at all, would
be small and dark and many jobs would be better done outside, as here.
This girl is busy with the scrubbing brush; possibly preparing
vegetables. These carefully made steps seem like an extension of the
cottage; and the sheltered corner next them is obviously used for storing
household equipment. Her rough clothes and bare head proclaim her a
working girl.

Plate 9 Water carrier. The big houses in this picture probably had
water laid on, but even by the early 1900s many cottagers would still
need to fetch their water from the pump or stream. The solitary aproned
girl on the left is taking her bucket down to fill from the river, watched
by a group of boys idling on the bridge. The lively group on the right,
intent on something in the shallows, also have time to enjoy the river,
unlike the sad figure approaching them.

Plate 10   Gleaners, 1857. Two gleaners with their spoils: in this case apparently they have collected a whole sheaf (more usually gleaners gathered fallen ears and would end up with bags of grain). The seated girl is stripping the grains off the stalks into her lap: probably her apron, like her companion's, would serve as a pocket. Gleanings might keep a family in flour for the winter (barley gleanings would be fed to the pig or poultry). The straw would not be wasted, serving as litter for the pig, perhaps; in some parts of the country it would be plaited and provided the raw material for hats, bonnets and basketry. Note their sturdy outdoor look, the layers of different clothes, their hats, and the stout booted foot on the right, easily visible beneath the short skirt.

Plate 11   Woman hop-picking, Hurstmonceaux. At hop-picking time, as for harvest, everyone could earn their bit. Whole families would take up employment together, all but the smallest helping. This picture, which is undated, comes from Hurstmonceaux, in a hop-growing district of Sussex.

Plate 12 Cockle-gathers at Stiffkey, Norfolk, early 1900s. Cockling
involved long walks as the distances in these Norfolk photographs
suggest. The work itself, on the sea's edge, was cold and bleak: these
women are much wrapped up but their legs had to be bare for wading
(clergymen denounced their tucked up skirts as immodest). Once their
sacks were full, they strapped them on their backs, and set off for the
long walk back.

Plate 13 Quarry radicalism in action. September 1909. This
photograph, which was issued as a postcard at the time, shows the
Conservative propaganda van after it had been tipped on its side—and
the speaker made to flee—during the 'People's Budget' election campaign.
This is the last remembered occasion when 'Quarry roughs' made their
appearance as a collective political force, and according to village
tradition they succeeded in tipping the van down a stonepit. The
photograph suggests that they were satisfied with a less complete
destruction than this. (I am grateful to Mr G. S. Jones of Kennington
who sent me the photograph in response to an appeal in the *Oxford
Times*.)

Plate 14 A group outside the 'Mason's Arms', circa 1905. The 'Mason's Arms' was the most plebeian of the four village pubs, a converted cottage at the time this photograph was taken with a drinking parlour in the front, a fish and chip shop in the middle, and a sweet shop in the rear. Behind the pub was the Mason's Pit where the gypsies drew up their caravans for winter. Those who drank there were said to be 'a little school' on their own. 'Everyone drunk out of the same pot', according to one affectionate memory of it. 'If you couldn't afford a pint you had a sup . . . everybody in the little tap room shared . . . didn't matter who was paying for it, the quart cup went round.' (This photograph was kindly lent by Donald Taylor.)

Plate 15   Headington Quarry Morris in the Cowley Road, circa 1900.
This photograph was taken outside the branch office of the Pearl
Assurance Company in Cowley Road, Oxford; a copy has been preserved
in the archives of the Company and was reproduced in the *Pearl
Magazine* for January 1962. So far as I know this is the only photograph
of the old Morris side to have survived. The fiddler at this time was
Mark Cox who can be seen on the extreme left of the picture; next to
him is the Fool, with the stick in his left hand, but the pig's bladder
which he carried on the end of it—if he carried it that day—is invisible
to the camera. The collector (whose box is now in the possession of Mrs
Polly Longford) is in the foreground. The photograph was probably
taken during Whit week when Quarry's Morris side made an annual
appearance in the streets of Oxford, as well as dancing in Quarry itself,
and making a tour of nearby villages.

Plate 16 *above* Quarry's long cottage gardens. These gardens were dug out of the waste, wherever there was an abandoned hollow or piece of waste. By the standards of the time—and even more of those today— they were quite unusually large, because land was freely available to those who asserted squatter's rights; gardens like this used to house a promiscuous variety of activities—laundry drying, poultry keeping, pig rearing as well as growing vegetables. Some are remembered as little orchards. Many of these gardens have now been built over in the post-1918 development of the village, but it is still possible in a few cases to trace their originally winding and irregular shape. (Photograph from W. J. Arkell, *Oxford Stone*, Faber, 1947.)

Plate 17 *below* The last of the brick works at Titup. Brickworks in Quarry settled on the eastern perimeter of the village, and especially about the detached hamlet of Titup on the old London Road. The bricks were all hand-made, but for a long time they survived the competition of the machine, and bricks were still being made at Titup in the inter-war years. (Photograph in the writer's possession.)

Plate 18   Preparing the bricks for the kiln, circa 1900. These
photographs were taken in a more up-to-date brickworks than any in
Quarry, but they are the only ones I have been able to find showing the
later phases of the work. In the first picture the bricks are in the hacks,
waiting to be seasoned. In Quarry the seasoning took place in the open
air, with the bricks being covered with straw. They remained the maker's
responsibility until they had been taken to the kilns: on a wet night he
had to make sure that they were sheltered. In the second picture they
are being wheeled to the kilns. The brickmaker's table, where the bricks
were shaped, was a very rough and ready shanty, with some slight
covering to shield the maker, on a hot day, from the glare of the sun.

Another way of coping with the shoe problem – especially in a big family – was by hand-me-downs.[117]

We had . . . shoes belonging to the older brother [one man told me]. I never had a new pair of shoes till I went to work. My eldest brother bought them for me and they was 'obnailed – well, that was the first pair of shoes I ever had and we walked to Oxford and do you know they was hard as this table.

Many Quarry homes in the 1900s still had their own 'foot-iron' (the Quarry name for the shoemaker's last) and it was usual, when shoes were wearing out, for them to be cobbled at home. 'They used to patch them up themselves, most of 'em.'[118] Tommy Webb, the carrier, used to make his children's shoes, as well as mending them, 'used to get a piece off of the 'orse-saddles, and . . . that was good leather . . . you could buy the rivets and studs then – used to make a good job of 'em.'[119] In Charlotte Webb's household shoe money was financed by the poaching activities of her sons:[120]

Used to have a cup, a pint mug on the shelf and in them days they'd allus keep a couple o' old lurcher dogs . . . and if they was a-going about – we'll say to Cuddesdon – they'd come with 'ee, and if they ketched a rabbit or a hare . . . Granny Webb . . . she'd allus sell that 'are or rabbit and put that money in a jug; and she'd go over Whiteheads at 'Eadington and have our shoes made – old Whitehead made 'em in them days – that's sixty, seventy years ago – old Whitehead used to make 'em . . . couldn't buy 'em in the shop at 'Eadington – and our Mam 'ud allus have our shoes made – Granny Webb . . . she used to save the money, what the dogs ketched the rabbits – and put the money, in a jug – to buy the shoes. That's what they used to do. I can remember now. And they never let them touch that money in that cup . . .

The part played by the children in the family economy varied greatly, depending on their number, sex and age – the young adolescent had more to contribute than the child of seven or eight. A lot depended upon the source of the family livelihood: there was much more for children to do if it was mainly Quarry-based (as in the case of brickmaking and the

HVL

laundry work). A lot depended too upon the nature and extent of the family sidelines. In a poacher's family it seems the girls were sometimes expected to take the rabbits from door to door[121] (Crowy Kerry's daughter went round to his customers regularly on Fridays);[122] and the same might be true when the men had been out totting: 'They used to go and get mushrooms and blackberries . . . and we used to have to go and sell them, all down Divinity . . . We used to . . . put them in these baskets.'[123] In a brickmaker's family the boys were called on to help at an early age, both in carrying up dinners, and on the work itself. 'I used to go up and help my old Dad', Dutchy Wharton recalls, 'used to take his breakfast up, and then stop. All the children done the same.'[124] Crowy Kerry used to go up after school. 'Us boys used to come up with our father . . . We used to have to go and tak' their tea up and then we stopped there till dark, sanding the mould and all that.'[125] In the family which took in washing – certainly the great majority of Quarry households at one time or another in the cycle of family life – girls worked alongside their mothers at a very early age, and it was a natural progression from this that when they came to leave school they continued to work in laundry, rather than enter into 'service' – the normal destiny of girls at Flora Thompson's North Oxfordshire hamlet of Lark Rise.

In a carrier's family children were being for ever called upon to mind the horse. Will Ward remembers spending hours with his father's horses while they grazed in Bayswater Brook,[126] and Waggle Ward did the same for his uncle's pony: 'He'd say to me "Goo and graze him lad, here's ha'penny and a long cord" . . . ha'penny they gave you in those days.'[127] Grassing is another well-remembered duty:[128]

> Me and George Baker cut every inch of that Sta-an Road
> . . . going down Bayswater . . . out to Beckley . . . going
> to'ards Stan – we've cut every inch of that for horses . . .
> when us was boys . . . every inch, with a scythe – used to
> put a little scythe – cut every inch o' that. Nobody 'ud
> stop you, not along the side of the road . . . Used to make
> a little rick – put it in a little rick sometimes – and if you
> didn't use it – any left over – you'd sell it . . .

Children took the horse out on their own at an early age.[129]

I used to do that when I was about eleven [one of them
recalls], drive a bloody horse down to Oxford, put a load on
Friday night of clean, then take another load down
Saturday and help him with the coal on the Saturday, and
then take a load of clean washing down . . . bring a load of
dirty washing back, Saturday night.

Waggle Ward started on the laundry cart even younger:[130]

We used to take them round the Banbury Road on a
Friday. Old Will Webb 'ud know . . . Me and him got lost
up there one day, up the Woodstock Road . . . somewhere
round the Parks . . . we didn't know where he was . . . I
started to cry . . . I waren't above seven or eight then.
Old Will, he's two year older'n me . . . He said, 'We shall
find it', 'ee says, 'Shut up' and I started crying. And I'll
tell 'ee, I can always remember – we was lost . . . all the
a'ternoon and Granny Webb found us . . . Granny Webb
found us in 'Ollywell, come and met us, walked and met us
from Quarry and found us – and I can see Granny Webb
now getting up in the cart to go back with us . . . I can
always remember when she found us, in 'Ollywell or
Broad Street . . . the cross-roads at the King's Arms.

Waggle Ward's mother had also worked on the cart when she
was a girl, and it was there that she started courting.[131]

That's how our Mam picked up with our Dad. She was
going down with the pony; well when she dropped the bit
of washing round there she drove round on the cricket
ground, on the New College cricket ground, to get a bag of
grass. Well our Dad was at work there, and when he loaded
the grass up he said 'That's all right', 'ee says – he give
her a sack of grass – Well, she went back and told Granny
Webb – used to have to pay about a penny a sack for it –
or ha'penny a sack – she said 'That chap give me that
grass', she said, 'I be going there again.' Well, she went
there again, he gave it her again, and she paired up with
him, and that's how our Mam found our Dad, on that
cricket ground . . .

Apart from employment within the family there were all
kinds of twopenny and threepenny jobs which children could

take up on their own, for example, minding cows on Shotover. In summer-time there was a good deal of employment for children in the fields, though usually for short periods at a time: shallot-pulling was one of the more severe: 'You could earn twopence or threepence of a Sat'day morning – but your hands were terrible after you'd finished with it ... sore as anything.'[132] At strawberry-picking time boys were employed at Pinch Plum Coppock's orchard 'before going to school in the morning';[133] in September some of them went walnut-bashing at Quarry manor. ('Youngster's job. Anybody who 'ud go up a tree, like a monkey ... go up the top and have the pole handed up to him.')[134] Some, too, turned temporarily trader, picking acorns on Shotover for sale to the village pig-keepers. (There was also a micro-trade in hogwash which children took part in: one village pig-keeper is remembered as paying 'a halfpenny and an apple' a bucket.)[135] May Day was a children's harvest, from the point of view of earnings, but the number who went out with their begging tins was limited by notions of family prestige: 'it was definitely the children of the poorer sort of people ... who went out', one man told me. It was the same (according to this account) with carol-singing at Christmas, when some went from door to door: 'The more respectable would keep away.'[136]

Within the village itself there were thus some of the elements of a secondary economy, supplementing wage labour, and sometimes taking its place. Earnings were built up higgledy-piggledy rather than by reliance upon a single weekly wage. As little as possible was bought in the shops, though there was a good deal of swapping between neighbours, and a rudimentary system of indigenous trade. Vegetables, including potatoes, so far as possible were home grown – 'in those days you *had* to grow your own food'[137] – and pickling helped to preserve them for the lean winter months. Pigs were a chief support of the cottage economy – 'That was the religion ... almost ... nearly everyone in Quarry had to have a couple of pigs'[138] – and a whole network of reciprocities and transactions grew up around the keeping of them. Children still played a big part in the family economy, though compulsory school-going inevitably curtailed it. As for women, their role as housekeepers was a very much more active one than it is today, for the household was to some extent self-supporting: production

and consumption, so far from being separated, went hand
in hand, bound together in the day-by-day necessities of
subsistence.

4 Totting and poaching, woodland and waste

Supplementary resources were to be found outside the village
as well as within. The immediate vicinity of Quarry was
imperfectly colonized, a humble-jumble of waste land and
grass-grown hollows, farmers' fields, and individually rented
'ground', sometimes cultivated but apt to revert to common
and waste. Clayhills, for instance, which bordered on the
Vicarage, had originally been a farm, but by the later nineteenth
century it became the waste extension of a nearby brickyard;
it was used for lime-burning and sometimes as a source of
brick-clay, but otherwise it escaped the control of its nominal
owners.[1] The village horse-keepers made free of Clayhills (and
Parson's Field, its neighbour),[2] which they used extensively
for grazing. It is also remembered as a good place to go 'timber-
hunting'[3] (there was a lot of wood in Clayhills), and a handy
spot for bird-catching and rabbiting: '. . . that was sort of
anybody's ground the Clayhills was in them days – there was no
owner to it . . . and we used to ketch these rabbits'.[4] Snuffer
Webb, an expert marksman, used to go there shooting blackbirds with his catapult when food at his mother's was short.
Waggle Ward, when he was a boy, went with him:[5]

> Used to go out on the Clayhills and ketch blackbirds
> an' thrushers and Granny Webb 'ud do 'em. Blackbirds
> and nothing else, no other bird . . . when Granny Webb
> used to do 'em you could see them little bits of fat running
> round the breasties . . . old Snuffer (I was only a boy,
> a-carrying) . . . he'd get his cat-i-polt like that . . . and
> then he'd stand and he'd see one right up the top of the
> bush, and . . . every time he'd near enough have 'em, down
> they come. I used to put 'em in a bag and then go back and
> Granny Webb 'ud do 'em . . . They used to joke – Granny
> Webb – our Mam did – she used to say 'This pie'll start

whistling when you bring him the oven' . . . Old Snuffer
Webb – that was my mother's brother – he could knock
them out of them trees – Clayhills – out of them big
bushes every time he shot nearly. Winter time. With all
the leaves off the 'edges, they be roosting there . . . You
didn't used to ha' to make a row, else they'd always go
out . . . Kept quiet and went against the wind . . . And I
can remember eatin' 'em. It was all right – waren't a big
bite on 'em but them old blackbirds when Granny Webb
used to do 'em, you could see all the fat, all round the
bodies like, yeller fat, you 'ud. Well . . . they eat snipe, and
a good . . . thrusher's as big as a snipe isn' he? But you
never eat starlings, never eat starlings, Granny Webb ud'nt.
Blackbirds, thrushers and foults – nothing else – they was
three things you could eat – we used to eat – and our
Granny Webb 'ud have a dozen in a pie . . . you get a
dozen thrushers in a pie – a dozen, and blackbirds, well
that was a bit of a feed, waren't it, when you come to
look at it, in them days.

The village was flanked on its eastern border by a wide tract
of woodland and waste, the substantial remnant of the royal
forest of Stowood and Shotover which had been disafforested in
1662 but which remained in its more or less wild state. It
started on Shotover itself, 'a roughish wooded tract, rather
formidable';[6] 'the highest hill or mountain between here and
the Urals', as Quarry children were informed by their headmaster in 1913.[7] Shotover plain, the broad open space, a mile in
length, at the top of the hill, had been reserved as common land
under the Disafforestation Act of 1662, and assigned to the
five parishes of Headington, Horspath, Marston, Wheatley and
Cowley.[8] It was used as grazing land by local cow-keepers, such
as Pinch Plum Coppock of Quarry, and Dadger Green of New
Headington, and provided the villagers with a generous supply
of tottings – 'people would go up there to scrounge what they
could . . . there was plenty of rabbits'.[9] The route from Quarry to
the top was also common land where the villagers went foraging
for blackberries, acorns ('it was . . . acorn trees . . . all the way
up the path')[10] and fuel: 'Everyone used to go up there and get
what they wanted – all their wood, and anything they could
scrounge . . . It was always known as the happy hunting ground

up there.'[11] As well as subsistence, Shotover also provided the
enterprising forager (or the desperate one) with 'an extra bob
or two'. Moss gathered from the ochre pits on the Wheatley
side of the hill,[12] acorns picked up on the drives of Colonel
Miller's estate ('all oak trees down them drives'),[13] or, less
hazardously, on Shotover Plain itself, holly branches and berries, sold to the dealers for Christmas,[14] could all provide the
hard-up labourer with 'a bit of a living'. So could ferns:[15]

> I'll tell you what my Uncle George used to do in the winter,
> when he was frozen out – he'd go up there and cut a great
> bundle of that fern up on Shotover Hill, and bring it down,
> and sell that to people for pigs, for litter – bob a bundle
> perhaps.

Apart from the plain at the top, the whole of Shotover was in
private ownership, part of the huge estate of Colonel Miller,
who, however, seems (like Charles I) to have suffered from the
'lewd and disorderly persons' in Quarry. Quarry poachers
exercised a kind of informal hegemony over part of it, and treated
the 'Wheatley gang' – their rivals from over the hill – as trespassers. It was a promising terrain. The 'Middle Ground' on
Shotover was said to be 'alive with rabbits';[16] so too was
Moonpiece (also part of Colonel Miller's estate), the scene of a
legendary encounter between Crowy Kerry's dog and one of
Colonel Miller's bulls.[17] Shotover Field, on the lower grounds,
was yet another part of Colonel Miller's estate which was said
to be 'good . . . for rabbits', and was used by the Quarry
poachers to train their dogs in. According to one old poacher,
paying a tribute to his dog, their enthusiasm was fully equal to
that of their masters:[18]

> . . . then they'd let the dogs loose and they'd go backwards
> and forwards the bloody field and bring the rabbits in –
> 'cos them dogs enjoyed that more than what we did – you
> wouldn't believe what they dogs was like at that time of
> day – they used to go bloody mad to go with us . . . We
> got in Shotover field, good place for rabbits at that time,
> we had an old dog called White Willie – he was a beautiful
> dog . . . well he got . . . left behind . . . and he found us
> right t'other side of the ochre pits – pleased as bloody
> punch he was a bloody smashing dog he was . . .

From the foot of Shotover down to Cowley there were four open commons – the Ridings, Slade Common, Open Magdalen and Open Brasenose – known collectively to villagers as the 'Moors'. Their wasteland character was expressed (and confirmed) by the uses they were put to: the kilns of Shotover brickworks smouldered at the northern end; in the middle, standing in open heath, was Cowley Barracks (built in the 1870s). Save for the allotment grounds at Titup, which were extensive, and for the glebe allotments at the bottom of what is today Windmill Road, very little of this land had been brought under regular cultivation. It is remembered as being 'very wild':[19] 'all open'[20] and almost entirely unfenced.

The Slade itself was partly occupied by gypsies. Their settlement there has a long history. The name 'Gypsy Lane' was already in use in 1861[21] and the MS. census returns of that year record the names of some of the more regularly settled gypsy families.[22] Earlier still the gypsies on the Slade were blamed for the supposed murder of Thomas Buller, a Cowley furze-cutter, who disappeared while making his way to Shotover on Pancake Day, 1844.[23] The settlement showed great tenacity – indeed traces of it can be seen on the Slade to this day. In the 1920s the Slade is remembered as being 'full of gypsies from one end to the other',[24] 'all caravans'.[25] A number of families used it as a regular winter camp and seem to have succeeded, over the years, in acquiring an informal title to the land on which their wagons were drawn up, staking out fences and putting up sheds or huts. One of them was the Bucklands, a well-known family of travelling showmen, who arrived in Quarry about the turn of the century. They became so well established on the ground that they are said to have been paid £200 by the City Corporation when some of their land was taken away for a road-widening scheme. (According to their own testimony, as well as that of the villagers, the Bucklands were accepted as part and parcel of Quarry life, even though they were away on their travels for part of the year.)[26]

The status of all these eastern borderlands was uncertain. None of them was officially a common, but common rights, though not upheld by law, were freely exercised over them. Open Magdalen, the storm centre of the disturbances of 1860–80, may be taken as a case in point. It had never been recognized in law as common land, and such rights as the villagers claimed on it had been supposedly extinguished for ever when the royal forest of Shotover (within whose boundary they fell) was disafforested in 1662. The last vestige of common rights on the Magdalen – the right of the Cowley commoners to walk their cattle along the driftway from Cowley to Shotover – was legislated away at the time of the Cowley enclosure of 1853. Nevertheless the land continued to bear the aspect of a common, and it was described in 1871 as being 'almost entirely covered with timber trees some of which are of great age, and underwood and thick brakes of furze bushes and thorns with very little grass except by the sides of the . . . driftway'.[27] The villagers had their own local name for the Magdalen – 'Open Elms' or 'Oaks and Elms'[28] (there is some uncertainty as to which name was generally in use); and when Richard Pether, who leased it from Magdalen College together with his farm, attempted to clear a portion of the land, he was met by a formidably protracted resistance.

Open Brasenose, which lay alongside the Open Magdalen, was another limb of the ancient royal forest, and it too escaped the control of its nominal owners. The land was simultaneously in private occupation and yet subject to commoners' rights. It was an extra-parochial common land, on which common rights were established by usage but denied by law: the right of the villagers to take a 'man's load' of furze bushes or brake, 'but not to take a cart within the boundary' – the last of the unambiguous rights – was taken away at the time of the Cowley enclosure of 1853.[29] The land was partly fenced, but it remained wholly uncultivated and peculiarly wild in appearance. In the 1870s Brasenose College attempted to begin a clearance, but after meeting stubborn resistance from the villagers (provocative trespass was its characteristic form) agreed, 'for the sake of peace', to leave about one-third of the common unenclosed. No very sustained attempt was made to enforce the college's authority over the remainder. The college bursar admitted as much in 1883: 'There had been a tacit acquiescence by the College in regard to the exercise of certain limited privileges or indulgences on the part of certain persons.'[30] John Chillingsworth, who leased the Open Brasenose from the college in the early 1880s, attempted to drive the villagers off, but he too seems to have been unsure about his rights – 'The place was a sort of enclosed common', his steward told the court, during

one of the prosecutions which he brought.[31] Abel Bicknell, one
of his successors, who had the tenancy of Brasenose Farm in the
1890s, seems to have been even more uncertain about his rights,
though this didn't stop him trying to enforce them. His evidence
in one of the prosecutions which he brought against George
'Pedgell' Webb (the most persistent of Quarry's trespassers)
shows how the notion of common right lingered about the
place:[32]

> Cross-examined by Mr Ballard – He believed the public
> had some sort of rights respecting the riding of Open
> Brasenose, but he could not say what those rights were.
> He was not aware that the inhabitants of Headington
> claimed the right to cut wood there, because the college
> had told him just the reverse. He might have heard people
> say that they had a right to the wood, but he did not
> remember having done so. They fancied they had a right,
> he knew.
> The Clerk: What right?
> Complainant – When I have spoken to them sometimes
> about cutting the wood they have said they have a right
> to the furze . . .
> – By whom are these claims made?
> – The right is claimed chiefly by the people of Headington
> Quarry.
> – Cottagers, I suppose?
> – Yes, sir.

The villagers themselves experienced no such uncertainties.
'They took it for granted, it was theirs.'[33] It was a 'proper
hunting ground' for rabbits; a favourite spot for wooding.[34]
They had their own village name for Open Brasenose ('Kimber's
Wood'[35]) and treated it 'like common land . . . they used to be
able to cut the wood in there, all the brushwood'.[36] Thirty and
forty years after the last vestiges of common rights had been
extinguished by the Cowley enclosure, poor cottagers could still
be seen coming out of the Brasenose carrying a man's load of
winter fuel. One man who had made particularly extensive use
of it was George 'Pedgell' Webb, who made a 'bit of a living' by
taking firing off Open Brasenose and hawking it round to his
fellow villagers. He claimed that he had been freely making use
of Open Brasenose for fifty years, and the nature of this interest

can be traced in a succession of police court prosecutions for
rabbiting, trespassing and wood-stealing. By the time of his last
arrest, in 1895, he was a very old man, but the spirit of defiance
was still strong:[37]

> Mr Bicknell said he was in the riding of Open Brasenose on
> the day named and saw the defendant coming away with a
> bundle of wood – blackthorn, whitethorn, and furze.
> Witness said to him, 'Then you have been for a bit more'
> and he replied that he should have as much wood as he
> wanted, or words to that effect. He had frequently seen the
> defendant leaving the riding with wood under his arm . . .
> P.C. Dodd said on the afternoon named he was on the old
> London-road near to the riding leading to Open Brasenose,
> and saw the defendant carrying a fag of wood. He asked
> Webb where he got the wood from, and he replied that he
> had taken it from Brasenose Common, that he had cut
> wood there for the past fifty years, and that if witness were
> there next day he would see him have some more probably,
> as the wood belonged to the poor of Headington.

The existence, so near to Quarry, of all this woodland and
waste, added an extra dimension to the village economy.
For the poorer class of cottager it was a major source of fuel
('everyone had a chopping block outside the back door').[38]
At the time of the dispute over the Magdalens it may well have
been the only one, and even at the end of the century, when
coal and coke were coming in, some fires were still being kept up
primarily with wood. 'Couldn't afford coal,' Fred Tolley recalls,
'just a half hundredweight a week – one nob a week . . .'[39] Men
are remembered coming down from Shotover dragging whole
branches of trees behind them:[40]

> great big fellers – strong as elephants they were – used to
> come a-carrying these trees down, just trim the branches
> off – carry the trunk down, saw it up . . . a good lump of
> wood and big lump of coal used to last all night in the
> old-fashioned grates, you know.

In Fred Tolley's family the mother and the children would
sometimes go out wooding together, the mother with the
jagging hook, to cut it down and trim, the children with a
truck laid on a pair of pram wheels to haul the load back home.

At other times it was left to the boys: 'A little gang of us, my brother, myself . . . a little gang . . . of boys. Made a day out of it . . . half a day . . . round Open Brasenose, Shotover, down the Ridings.'[41]

The wasteland helped to give variety to the Quarry diet, as well as providing food at little or no cost. The meadows by Open Brasenose (Kimber's Wood), for instance, were said to be 'tremendous' for mushrooming,[42] and there was another good field for mushrooms 'all round Broad Oak – bottom o' Shotover Hill'.[43] Watercress, picked at Bayswater Brook, was a popular relish (in Quarry as in other working-class communities) and, for those who sent their children out to look for it, free. (It was also sometimes exchanged in the pub for a sup, or quart, of beer.) Blackberries from Shotover, used alone or in combination with other fruit, such as apples or gooseberries, served to diversify the village jam. As for rabbits, they took their place at the family table in place of butcher's meat, and were a chief ingredient of 'shackles', the Quarry hot-pot. ('. . . Taters, swedes, turnips and all that, rabbits . . . couple o' rabbits legs . . . all in together, shackles . . . that was nice in the winter, there weren't much left'.)[44] 'Two or three times a week we would dine off rabbits,' Fred Tolley recalls. 'It was our staple diet, nothing better.'[45] '. . . It was the real stuff,' recalls Johnny Buckland, 'when you'd eat it, it would stick to your ribs, and now we don't know what's tinned up for us, do we? . . . Rabbit, bit o' bacon boiled with it a few suety dumplings, you had . . . a real 'olesome dinner.'[46]

Quarry poachers – those who made a 'bit of a living at it', and went out at night in gangs – enjoyed a ready local market for their hauls, though the larger ones were usually disposed of to the Oxford dealers. Some hawked their rabbits from door to door ('they used to keep them on a stick . . . and they'd come to the door and say "could you do with a rabbit?" . . . sixpence or ninepence, then, that made up a good hot pot');[47] some swapped them for beer in pubs. The regular poachers were well known to their fellow villagers, and orders were put in to them, by housewives, in much the same way as at a shop:[48]

We had a job to get one even when we wanted one.
[Mrs Auger recalls] . . . I don't know what they done with them. I used to go round . . . and ask them to . . . save me

one. Crowy lived down there, didn't he, along by Grampy?
– down in that cottage there . . . I'd go to him . . . and ask
if he'd got a rabbit . . . He'd say 'No, but I might have one
tomorrow.' Then if I got one I'd go round to Bessie
Barrett's, where they got the pig meat, and get a piece of
pork to go with it. Well, you see you'd got to ask him.
Sometimes he'd got one, and sometimes he 'adn't. P'raps
he hadn't been out, because he didn't feel well.

Crowy Kerry had regular customers, and sent his daughter
round with his catch:[50]

She used to take my rabbits all round Quarry to various
houses, they used to order them . . . There was Joe Bush
in Green Road, he used to order two . . . a week – that
was a shillin' a piece, that was two shillin' – well that two
shillin' was money at that time of day, now today it's
nothing.

One set of men who profited from the waste were the village
horse-keepers – the carriers, haggle-cart men and horse-
dealers – who were able to feed their horses at what one of their
descendants ironically describes as 'minimum cost'.[50] The
entire hinterland of the village – and the waste lots within
it – were treated by them as a potential source of fodder.
Horses were grazed wherever a patch of rough pasture offered
itself, whether on the open common, by roadside wastes,[51] or
(overnight) in other people's fields ('somebody had to get up
early to get 'em out').[52]

There was three ways they used to do it – I know, 'cos I
used to help our old man and that do it – one of them was
slip 'em in somebody else's field at night, get 'em out early
in the morning – the second one was to 'obble 'em –
Shotover Plain that was – tie their front feet together . . .
leave them just that little bit so, so that they could only
move their feet a little bit at a time – and the other was
penning 'em, where you put 'em on a long chain. There was
billions of places round here to put them out . . . top of
Magdalen Pit, there was grass there . . . You got some
more along Quarry Lane, you got Shotover . . . Really they
didn't want to do a lot of putting 'em in other people's
fields because there was so much waste ground round here.

The local cow-keepers also made use of the wastes, though by the end of the century they were more inclined to rent the use – or partial use – of a field. 'Nearly all the parish', according to George Coppock, testifying before the Bullington Petty Sessions in 1871, were used to turning out their cattle on the Open Magdalen when he was a boy, about 1810, and he himself had had the job of minding his grandfather's cows while they grazed there ('every day all the summer through').[53] Cattle were still being pastured on the Magdalen in the 1860s, and the attempt to stop them doing so was one of the immediate causes of the disturbances of those years (Cowley cow-keepers, too, were involved, and they were still stoutly maintaining their rights on the Magdalen in 1892).[54] Shotover Plain was also extensively used for grazing cows, and so, to some extent, were the Moors.[55] In Edwardian times the only cow-keeper who relied on common rights entirely was Dadger Green of New Headington, who had six cows and a local trade in milk:[56]

He didn't have any fields – he used to take them either down by the Warneford Asylum . . . where the grass is, or Shotover, on the roadsides. Up the top, on the Plain. There was plenty of grass on the sides, you didn't have to go all the way up to the top. He used to give the kids threepence to take them out.

Another class who made extensive use of the waste were the gypsies, whose settlement in Quarry – as already suggested – must be largely attributed to it. The Moors provided them not only with somewhere to live, rent free and untroubled by the property-conscious farmer, but also with rough pasture for their horses (' 'cos that was grazing ground . . . common land'),[57] 'Black Sally' (the wood from which they made their clothes pegs and skewers), and the furze and underwood which kept their fires alight.[58]

The village totters – those who went foraging in the surrounding countryside 'to make an extra bob or two' – were yet another class of men who were very well served by the waste. Clayhills, with all its opportunities, was only fifty yards from the 'Mason's Arms', Shotover less than a mile away. Shotover was a favourite haunt of those who went out catching song-birds. So was the Open Brasenose:[59]

Most that I can remember is people going down there
catching birds, like bullfinches. They used to go down there
and set these traps. Song birds. Sell them – linnets – quite
a few of 'em used to do it. Flog 'em down the town or
around – everybody kep' a bird in a cage . . . My two
brothers . . . was devils at it, always going out with these
blokes catching birds . . . Another thing they used to do
was to go with nets at night, and wait till it was dark, and
then go up and bash the tree from the opposite side where
the nets was held and the birds would come out and go
into the net . . . There was a greater variety of song-birds
in them days than what there is now.

Under the beech trees on Shotover was said to be the best
place for gathering leaf-mould, because there were so many
hollows for the leaves to gather and rot. Stunt Kerry and
Waggle Ward used to collect it there and take it down to the
florists in Oxford: 'That 'ud be about a tanner a bag . . . down
in Oxford . . . You could always sell leaf mould.'[60] Horse-radish
was another saleable tot which lay easily to hand, though
digging it out might require the permission of a farmer: 'You
could allus go and dig horse-radish up round Harry Lord's
farm . . . in them old gardens or underneath the hedge.'[61] Those
who went hollying travelled further. Shotover, according to one
of them, 'weren't a good place for holly' because it never grew
berries. The nearest berried holly was at Elsfield, though even
here the crop was variable (some years there were no berries,
and the holly had to be faked up with 'ha-azes'):[62]

We used to get a lot 'o holly from Peg Top Farm – all big
holly trees there – and you'd get some years they was
berried red all over . . . the people knowed that it was an
old broken-down lonely farm, and they knowed this holly
used to grow there . . . they'd go out with a pony and cart
at night and have a holly tree in him – load him right up
you know . . . hawk it round Oxford, hawk it to these
shops.

A good deal of briaring was done locally – 'down here in the
Ridings, Shotover . . . or down Bayswater'[63] – but those who
did it on a larger scale went further afield, partly on account of
the competition (briars were one of the most valuable of tots,

and they could be sold locally to Mattocks, the rose-growers of New Headington). Stunt Kerry and his little clique went all over the place on their raids:[64]

> Down into Menmash, Horton-cum-Studley, all round there – Worminghall – all up there, we used to drove a donkey there . . . you'd . . . put a bridle on him – or turn him up this lane – or . . . peg him – then you'd be a-briaring all day long . . . When you'd cut a dozen you'd carry them back and put 'em in the cart . . . if you got say three or four or five dozen, well you had five or six bob . . . that was good money in them days, waren't it?

Quarry poachers, too, sometimes travelled, though Elsfield (where Robert Horwood was arrested on four separate occasions between May 1877 and April 1879[65]), Sandford Brake[66] and Otmoor seem to have represented the limits of their expeditions. Horton Wood, at Horton-cum-Studley, was one of Crowy Kerry's favourite resorts and another poacher remembers taking as many as forty or fifty rabbits there in one night:[67] 'They was good rabbits, they was, come off the clay ground, they was fat. Oh! beautiful rabbits.'[68]

> Horton Cover . . . was alive with rabbits at that time . . . we used to string them up and work our way back home – work all the covers back – Holly Wood and all that . . . work our way back home . . . before morning – I've knowed the time we had, I think it was close on 20 rabbits a-piece to carry from Waterperry Wood – 20 rabbits a-piece, I should think, close on 20 we had a-piece – and we was all buggered up when we got home.[69]

But for the most part the poachers kept to the near vicinity of Quarry, with Colonel Miller's estate on Shotover as their Mecca.

'Mushrooming', 'briaring' or 'cressing' were sometimes the object of an expedition, sometimes an alibi for poaching. 'They couldn't summon you,' an old poacher explained, 'not for going about in the fields.'[70] So far as the poachers were concerned – the regular poachers who went to work in gangs – these activities were all of a piece, and one led on naturally to another:[71]

Us old Quarriers, used to get moss, horse-radish, mushrooms
. . . moss – I be going back sixty years you know, getting
that moss – and leaf mould – Us clique, our old rabbiting
clique, . . . well we *knowed* where to go and get it – when
you'd been a-rabbiting . . . You'd see it and you'd think
'Look at all this moss' or 'look at all this leaf-mould' –
well that's what we used to gu-o and do, especially little
Stunt . . . If you were rabbiting, you'd find a mushroom
field – 'cos you could, see – they'd come back and say
'Oh-oh, we come across Broad Oak last night, and it was
white', they 'ud say. Well, you was there the next mornin',
weren't ee? – that's how we used to find out about all these
things, see. The briars a-comes in it. The leaf mould comes
in it – see my meaning? – all in the line of gettin' a living
in them days – nothing else to do.

By and large these activities were seasonal, and confined, for
the most part, to the autumn and winter months. Autumn was
the totter's harvest, when the acorns fell from the trees, and the
hedges grew heavy with blackberries. Farmers' fields temporarily reverted to common and were open to the gleaners. Mushrooms came up 'only . . . September, just a certain time then
it was finished with'.[72] Fern-cutting began 'p'raps October . . .
about when it was going off' ('got to wait till it's dried off; you
udn't go cut it when it was . . . heavy').[73] The bird-catching
season started in September and finished in March: 'When they
was breeding they didn't catch them, it was close season then.
When they went out hedge-bashing, that was winter-time.'[74]
Poaching too began in September and October, though the
autumn season was a short one and came to an end when the
frosts drove the rabbits to ground. Hollying, which was timed
to meet the Christmas trade, was the last autumn harvest.
Later on things grew more difficult, and if the winter was a
harsh one, every class of tot grew scarce: 'That was when they
used to raid the Clayhills and Shotover with the axe – and the
swede fields – and the potato clamps. They had to have something to eat, and they got it.'[75]

So far as the standard of life is concerned, it is difficult to
assess the value of these extras in monetary terms, to 'quantify'
in a way that the economic historian might feel professionally
obliged to demand, or to incorporate them in the week-by-week

household budget. A good deal of totting was for immediate consumption; but often too it provided a 'latch-opener' in the pub, enabling the totter to pay his round.[76] Watercress, when Saccy Horwood gathered it at Ewelme, or from the Holton stonepits, sold for twopence a bunch at the 'Six Bells' on a Sunday morning.[77] (Figures in the paragraph refer to remembered prices in the 1900s.) Ferns, sold to the village pig-keepers for litter, are remembered as fetching ''bout sixpence' for the bundle ('One bundle, that's all they'd want for a week or a fortnight').[78] Fiddler King, a publican on the Cowley Road who kept pigs, paid . . . ' 'bout a shilling a bushel' for acorns;[79] Piggy Baker, in Quarry itself, was said to pay less ('he'd give 'ee about a penny or twopence'[80]). Horse-radishes, sold to Cooper's, the marmalade people in Oxford, fetched a higher price than this, and were more difficult to get, but the rewards, even for a successful expedition, were still quite modest: 'If you had a pound a hundredweight there, you was a millionaire.'[81] A load of holly fetched 'half a crown perhaps' if sold to a grocer in St Clements;[82] if it was sold to a London dealer the price depended on the state of the crop.[83] 'Old Mattock', the rose-grower in New Headington, bought briars at a penny each. ('You'd tie 'em up in a dozen – that 'ud be a shilling . . . p'raps . . . you might get a couple or three dozen.')[84]

Poaching incomes were also modest, despite the fame of Quarry's poachers. Quarry poaching was for rabbits only, never game, and they were disposed of in a comparatively homespun way. The individual rabbit sold at prices variously remembered as from fourpence to a shilling, with a penny (or according to one account threepence) for the skin (Joe Brockhall, a ragaboner from St Thomas's, used to come up to Quarry to buy skins).[85] Eight or nine rabbits apiece was reckoned a good haul by those who went out with the long nets ('the old man used to sell t'others, and then he'd keep a couple to ate').[86] Larger hauls were disposed of through Milky Allen, a Wheatley fence who had a milk round in St Clements. He was a hard bargainer:[87]

There was an old milkman in Wheatley called Milky Allen, and 'ee come trotting by with his 'o-orse, a-going to Oxford . . . used to put these rabbits in a pram, and . . . stand up on the London Road – where the Shotover Arms

is now – underneath the 'edge – and wait . . . for old
Milky . . . to come driving by with his 'orse and float . . .
They got – ah – fifty, sixty, 'undred at the time. I've took
them, and our Ma have . . . allus stick 'em under the
pram – and nobody couldn't see 'em, with a little old bit
of strap over 'em – laid in the pram . . . you know these
old-fashioned prams, you could push 'em straight out of the
pits . . . Old Saccy Horwood 'ud be waiting there – that's
a good many years ago – old Saccy'd be waiting with his
'n . . . either in a truck or a pram. And we used to sell
Uncle Dusty's for him, his rabbits . . . and you'd see old
Teddy Hooper's wife, 'cos their kids weren't as old as
ours . . . and you could see them waiting for Milky Allen
to come by to pick these rabbits up . . . Old Saccy waiting
there, old Jessie Hooper's, waiting with the pram, and
our Mam. He'd have a look at 'em, run through 'em and
. . . offer you a price – no matter what he offered you,
they'd give it . . . him, because they was only waiting for
the threepence each . . . You'd be lucky if you had a tanner
apiece off of Milky Allen. Then when Uncle Dusty used
to walk up at night on his 'lotment . . . I used to have to
walk up . . . and give him his bit o' money.

Poaching is no more easy than totting to assess, so far as
household incomes are concerned. Some of the rabbits were
eaten at home, some were swapped in the pub, some given away
as presents – transactions which, by their nature, escape the
quantifier's grasp. But it would be absurd, for this reason, to
discount it as a component in the standard of life. In Charlotte
Webb's household poaching was treated as 'sort of a sideline',
but it kept the family in shoes, as well as supplying the table
with meat:

We used to ketch these rabbits – and if you took a rabbit
home Granny Webb 'ud take the insides off – out of this
rabbit . . . what we used to call gut him – gut this rabbit –
and she'd have a customer for that rabbit, to sell it –
that tuppence 'ud gu-o in the cup, to buy their shoes, help
buy their shoes, I can remember as if it was yesterday.

For Charlotte herself there was the additional comfort of a drop
of beer. 'Allus used to take 'em to Bill Goodall, kept the Public

there in them days – old Bill Goodall, liked a rabbit, and Granny Webb used to have her drop of beer – I've fetched her beer in a jug from there.'[88]

Poaching, despite some legendary hauls, was never a full-time occupation. Crowy Kerry, 'one of the best poachers ever born', went in for it in the autumn, when employment in the building trade was slack. Bob Gooldame, who had the reputation of being a very good poacher, and who also collected mushrooms, turned to these activities when there was nothing else to do: ' 'Course, he'd go to work if he had the chance, but this was when they were out of work.'[89] Dusty Webb, a very famous poacher in Edwardian times – 'big man, tall man, black hair, more like Italian' – could make as much as seven shillings for a good night's work, according to Waggle Ward, who used to collect his money. But his poaching was very definitely an extra, and he combined it with gardening on his allotment, as well as with a full-time job on Oxford sewers.[90]

> Uncle Dusty . . . he had allotment on Quarry Field,
> when he lived in St Thomas's, and he used to come
> up a-digging, and if the wind was a-blowin' at night,
> he'd leave that digging, and he'd go a-rabbiting all night –
> he'd walk from there, when he come from rabbiting – he'd
> have a cup of tea in Granny Webb's – he'd walk back down
> St Thomas's, he 'ood, and he'd go to work all day, and
> he'd be a-digging on the allotment at night in Quarry. Tell
> me where another man 'ud do that today? They ain't born
> to do it. They was bred different – horses they was, I
> reckon. That's the truth, what I be saying, it is, it's the
> truth – you can write that down what 'ee done, and I
> ain't ashamed for anybody to read it – any old 'uns 'd
> prove it. Old Dutchy Wharton could prove that and old
> Crowy could, but who else is there to prove it, what I be
> telling you? . . . that Uncle Dusty would walk from St
> Thomas's to Quarry, on his 'lotment, if the wind was
> a-blowing he'd go rabbiting all night, and he'd come back –
> carry about twenty rabbits on his shoulder – all round
> Waterperry and Shotover – he'd come back, he'd leave
> these rabbits there, and he'd walk to St Thomas's again
> in the mornin', and he'd go to work all day, and he'd be up
> there diggin' at night . . . that's what Uncle Dusty used to

do. My Mam's uncle that was. He was a man and a half, he
was . . . a man and a half . . .

Poaching on a large scale was confined to particular gangs –
there were three of them in the village in the 1900s. But there
were all kinds of men who went in for it in a smaller way. Their
poaching was incidental to other activities, such as harvesting,[91]
or well-digging, or walking to work. Building workers, for
instance, would put down a wire or two in the morning on their
way to work in the hope of collecting the odd rabbit on the way
back. Those who went out for a walk with the dog kept a
weather eye on the hedgerows. Johnny Buckland, who had an
old gingery dog called Mud, was often in luck: 'He'd kill every
hare he run after . . . I'd put him in my pocket and come
home . . .'[92] Waggle Ward recalls how when he was sent
out 'grassing' the dogs would do the rabbiting all on their
own:[93]

. . . the horse 'ud be a-grazing . . . when we was grass-
cutting . . . and when you went back . . . there 'ud be a
couple of hares which had been ketched – put 'em in
theirselves, these dogs 'ud – you can tell what sort of dogs
we had in them days.

Boys in Quarry got their first taste of poaching in this more or
less impromptu way. Those who went cow-minding on Shotover
'did a bit of rabbiting' while the cows were grazing or lying
down to rest: 'The old cows . . . they wouldn't take no notice of
anybody, just munch away – they wouldn't walk away while
there was any food.'[94] The boys in Charlotte Webb's household
dovetailed poaching with their laundry-carrying to and from
Cuddesdon College: 'That's why we come back over Shotover
Hill – we four – because old Stunt was a proper dog man, and
there was – Oh! hundreds and hundreds of rabbits over Shotover
Hill – plenty on 'em . . .'[95]

Totting, too, even for those who made a speciality of it,
seems usually to have gone hand in hand with other activities.
Stunt Kerry, for instance, 'made a living' out of leaf-mould and
moss ('in the winter time'), and recruited a little clique of
followers ('they'd sell that in the market . . . to the wreath-
makers and the florists');[96] but he kept up a regular coke round,
and also did a little laundry-carrying. Bobby Cooper used to

'wander round' collecting herbs, and made up patent medicines himself, as well as supplying Lloyd's, the Oxford herbalist: he also 'used to work on the buildings'.[97] George Cooper, who work-ed on the ochre pits at Shotover,[98]

> got a living out of collecting fossils, up on Shotover, and animals and all that. He used to sell them to the Colleges – that was a favourite trick round here – getting the fossils out of the stone . . . used to have them outside his back door on a little table.

Even Saccy Horwood, who was driven by ill-health to a more or less complete reliance on totting (in his young manhood he had been a morris-dancer), had a number of strings to his bow. His totting activities were far-flung and stretched from catching snakes on the brickfields – which he sold to the university laboratories – to ragaboning and collecting red ivy and moss.[99] But he traded in nuts and oranges as well, 'all . . . round the pubs'; sold fish;[100] made nets and sold them for use in the kitchen;[101] grew potatoes which he sold down in Oxford (especially at the time of St Giles's Fair);[102] and at one time he also put on a weekly open-air show in Quarry itself – 'Saccy in the Tub' – which is still affectionately recalled by older villagers.[103]

The most famous village totter in the early 1900s was James 'Dead 'n' Green – an old man of about seventy years of age when people first remember him. His activities can be tracked in the records of the Bullingdon Petty Sessions, where he made the first of his frequent appearances in 1876[104] (six convictions were recorded against him in 1886 and at least five in the previous year).[105] He is remembered by older villagers as 'a bit of a gypsy' who used to go round with a sack on his back 'and you never knew what he got in his sack . . . could be anything'.[106] He had a cottage by the New Inn, on the turnpike road.[107] His speciality was 'briaring',[108] but the police court records show him also quite often trespassing for rabbits (the magistrate in 1898 rebuked him with having a 'terribly black list' against his name for this offence),[109] as well as occasionally for more humble prey (he was brought up before the courts for stealing turnips in 1887,[110] and for taking 'a quantity of cabbage' from Mr Morrell's estate, in 1899).[111] He seems to have worked at a variety of jobs. When he was arrested in 1908 he said that he was engaged 'every day in the pig-yard'[112] (possibly this was Coleman the blacksmith's pig-yard on the London Road); he is also remembered as taking on thrashing jobs in the winter, together with his brother Chaffy, 'then in between that he'd go briaring and mushrooming and watercressing'.[113]

A certain number of men – older men, it seems, especially – did contrive to make a kind of compound living from all these 'dibs' and 'dabs'. One was George 'Pedgell' Webb, the champion of cottager's rights on the Open Brasenose and the Open Magdalen, and from his case one can see how totting and foraging on the waste could be combined with the village-based resources of the cottage economy (gardening, pig-keeping, 'penny capitalism'). He was referred to as a 'labourer' when he was prosecuted for his trespassing (the same was true of Dead 'n' Green), but he was known in Quarry itself as (among other things) an itinerant hawker, selling nuts and oranges on Quarry Rec. 'He used to come up in the Recreation there, Saturdays, with his oranges and nuts – carried in . . . a carpet bag.'[114] He gathered faggots from the Open Brasenose and the Open Magdalen to sell round the village (from the evidence given at his prosecution in 1895, he seems to have gone to the woods daily).[115] He had an allotment at Titup, where he grew vegetables and kept pigs; he cured his own bacon at home. ('. . . You could smell that when you was in school . . . old Pedgell Webb's bacon. Home cured and that'.[116]) According to Will and Bert Webb, his nephews, he also dealt from time to time in horses '. . . buy in the market and then bring it back and sell it to somebody'.[117] After his wife's death in 1902 he went to Charlotte Webb, a relative, for his meals. Waggle Ward, who was brought up in that household, remembers how he used to bring his contribution to the table:[118]

> Old Uncle George – Pedgell Webb – used to have a big 'lotment up there and 'ee used to have plenty of carrots, plenty of swedes – well that was a good feed, good rabbit – they'd ketch their own rabbits – and old Pedgell used to have a big 'lotment at Titup 'ee used to, and 'ee used to bring Granny Webb all this green stuff home . . . I can just remember old Pedgell Webb.

His livelihood may well have been precarious, but he was able to leave enough money at his death for one of his nephews to be indentured to a trade – something for which he is still remembered in the village.[119]

As mentioned earlier, a number of men made a 'bit of a living' catching song-birds. Snooks Smith, for instance, 'used to go about ketching birds – goldfinches and that – and he'd send 'em to London';[120] Saccy Horwood, alongside his other totting activities, 'used to ketch a few birds . . . and send away to London'. 'Sometimes our old Dad used to be a bird catcher as well: used to catch goldfinches, bullfinches, linnets . . . used to have a little aviary at the bottom . . . put them on a train and sell them different places.'[121] Braddy Webb, who worked at Taylor's brickyard on Shotover (and in later years 'on the buildings') used to get his living catching birds 'and then all summer he used to go in the brickyards and work'.[122] He not only went out catching birds, but constructed a sort of triangular trade on the basis of them:[123]

> Braddy had always got a cage full of birds – he'd get some
> sent down from London – canaries and all – of course you
> couldn't catch canaries, only bullfinches. He send them off
> and then they'd send him some canaries – and then he'd
> sell 'em . . . Anyone 'ud want to buy one, they'd go there
> and buy one.

Harry Gurl, who worked at stone-digging in the summer, was another man who made a winter livelihood of birds:[124]

> Uncle Harry he didn't have a regular job. He worked with
> Dad all the summer, and then he'd go bird catching all
> winter. He made a livin' at it anyway . . . All over the
> place he used to go bird catching – nights and all – I've
> been with him at nights – with his clap-nets as he called
> them – two sticks – and when the birds was in he'd clap
> them on together – they used to come down the net . . .
> shoot them down the net into the bag at the bottom.
> That was up Shotover Hill . . . up in the park there. I
> never could understand how he could see to catch 'em.
> He'd have them nets done between them bushes like a
> flash of greased lightning . . .

For most Quarry villagers, totting was a more occasional resource than this. It was something taken up by fits and starts, sometimes in the search for 'extras', sometimes, as in a bad winter, a last resort. It is difficult to speak with confidence of how much it contributed to the standard of life, but there is no doubt about the importance of its social and moral effects. The notion of common rights was built in to the cottager's economy, and so too was that of personal independence: it was possible to make a 'bit of a living' even when wage-paid labour gave out, and even when there was no money, to keep the table supplied with food, and have enough fuel to feed the fire.

Perhaps it is this which helps to explain why Quarry, though 'rough' by the standards of more regulated communities, seems to have escaped the kind of destitution so familiar in the late Victorian countryside and so rampant in the towns. Subsistence never gave out, however severe the season, nor was charity ever called upon to take its place – there was little available save that which the working population of the village provided for themselves. 'Practically but very few of the Parishioners are Paupers,' runs a note in the archives of Holy Trinity, probably written in the 1870s, 'seldom more than ½ dozen or so in receipt of Parish relief.'[125] The MS. census returns for Headington workhouse bear this out – there is a remarkable paucity of Quarry names – and so do older villagers: in all the hardships which they speak about, no mention is made of those two great standbys of the out-of-work elsewhere: the workhouse and parish relief.

5   *Wage labour and capital*

Capitalism in the nineteenth century was an uneven development, in the countryside no less than in the towns, and Quarry was one of those dark corners of the kingdom – like the East End of London – which had been imperfectly colonized, from an economic and industrial as well as from a cultural and social point of view. Numbers of villagers escaped the servitudes of wage labour altogether, and there were many more for whom employment was characteristically short term and indirect. Within the village nothing like a capitalist class

emerged. In building the smaller jobs were often taken on by
pairs of mates, or by individuals acting on their own, or with a
helper. Stone-digging work and navvying were often in the
hands of 'companionships' – self-selecting bands of men, linked
to one another by ties of friendship or blood and sometimes
both. The well-diggers ran the job themselves, with no one
giving orders: so did the rabbit-catchers. Even in the brickyards labour was far from a simple commodity, and there
were lines of kinship which cut across those of class. The same
was even more true of cottage laundries, where family labour
took the place of the absent proletariat; on the farms, where
wage-paid labour was an exception rather than the rule; and in
the carrying trades.

Quarry farming was in the hands of small farmers who
worked the land, for the most part, with their own labour, and
that of their families, and called in outsiders only when there
was a rush of work.[1]

> These farmers – well smallholders a lot of them were, but
> I mean they called them farmers – if they got a crop, just
> been cut, say, and it didn't look too promising, they'd
> come round the village and rope anybody in – don't
> matter – women, *anyone* . . . as long as they got it in.

At the time of the 1861 census there was only one farmer with
more than three servants in his employ – Richard Pether at
Wood Farm who is recorded as having twelve men and four
boys working for him.[2] By 1900 there were none. Edward
Bannister, 'a little short man',[3] styled himself a 'dairyman' but
he used to fetch the cows in himself (he was to be seen milking
them at 4 a.m.)[4] and he sold the milk round the village in a
bucket.[5] His 'farm' was made up of two separated fields (one
of them, known as the 'Workhouse Piece' was rented from the
parish). The Thorntons, who had an orchard in the Pitts, are
said to have stayed up all night 'hollerin up . . . with the rattle'
to keep the birds off their cherries.[6] George Lord worked his
farm with his own labour and that of his sons – 'proper country
boys'.[7] Muddy Clarke, an old man when Will Webb was a boy,
'did a bit of market gardening and that'; he had a little field at
the back of the workhouse (possibly the one which Bannister
rented in later years) and sold his produce from a donkey-cart.[8]
Henry Harris, who farmed Monk's Farm, was a dairyman

whose 'labourers' were himself, his wife's sister, and his wife, who carried the milk down to the village on yokes.[9]

Employment in the laundries was also a matter of family relationships, though the networks – in the case of the larger ones – extended farther than they did on the farms. The laundry-woman relied, for the most part, on her own labour and that of her daughters; husbands too were drawn in, to take on the fetching and carrying, and sometimes other relatives as well. Wages for extra labour were low – 2d. an hour is the best remembered rate in the 1900s (or in some accounts 2s. a day) – but such work was very different in character, and preferred, to going out to service, or charing for one of the big houses on Headington Hill. In some cases at least, the extra labour seems to have been recruited on the basis of sharing rather than of profit: 'They used to gang up together, these women in the village, and they'd take big baskets.'[10] The distinction between the laundrywoman and the wage labourer was by no means hard and fast, as one can see from the case of Mrs Auger, the blacksmith's wife. Like her husband, she went out to work for others at one stage in her life and worked on her own at another.[11]

> ... our Mam, she went out to work a bit – two bob a day – from eight to eight – washin' and ironin'. That was in the village. Narroway. And then ... she 'ad a 'amper or two she done at home ... she went out and then she done some at home at the finish.

Whether or not a woman set up on her own depended upon family circumstances as much as anything else; the woman with a large family of daughters was particularly well placed; the availability of free transport may also have played a part – the family with a horse, or a pony, or a donkey and cart was better able to take on big washings than the family without.

The carrying trade, too, was very much a family affair, with one man and a boy – or sometimes two brothers or cousins – as the basic work force and other relatives giving a hand from time to time. In a large family, like the Webbs or the Kerrys, the work was widely shared; Charlie Jones seems to have worked in tandem with his brother, Jewbell, sometimes employing a nephew besides; Georgie Boulter, a newcomer to the village, employed a boy.

Little capital was required to start enterprises such as these. The launderer needed nothing except a garden to serve as a drying-ground, and a willing band of helpers if more than a 'family's washing' was to be taken in. The brickmaker, too, in the days of hand-made bricks, required very little in the way of 'plant', and perhaps this is one reason why so many farmers tried their hand at it in the nineteenth century, if they chanced to have clay on their land. Once the kiln had been built (and some of them were rough and ready affairs) everything depended on manual labour: there was not even a pugging machine for processing the clay. The carriers often got a start within the family, like Tommy Webb, whose first horse was a grey pony given, or left to him, by his uncle Toby (according to family tradition he began as a carrier at the age of eleven, after his father and mother 'died off'),[12] or Waggle Ward, who started up a coke round with his uncle Nobby's donkey. A horse could be maintained at 'minimum cost' since grass could be cut from the roadsides and grazing was free; it was also comparatively cheap to replace a horse because of the amount of horse-dealings which went on in the village, partly through the influence of the gypsies. (All the same, it could be a strain: when one of Tommy Webb's ponies died there was a collection 'round the Quarry' to help him buy a replacement.)[13]

Production on the farms was for subsistence rather than for surplus or for profit. 'It was a scratch all the time', I was told by Bill Trafford, who spent his early boyhood on Quarry Farm, then in the tenancy of his grandfather. 'You used to keep a few fowl, a couple of pigs – that sort of thing – and that was half your livin'.'[14] The brickyards produced more in the way of surplus value, and unlike Quarry's other local enterprises they were definitely geared to profit. Even so they failed to grow as capitalist firms, perhaps because so little was demanded of the employer in the way of management, supervision, or capital expenditure. Henry Hedges' works on Shotover, 'from which large quantities of bricks of superior quality are made', was up for auction in 1868.[15] John Coppock's works, the largest in the village at one time, 'petered out',[16] being built up by the father (who was also active in adding to his land),[17] and dwindling under his son, John Coppock, jun., who according to some gave more attention to poultry-keeping and sport. Jack Phillips's brickyard, which he had inherited from his mother, came to an end when his son went away to be a farmer. George Taylor's was sold up at his death.

No dynasty of brickmasters appeared, even in the heyday of the industry's local prosperity, nor was there a decisive separation of wage labour and capital. The children of the brickmasters were not segregated from the rest of the village for the purposes of education or social grooming, but went to work alongside the 'roughs'. All four sons of George Taylor, the Methodist brickmaker, worked as labourers in his yard, and they were by no means trained up to take the business over. One of them, Walter, was killed in the Vicarage Pit (an accident variously attributed to an explosion or a fall of stone[18]). Two others, Ferret and Beautiful, were famous village 'roughs'[19] (both of them joined up with the village poachers; Ferret was an expert with the dogs, which may be where he got his nickname; he was in jail when war was declared in 1914). The fourth son, Reg went off to be a policeman in St Helens, after serving in the 1914–18 war.[20] Ellen Phillips's three sons also worked in her yard, one of them being 'the sort of second boss', but another is remembered as 'an odd feller' 'just helping in the yard here and there'.[21] Jack Phillips, 'a great big tough quarryman' who inherited the yard,[22] had his brothers, nephew and his son working for him, although the son eventually left to be a farmer.

Road haulage, a major element in the Quarry economy on account of the laundries, the brickworks and the quarries, provides another example of the failure of capitalism to grow, even in apparently favourable conditions. Despite the new opportunities of the later nineteenth century, it stayed at the level of the man with the horse and cart. When demand expanded all that happened was that more individual carriers started up, so that in Edwardian times all kinds of men were getting a 'bit of a living' from it (the husbands of the laundry-women, for example), quite apart from those who followed it as their trade. The carrying businesses themselves were fissiparous; if a second horse was added it might be to give a second member of the family a start rather than as a stepping-stone to growth. The same was true of laundries: when business increased the industry expanded sideways, with more and more homes taking in washing, but no large firms developing. The growth of retail trade in the village, another feature of the late nineteenth- and early twentieth-century years, had a similar effect: instead of trading activity being concentrated it was diffused. There were few shops in the village, and none purpose-built,[23] but numbers of working men and women ran little trading sidelines, sometimes from the kitchen, sometimes from the parlour, sometimes from a shed, or else, like some of the poachers, by door-to-door sales or transactions in the pub. In the building industry, too, with its multiplicity of small-scale and subcontracted jobs, activity was apt to be dispersed instead of falling into the hands of a few master builders (there were none in Quarry itself, though there were plenty of men who took up jobs on their own, or worked with a mate).

Businesses in Quarry – like other forms of livelihood – were usually made up of a mix of different activities. Harry Coleman, the blacksmith, for instance, kept a pigyard for speculative breeding, and a bacon shop (later turned into a café) for the sale of hog's puddings; he was also 'a bit of a saddlemaker'.[24] The Corby brothers, wheelwrights, also made coffins, kept cows and sold milk at their house; they added another string to their bow by acting as undertakers at village funerals; and yet another by shoeing horses.[25] Retail businesses were usually run in tandem with other activities rather than as a single-minded pursuit. William Coppock, the grocer, for instance, was also a fruit-grower with a well-protected orchard behind his home, grazed his cows on Haines's Field, and had a cowshed and a little dairy by his shop.[26] (He was styled 'butcher & farmer' in the census of 1871;[27] appears as 'grocer & post office' in Kelly's *Directory* for 1890–1; and 'grocer & rate collector' in that for 1896–7; the *Shrimpton's Oxford Directory* entry for him, in 1875, has his occupation as that of 'farmer & general dealer'.)[28] Stephen Goodgame, as well as running a little general store – coals, sweets and pickled onions are among its remembered lines[29] – 'also used to grow a bit of fruit and stuff to sell . . . mostly strawberries, raspberries, gooseberries . . .'[30] (he had a large garden ground in the neighbourhood of the Pitts); earlier he had been licensee of the 'Chequers' and was at one time styled a 'stone merchant' as well.[31] Tommy Trafford, who began life as a stone-digger,[32] was listed as a 'coal merchant & carman' in Kelly's *Directory* for 1902; about this time he also took on the tenancy of Quarry Farm; in 1908 he lost the tenancy of the farm and returned to his coal business (the coal business failed in 1914, after a long, hard winter, and his son went off to work in a saw mill[33]).

The brickmasters, perhaps as a form of double-banking, were usually something else besides. Henry Hedges, for instance, a well-known figure of the 1850s and 1860s, is variously referred to in the directories as a 'farmer', 'beer retailer' and 'brick burner'; he was also a cow-keeper and it was in this last capacity that he played a leading part in the cottagers' fight for the Open Magdalens.[34] George Coppock, a 'brick merchant' according to the census of 1871, and later on the owner of a brickworks on Shotover, kept the 'Six Bells' as well, and at one stage he appears also to have been a farmer.[35] Jack Phillips is described as a 'farmer & brick maker' in Kelly's *Directory* for 1910–11;[36] George Taylor, the other big brickmaster at that time, is also remembered as one who 'used to grow corn and that;[37] John Coppock, jun., was described to me by one who knew him as 'a bit of all sorts';[38] apart from running his brickyard he bred ducks, which he attended to himself (Will Smith as a boy used to watch him taking them to the pond[39]), and sold 'quite a lot of eggs' at the Manor House[40] (he also sold walnuts there when there was a fall from the trees).

Businesses in Quarry remained anchored, by and large, to individual activity and family circumstance; they did not blossom out into firms; nor were they built up and improved upon, as premises or plant, from one generation to the next. Farms changed hands frequently, and none of the names which appear in the directories of the 1850s are in those of the 1900s. The brickworks seem to have progressed by fits and starts rather than on a steady upward curve: none of them stayed in a family for more than two generations and some had only a brief existence – like that of Simeon ('Simmy') Phipps, a man who was in trouble with the School Board in the 1870s for failing to send his children to school, and who is said to have taken to drink.[41] He appears in Kelly's *Directory* for 1877 as a brickmaker,[42] but in 1908 a newspaper paragraph refers to him as a 'labourer':[43] the brickyard, by the time living memory begins, had disappeared. Shops – those few which existed – were comparatively short-lived; quite a number of people tried their hand at them but then moved on to something else, like Charles Snow, 'stone merchant' and 'beer retailer' at the time of the census of 1861,[44] who was a working

stonemason at the time of writing his diary in 1882–3; or
Harry Stiles, who turns up in the MS. census returns succes-
sively as a stone-digger (1851), a grocer (1861), and then a
baker (1871); or George Stiles, who appears briefly as a baker
in the census of 1871 but then emigrated to Canada;[45] or Harry
Coleman, who is entered as a 'grocer' in the directories of the
1880s and early 1890s and then starts to figure as a blacksmith
in 1896–7, the occupation for which he is remembered in the
village today.[46] Others turned to shop-keeping comparatively
late in life, and when they died the shop died with them, as
in the case of Emma Webb's little sweet shop in School Place.
Most of the shop-keepers mentioned in the MS. census returns
of 1841–71 (one in 1841; five in 1851; eight in 1861; ten in 1871)
appear on one occasion only, the publicans showing more
stability than the rest.[47]

There was plenty of individual enterprise in Quarry, but
it was apt to be dispersed in a variety of directions rather than
concentrated in a single whole. The villagers were good at
making ends meet, often in trying conditions, but not, it seems
at making money. They lacked the capitalist instinct for getting
rich at other people's expense, or on the basis of other people's
labour. They made the best of their environment, but they did
not overstep its limits, or treat it as a point of take-off. Quarry
poachers were expert in the field, but careless when it came
to marketing their hauls, and in their poaching itself they
stuck to rabbits instead of venturing further afield for game.
The haggle-cart men and the carriers conducted their businesses
as a source of immediate livelihood rather than for surplus or
for profits: none of them attempted to build up a fleet of vans.
No captain of industry rose from the villagers' ranks to make
a career of his trade (Jackie Snow, 'the village Lord Nuffield',
was a working nobbler all his life, and the money which he
left to the Wingfield Hospital is generally attributed to an
exceptional frugality rather than to speculative prowess[48]).
There was no local contractor to make a fortune out of construction work, haulage, or navvying. No steam laundries were
introduced into Quarry (there was a well-established one at
Littlemore):[49] the industry remained at the level of the cottage
shed even though the volume of trade grew by leaps and
bounds.

The working class in Quarry was very far from being made up

of wage labourers alone. Numbers of villagers – at one time
or another – were self-employed, and there were many more
who contrived to make a 'bit of a livelihood' on their own,
even if they also worked for wages. There seems little doubt
that the category of the self-employed was one which *grew*
in nineteenth-century Quarry (especially in the latter years),
partly because of the rise of laundry work, partly because of
the growth of the village itself, which provided so many opportunities for the totter, the carrier, and the dealer. Another
influence was that of the gypsies, who established a regular
settlement in the village some time between 1859 and 1861 (no
fewer than four separate households of North Oxfordshire
Smiths appear in the census returns for 1861), and who were
accepted as part and parcel of village life, even though they
travelled away in the summer.[50] The gypsies always worked
in some sort for themselves, whether hawking their baskets
and skewers (the chief source of livelihood for the Quarry
community when F. H. Groome came upon them in 1872),[51]
putting on their shows (like the Bucklands with their pony
roundabout and Razzle Smith with his hoop-la[52]), or taking
on fruit-picking and harvest jobs. Like the Slade gypsies of
the 1920s: 'They always worked as a group, for *themselves* –
doing those sort of jobs they would be paid on results, wouldn't
they? They could leave when they liked and start when they
liked – it's not like working for a farmer.'[53]

The self-employed were not a distinct social class, but were to
be found at each social level and in every category of skill.
Some were quite poor, and forced to work on their own account
because nothing else was available to them – Saccy Horwood,
for instance, a morris-dancer in his youth, seems to have turned
to totting when his health broke down. Others, like the Corby
brothers, who cut and hauled their own timber and employed
one or two men in their saw-pit, or Stephen Goodgame, a 'well
respected man' (see p. 161), with his little coal and vegetable
shop, and also his 'tidy bit' of ground, were comfortably
off. The same variations in fortune are to be found among the
village laundrywomen: in some cases they were engaged in a
hard struggle to bring up a family 'on the wash-tub', in others –
as with Mrs Narroway, whose husband was a jobbing builder –
the household was well placed. Setting up on one's own was
often a phase in the struggle to produce the means of subsistence

rather than the start of a life-long career. For some it was a form of double-banking, an insurance against the lowness or uncertainties of pay. For Harry Gurl and Braddy Webb, the bird-catchers, it was a sort of winter job, something to fall back on when wage-paid labour gave out. Wage labour and individual enterprise were not necessarily alternatives: often they were two sides of the same coin.

The labourer in Quarry was very differently placed from the farm 'servant' or the factory 'hand'. He was accustomed to find his livelihood in a variety of ways, rather than by confining himself to an individual master, or a particular line of trade; his employments were often short-lived, and his prospects, from month to month, precarious. But he enjoyed an element of real personal freedom in his work. He did not have to answer to the time-keeper's watch or the foreman's beck and call: his time was very much his own, with bursts of hard work alternating with spells of idleness. He moved with comparative ease between a variety of employments, depending upon the state of trade, and the opportunities available. Often he followed two or three different callings in the course of a year, or even simultaneously. He might work for a farmer at busy times, such as harvest; engage himself for a mowing job, or at hedge-laying or thrashing; take up a few weeks' work in a navvying gang (land-draining, well-sinking or digging ditches), dovetailing such jobs, as far as he was able, with longer stretches of work at the brickmaking, on the building, or in the quarries. The drainer, the well-digger and the hod-carrier might thus be one and the same man at different seasons of the year. William Green had even more strings to his bow, 'a navvy when there was navvying to be done, or a farm labourer – a sort of handyman – everyone was – getting whatever they could: he was a bit of a horse doctor too . . . bit of rabbitin wasn't amiss'.[54]

Virtually the only class of labour with regular employment in Quarry – at least among wage labourers – were the men who worked in the brickyards, or at least the nucleus who remained in the work all the year round (some men worked there only in the summer-time, while the making season was on). Stone-digging was much more irregular and employment on it was often short-term. Farming jobs in the 1900s were usually short-lived, a matter of working odd days at the busiest time of the year – going out mowing 'in the spring', taking on

haymaking 'to get an extra bob or two' or doing 'a bit harvesting'. 'They'd have a day, p'raps, and then they'd go back to
brickmaking.'[55] The class of regular farm servants, by no means
numerous even at mid-century, was by the end of the century
extinct, though boys still found employment as farm hands as a
first job on leaving school.

The industrial development of Quarry in the second half of
the nineteenth century seems to have made work more irregular
rather than less, by diversifying the field for labouring employment, and giving rise to a class of free-lance navvies, who worked
sometimes at well-digging and field-draining, sometimes at
sewerage, sometimes on footings or at hod-carrying. They
moved easily between employment in the country, in the suburbs of Oxford, and in the town itself. In the building industry
regular weekly work was difficult to obtain even for the man
who sought it out; there were no such things as permanent
situations, even with the larger building firms, except for the
foreman, and one or two leading hands. Engagements lasted
only so long as the builder had a job in hand. 'When you had
finished that was it. When the job was finished, you finished,
unless they'd got . . . work following on.'[56] A spell of unemployment (sardonically referred to in the trade as 'being a gentleman')[57] was always on the horizon.[58]

Unless you was an old hand on a building firm you'd got
no chance at all, 'cos you'd be out of work as soon as you
got up on the roof . . . the older men finished it. They'd
got the old regular staff, the 'old codgers'. The others were
in and out . . . p'raps a day – two or three days – while
they got over a certain job.

In winter virtually every class of building labour – the craftsman
no less than the hod-carrier or the navvy – was liable to be
thrown out of work. It was accepted in the local trade as
inevitable:[59]

. . . it was all seasonal the building trade was – sort of a
summer job . . . come the winter time – you see now they
build any time – but if there was frost about the building
stopped – they wouldn't allow 'em to build in the frost,
you see – course they've got means now . . . stuff they
mix up . . . with the mortar . . . they couldn't do that

years ago . . . The consequence was you was all out of work
when it come frosty. Autumn time they started [to travel]
when the leaves begin to fall – they used to sing an old
song 'God bless the painters when the leaves begin to fall'
'cos they reckoned all the painters was out of work when
the leaves started falling. Sort of leg-pull for the painters
when the summer was coming to an end.

Bricklayers were always on the look-out for a job. A big
contract could keep them employed for months at a time, but
even in a rich town like Oxford they were occasional, and things
seem to have been particularly grim during the building slump
of the 1900s.[60]

You had to travel – get your own job – didn't work for any
one employer – when you were on a job in those days,
when it was finished, you finished, unless there was some
more work to go to – if not – you'd go and look for it. . . If
you seen a building just a-going up – starting – you asked
for a job. Walk in – see the foreman – ask if there was any
vacancies for a bricklayer and . . . if he did want one . . .
you could start in the morning.

Bricklayers kept a weather eye on the brick-carts. 'In them
days, say a load of bricks come out – they used to pull 'em with
'orses – the bricklayers used to follow the horse and cart, to see
. . . if they wanted a bricklayer.'[61] One Quarry bricklayer,
desperate for a job, is said to have ended up in Birmingham,
travelling with the bricks on the canal.[62]

Amongst the house carpenters 'there was very few had a
regular job'.

You was a journeyman, you see, you had to journey for
the job. You were on the job, as long as the job lasted . . .
perhaps six months – six weeks . . . according to how big
the job was, see, or whether you suited or not . . .

Carpenters, like bricklayers, had to be for ever on the look-out
for an opening:[63]

It was a sort of grapevine, it used to go all round . . .
'big job coming out so and so' – you used to keep your
eye on that job – say you were working somewhere else
[you'd think], 'Well that'll be ready about so and so' –
see – well, if your job petered out you'd be round . . .

Stonemasons, the most aristocratic of Quarry's tradesmen, were less susceptible to fluctuations in the building trade because of the amount of college stonework (possibly, too, because of a rising municipal demand for the inferior classes of work), but for them, too, employment was often short-term, and seasonally they suffered even sharper vicissitudes than people in the other building trades. The Long Vacation was the stonemason's 'harvest', 'when the toffs was all down'.[64] With the start of the Michaelmas term, work in the yards grew slack. 'You was done . . . when October come. You'd to clear out the colleges – couldn't work in there like they do now – any time they be there – you had to clear out.'[65] When winter set in the moisture began to freeze in the stone, and stoppages in the trade were general. In a bad winter the mason might find himself in real distress: 'My old gramp told me that they used to go out on Shotover shooting a bird – anything to make a pie . . . you got to that stage.'[66]

Even in a well-established mason's yard there were few regular hands: 'a builder may have sixty masons employed this year, and next year only six'.[67] High earnings were punctuated by a frequent occurrence of the 'sack'. This can be seen quite clearly in the stonemason's diary for 1882–3, preserved in the Vallis family. Charles Snow, the writer of the diary (Mr Vallis's grandfather), was a man who earned good money when he was in work, 30s. to 35s. a week which in 1882 was an artisan's wage; he was a leading Methodist and a respected local figure. His diary, with its careful detail of expenditure, does not suggest a man who by preference would take to irregular ways. But he had no regular employment, in the modern sense of the term, and he spent a portion of the year – when no employment was available – tending his garden (an extensive affair), or taking small jobs on his own account. Here are some entries from the diary for 1882 (entries stop in July):[68]

5.1.82.	Friday.	went to Oriel to work.
9.1.82.	Monday.	begin putting up chimney at Oriel Coll.
19.1.82.	Thursday.	had the sack from Oriel.
28.1.82.	Saturday.	planted Mr Blake's flowers.
2.2.82.	Thursday.	killed pig 9 stone 10 lbs 10/6 4-19-6.

3.3.82.	Friday.	went to work at Oriel Coll. roughing steps.
24.4.82.	Monday.	went to Hollywell & Jericho.
29.4.82.	Saturday.	wt day had the sack
10.5.82.		went to work Bodlyon
10.7.82.		went to University coll. to work.

In the Oxford building trade it was said that a man 'wasn't a tradesman' until he had been to London.[69] One of those who went there was Bert Coppock, a bricklayer now in his eighties. He got a job there almost immediately ('Home for Fallen Women Hospital – somewhere round Baker Street way'), and stayed on it for seven months: 'I got fed up really ... You'd got two homes to keep, that made a lot of difference in your money.'[70] It was quite common in the building trade for men to travel away: 'Most of it was local, perhaps twenty mile out or ten mile out, but if it come to a bad turn they'd have to go down to Bournemouth, anywhere there was a job on.'[71] Jobs were often at a distance, even with local firms as the employers, and if it was far to travel men would sleep away for the week and come back to Quarry for the Sunday: Vic Morris stayed away for fortnights at a time when he was bricklaying for Magdalen College. 'Stratford-on-Avon ... Chalgrove, Lower Quinton ... Gloucester ... home Saturday, back Monday morning.'[72] Some travelled away for longer periods. Walter Bushnell, a stonemason, 'used to go anywhere'. 'He was a rover ... used to walk miles and miles to get a job ... I know he walked from here to Aldershot to get a job once.'[73] George Coppock, a bricklayer, 'worked several viaducts down the country'. His brother Tom, a carpenter, 'built a lot at Maidenhead' working for Cooper's of Reading (he married and settled there for a time and then came back to Oxford, though not, it seems, to Quarry).[74] Jack Gurl, a bricklayer, 'went away for years up-country – that's how he got the name Yorky'.[75] Bill Slaymaker, another bricklayer, was one of 'several' who went from Quarry and the neighbourhood to work on the 'Tuppenny Tube' (the Central London Railway – know as the Central Line today – which was built and opened between 1900 and 1904): 'He stopped in London, his wife was here.'[76]

Quarry labourers do not seem to have travelled away as often as the bricklayers and the carpenters, but when they did

go they travelled far. One man ('a great big feller, so they said
. . . always in trouble with summat') went away to work on the
Manchester Ship Canal and is said to have died of pneumonia
there 'layin' rough and that'[77] (the canal was opened at
Manchester in 1894, but navvying work continued on it for
some years). Barrel Kerry, in later years a scaffolder with
Kingerlee, the Oxford builders, went to Yorkshire, 'up
Scarborough way', and worked there for some time before
returning to Quarry.[78] Steve Gurl[79]

> led a rough life after his wife died, he travelled the country
> all over the place, then come back occasionally . . . the last
> ten years of his life he worked with me in the pit – along
> with Dad and me, Magdalen pit.

Barry Jones, 'a sort of ganger', had a little clique of followers
whom he took with him on his jobs – 'navvying work, digging
trenches' – one of them 'off Durham way', another on the
Derwent water track at Derby[80] (later on Jones settled down in
Quarry and took on sewering and draining work in the
locality).[81] Snooks Smith and Scabs Gurl went off with him on
one of his London jobs, sleeping up at Tommy Webb's when
they came back to Quarry.[82] Teddy Hooper 'stopped up there
a bit' on the Derwent job.[83] At least two other Quarry
labourers were there as well: Dusty Wright and Beautiful
Taylor. They left Quarry on 11 June 1909, worked on the
Derwent water track until the end of August (Wright had
'some relation' at Ilkeston),[84] and then moved on north into
Lancashire, returning to Quarry on Christmas Eve. (When they
returned home they were immediately arrested and charged
with stealing ducks, but when the case came before the court
they were acquitted.)[85]

When winter came round, almost every class of Quarry
labour suffered from 'broken' weeks, the carpenter and the
stonemason even more, perhaps, than the free-lance navvy. The
degree of irregularity varied from trade to trade, and it was
also affected by individual disposition and family circumstance.
At one end of the spectrum were those who worked on the
brickyards all the year round, but even their trade was seasonal
with poor pay in winter and many days off work. At the other
were those who made their living, like Mark Cox, the morris-
dancer, in 'dibs and dabs', with nothing very regular, but

whatever came their way – 'this sort of odd man out, anybody's man that wanted him – or the biggest pay, if it happened to be that way'.[86] Character and circumstance reciprocated one another's influence, and bred in Quarry a sort of working-class Bohemian, individualist in the first place by necessity, but later on by choice and habit too – a man with a definite aversion to pinning himself down in one place. This is why Will Gurl turned down the offer of a permanent situation as maintenance man at Cowley Barracks. According to Bert Gurl, his nephew, 'He wouldn't have that 'cos it was a regular job, what he wanted was a job where he could earn a pound or two and then have a week on the booze.'[87]

The Great War did as much as anything to change this condition. It acted on Quarry men as it did on so many of those whose impetuous patriotism is recorded on the war memorials of our town and village greens: 'Terrific amount of men went out of this village and . . . a terrific lot didn't come back.'[88]

One of those who disappeared in the war was Dusty Wright, who is remembered by one who knew him as 'just a rough and ready bloke . . . straight as a die'. He was a 'little bit of a gypsy' and 'had a way of getting about without work'. When the war broke out he was doing time in Oxford jail: 'either poaching or fighting'.[89]

There was two inside, in jail, and when the war broke out they volunteered to go straight over. They let 'em out to go. They never come back. Old Dusty Wright, as we called him, and Ferret Taylor. Never come back. And they was blokes like – that when they was out there fightin' – if they see a German, they'd be after 'im – wouldn't wait to be told – they was that type of feller, and they both went west.

Even before the war there had been plenty of signs of change. At Titup, an outlying portion of the village, a number of men were engaged in what was described to me as 'more modern' occupations – 'sort of breakaway from the trades in Quarry' – such as employment on the tramways, or at John Allen's Steam Plough Factory in Cowley: three Titup men had jobs at the Clarendon Press.[90] In Quarry itself the number of men with apprenticed jobs in the building trade was increasing: two or three local men were well placed with the Oxford builders, as foremen or leading hands. The domestic economy was changing, too, with more being bought in the shops or via the carriers and dealers (coals and coke, for instance, seem largely to have supplanted wood as the chief domestic fuel). The arrival in the village of Bessie Barrett, the pork butcher, whose cheap savouries are still affectionately remembered today, ushered in a real change.[91] Pigs were still fatted; but the killing and the cooking and preserving of their meat was less often a household responsibility; the production of hog puddings and other delicacies was increasingly left to her as the specialist; and pig-raising was a way of paying off debts rather than meeting household needs.

After the war the balance of 'modern' and 'traditional' kinds of work was decisively altered, though not all of a sudden (there were still well-digging gangs in the village in the 1920s, and gypsies in the Mason's Pit). The coming of the motor works at Cowley provided Quarry's menfolk, for the first time, with work which lasted all the year round. Flimpy Webb, the poacher, went to work for Morris's 'when they started';[92] so did Dimmy Wright, who had been 'more of a horse dealer' before the war.[93] Will Gurl, the free-lance bricklayer, went off to Pressed Steel.[94] The coming of buses seems to have encouraged school-leavers to take up jobs in Oxford, rather than working in and about Quarry. Machine-made bricks put Quarry's brickyards out of business; the stonepits closed one by one, though the Magdalen Pit on the London Road continued to be worked in a small way down to 1949. Horses, commandeered for war service in 1914, and later on displaced by lorries, 'died out'.[95] The girdle of waste land and allotment ground was eaten up by the speculative builder. Pigs disappeared from the gardens, laundry from the sheds. Quarry was linked to Old Headington by a grid of built-up roads, and in 1936 it was swallowed up in the Oxford city boundaries. The village of the well-diggers and the morris-dancers gave way to one in which men clocked in for work in the morning, and took home a weekly wage. Women no longer worked together in family-based gangs, and instead of having to produce their subsistence, they could buy it in the shops.

Notes

1 'Quarry roughs'

1 Oxford Town Hall muniments, Y/49, Memorial to the Directors of the Oxford, Worcester & Wolverhampton Railway, 12 March 1852. 'From the manufacture of bricks being extensively carried on in the parish the consumption of coals is considerable, the brickyards alone consuming not less than 1,500 tons annually.'

2 HQT, Longford, fol. 1.
(HQT = Headington Quarry Transcripts. These are transcripts of recordings made by the writer in Quarry chiefly in 1969–70, and will be deposited, together with the recordings, in the Oxford County Museum at Woodstock when the research is completed; the transcripts have been checked against the original recording where extensive quotation or reference has been used in this text.)

3 *Oxford Times*, 28 March 1908, p. 5, col. 3.

4 Oxford Town Hall muniments, Headington parish council minute book, 20 July, 14 September 1896.

5 HQT, Webb, fol. c. 3.

6 HQT, F. Coppock, fol. 11. b. 3. cf. Also Webb, fol. c.4.

7 HQT, Lee, fol. 3.

8 'Went on Shotover hill to see soldiers', writes Charles Snow, the stonemason, in a diary entry for 2 March 1882. This diary is an invaluable, though all too brief, witness to life in Quarry in the nineteenth century. It runs from 1882 and is full of detail while it lasts. I am exceedingly grateful to Mr A. E. Vallis for letting me see it, as also for the MS. account of Quarry written by his grandfather.

9 For the opening of the waterworks, see the account in *Oxford Times*, 29 September 1877, p. 8, cols 1–3.

10 Bodleian Library, MS. Top. Oxon., d. 191, fol. 75^r, and HQT, Webb, fol. a. 13.

11 HQT, Vallis, fols b. 2–3.

12 *Oxford Times*, 16 October 1909, p. 9, col. 5.

13 HQT, J. Kerry, fol. a. 4.

14 O. E. Evans, 'The manor of Headington', *Oxfordshire Archaeological Society Report*, Long Compton, 1929, p. 201.

15 Vallis papers, MS. account of Quarry, fol. 1.

16 HQT, W. Kerry, fol. b. 1.

17 HQT, Webb, fol. b. 2.

18 HQT, Morris and Coppock, fol. 5.

19 HQT, Webb, fol. b. 1.

20 HQT, Longford, fols 12–13.

21 Charity Commission archives, file no. 1585.

22 Oxford Town Hall muniments, printed paper on Headington
   Charities.
23 HQT, Hay, fol. 10.
24 HQT, W. Kerry, fol. b. 5.
25 HQT, Mrs Gurl, fol. 3.
26 W. J. Arkell, *Oxford Stone*, London, 1947, p. 43.
27 HQT, Morris and Coppock, fol. 5.
28 Bodleian Library, MS. Top. Oxon., c.272, Oxford Board of Health
   minute book, 27 August 1832.
29 *Oxford Times*, 14 November 1908, p. 5, col. 8.
30 Ibid., 24 October 1908, p. 3, col. 6.
31 Public Record Office (hereafter PRO) RG 9/890/516.
32 Holy Trinity archives, parochial accounts, Headington Quarry,
   1870–91.
33 HQT, Webb fol. d. 2.
34 HQT, Longford, fol. 9.
35 HQT, Webb, fol. d. 1.
36 Ronald Blythe, *Akenfield*, London, 1969, pp. 16–17.
37 Holy Trinity archives, Headington Quarry Infants School log
   book, 7 January 1918; HQT, J. A. Coppock, fol. b. 10; Vallis,
   fol. c. 2.
38 Holy Trinity archives, *Headington Quarry Parish Magazine*,
   May, June 1893 for an epidemic of school window-smashing.
39 Quarry people kept time not by the church clock, but by the
   workhouse bell. HQT, Masters, fol. 1.
40 HQT, Webb, fol. d. 2.
41 HQT, Edney, fol. b. 6.
42 I have discussed the showmen in 'The gypsies in Headington
   Quarry', an unpublished chapter of this study; for old Mother
   Dolloway, HQT, Webb, fol. c. 8.
43 *Headington Quarry and Shotover, a History*, compiled by G. A.
   Coppock and B. M. Hill, Oxford, 1933, p. 67.
44 Vallis papers, MS. account of Quarry, fol. 3.
45 HQT, Phillips and Gurl, fol. 1.
46 HQT, East, fol. 2.
47 HQT, Buckland, fol. a. 1.
48 Vallis papers, MS. account of Quarry, fol. 2.
49 HQT, Mrs Gurl, fol. 2.
50 HQT, Tolley, fol. c. 4.
51 HQT, J. Kerry, fol. a. 11.
52 HQT, Phillips and Gurl, fol. 1; Cooper, fol. b. 7.
53 HQT, L. Coppock, fol. 3.
54 HQT, J. Kerry, fol. a. 10; Phillips and Gurl, fol. 1.
55 *Oxford Times*, 7 October 1905, p. 9. Cf. also *Jackson's Oxford
   Journal*, 1 August 1896, p. 6, col. 4.
56 Mrs G. Kerry interviewed by Bernard Reaney, 9 August 1969.
57 Mr Walker, an Oxford taxi-driver, in conversation with the
   writer, 12 October 1970. Mr Walker spent his childhood years in
   Oakleigh.

58 HQT, Edney, fol. a. 1.

59 HQT, W. Kerry, fols a. 1–2. Other strangers said to have suffered humiliation in Quarry include Del Nevo, the Oxford ice-cream man, and Laing, the master of the local hunt.

60 *Oxford Times*, 30 June 1877, supplement, p. 1; 2 November 1878, p. 3, col. 5; 21 February 1880, p. 3, col. 5.

61 *Jackson's Oxford Journal*, 15 December 1894, p. 6, col. 7.

62 *Oxford Times*, 15 March 1879, p. 8, col. 1 (cf. also ibid., 8 February 1879, p. 8, col. 1); *Jackson's Oxford Journal*, 22 August 1896, p. 7); for a youthful group of Quarry incendiaries, *Jackson's Oxford Journal*, 6 April 1895, p. 6, col. 5.

63 Holy Trinity archives, Headington Quarry School log book 8 January 1929.

64 Holy Trinity archives, school diary and scrapbook, 1864–1903; school committee minute book, p. 45, 12 October 1892; and ibid., p. 77, for a court report of 28 November 1896; *Headington Quarry Parish Magazine*, May, June 1893. For some personal memories of Bickley's cruelties, HQT, J. Kerry, fols a. 4–5; Webb, fol. d. 1; for window-smashing and resistance, HQT, L. Coppock, fols 2–4; J. Kerry, fols a. 4–5; Webb, fol. d. 1.

65 ' . . . The steps taken by Mr. Bickley on his arrival to enforce stricter discipline were thoroughly approved.' School committee minute book, 1 April 1895.

66 For Emma Parsons' assault on Mr Bickley (' . . . she struck him on the face . . . seized him by the whiskers, some of which she pulled out' and followed him into the playground 'where she scratched his face'), Holy Trinity archives, school notebook and minute book, 1864–1903, p. 72, cutting dated p. 72; for Mark Cox's assault on him, *Oxford Chronicle*, 21 September 1895, p. 5, col. 4.; for a grim memory of Bickley, HQT, Webb, fol. d. 1.; and for a more favourable one, HQT, Tolley, fol. 6.; for the very adverse opinion of Mr Bickley by the school inspector, Headington Quarry Mixed School log book, 29 February 1920.

67 *Headington Quarry Parish Magazine*, June 1893.

68 HQT, Webb, fol. c. 11.

69 HQT, Edney, fol. b. 5.

70 HQT, Wright and Jones, fols 9–10.

71 HQT, Hay, fol. 1.

72 *Victoria County History of Oxfordshire*, v, pp. 163–4.

73 Bodleian Library, MS. D. D. Par. Headington, E. 1., Headington vestry minute book, 1818–35, fol. 2m and entries for 13 November 1823, 8 October 1829.

74 *Oxford Times*, 6 October 1877, p. 5, col. 1; 13 October 1877, p. 2, col. 6; 11 October 1879, p. 3, col. 5; 17 November 1877, p. 2, col. 1.

75 HQT, Cooper, fol. a. 4. Arthur Kerry, suspected of poaching in 1912, was also accused of 'allowing a dog to stray on the highway without having a collar' (*Oxford Times*, 19 July 1910, p. 8, col. 6).

76 HQT, East, fol. 11.

77 HQT, Ward, fol. b. 14.
78 HQT, East, fol. 11.
79 HQT, Edney, fol. b. 3.
80 HQT, Webb, fol. c. 10.
81 HQT, B. Horwood, fol. 2.
82 HQT, J. Kerry, fol. b. 1.
83 HQT, P. Phillips, fol. 9.
84 HQT, J. Kerry, fol. a. 7; B. Trafford, fols, 9–10; conversation with the Rev. Head, June 1969.
85 HQT, Ward, fol. a. 1. For other versions of this story: HQT, Longford, fols 3–4; Webb, fols b. 6, c. 3; Tolley, fol. b. 3.
86 *Oxford Times*, 21 April 1894.
87 Ibid.
88 HQT, Blagrove, fol. 1.
89 'Memories of Old Quarry', *Oxford Times*, 19 December 1969, p. 14, col. 6.
90 Bodleian Library, G. A. Oxon, C. 317/21.
91 *Jackson's Oxford Journal*, 16 July 1892, p. 8, col. 2; for the 1892 disturbances generally, Holy Trinity archives, paper dated 1 July 1892 and signed by the Rev. C. F. H. Johnston, vicar.
92 *Oxford Times*, 18 September 1909, p. 9, cols 1–4.
93 Bodleian Library, MS. Top. Oxon., d. 444, fol. 62^r.
94 *Oxford Times*, 25 September 1909, p. 12, col. 7.
95 Ibid., p. 9, col. 7.
96 Ibid., 18 September 1909, p. 12, col. 5. I am exceedingly grateful to Mr G. S. Jones of Kennington who sent me a copy of the postcard, following an appeal in the columns of the *Oxford Times*. For a personal recollection of the riot, HQT, Vallis, fols. c. 3–4.
97 Bodleian Library, MS. Oxford Diocesan papers, c. 657, fols 21^r, 21^v, 22^r.
98 *Jackson's Oxford Journal*, 11 July 1807, p. 3, col. 2.
99 HQT, Baker, fol. 3.
100 Jack Holland, Alun Howkins, Raphael Samuel, *Headington Quarry and the Fight for the Open Magdalens*, History Workshop pamphlet (forthcoming).
101 *Oxford Times*, 2 September 1871, for a mass trespass; Oxfordshire Record Office, Misc. Mor. IV/I and *Oxford Chronicle*, 17 April 1880, for the incendiary fire of 1880.
102 HQT, Wright and Jones, fol. 5; J. Kerry, fol. b. 3.
103 HQT, Wright and Jones, fol. 5.
104 Ibid., and conversation with Cliff Gurl, June 1969.
105 *Oxford Times*, 28 September 1878, p. 3, col. 4; 26 October 1878, p. 3, col. 5.
106 HQT, F. Coppock, fol. b. 3.
107 For documents on the exchange, Charity Commission archives, file no. 15857.
108 HQT, Baker, fol. 4. There is a copy of the transfer agreement in the Oxfordshire Record Office.

109 HQT, Blagrove, fols 1–2.
110 *Oxford Times*, 25 October 1913, p. 7, col. 5: Headington parish council minute book, 20 October 1913.
111 HQT, J. A. Coppock, fol. a. 6.
112 HQT, Wharton, fol. 2.
113 HQT, Stowe, fol. 3.
114 HQT, Wright, fols 8–9, 12.
115 HQT, Montgomery and Coppock, fols 5–6.
116 P.P. 1865 XXVI, *7th Report, Medical Officer of the Privy Council*, Appendix 6, Dr Hunter's report on rural housing, p. 256.
117 Notes on a perambulation with the Rev. Head, June 1969.
118 HQT, East, fol. 9.
119 Letter to the writer from Simon Nowell-Smith, the present owner of Quarry Manor, 9 April 1970.
120 HQT, Smith, fol. 3.
121 HQT, J. Kerry, fol. b. 3.
122 HQT, J. A. Coppock, fol. a. 2; Smith, fol. 3; Edney, fols b. 1–2.
123 HQT, Edney, fol. b. 1; Kimber, fol. 1.; L. Coppock, fol. 1.
124 HQT, Kimber, fol. 1.
125 HQT, Blagrove, fol. 3.
126 HQT, J. Kerry, fol. b. 3.
127 *Oxford Times*, 3 April 1909, p. 12, col. 5.
128 HQT, Kimber, fol. 5; *St Andrew's Parish Magazine*, December 1871, p. 185; March 1876, p. 437; March 1880, p. 18; April 1885, p. 201; and entries at November 1885, May 1888, March 1889.
129 *St Andrew's Parish Magazine*, passim.
130 Samuel Wilberforce, *A Sermon Preached . . . on Behalf of a proposed Church . . . at Headington Quarry*, Oxford, 1847.
131 Holy Trinity archives, *Headington Quarry Parish Magazine*, April 1893.
132 The Rev. R. H. Head in conversation with the writer.
133 Bodleian Library, *Society for Augmenting Small Benefices in the Diocese of Oxford*, 4th Report, Eton, 1865, p. 8.
134 Bodleian Library, MS. Oxford Diocesan papers, c. 332, fol. 222^v; c, 335, fol. 186^r; d. 179, fol. 197^v.
135 Vallis papers, MS. account of Quarry.
136 Coppock papers, MS. notes on Quarry; and Vicarage tradition as passed down to the present incumbent.
137 A list of the early incumbents is preserved in Holy Trinity archives.
138 Coppock papers, Coppock family tree.
139 Bodleian Library, MS. Oxford Diocesan papers, c. 645, fols 26, 30; Vallis papers, MS. account of Quarry, fol. 2^r.
140 Vallis papers, MS. account of Quarry, fol. 8^r.
141 HQT, Vallis, fols c. 4, 6.
142 PRO, HO 107/877.
143 PRO, HO 107/1727.
144 PRO, RG 9/890/516.

145 PRO, RG 10/1434/20.
146 Holy Trinity archives, school note book and minute book,
1864–1903, entry dated 5 June 1897. In Edwardian times
gentlemen's residences began to be built nearby, and one or two
of their inhabitants began to take an interest in the Quarry.
Shotover Lodge is recorded in a directory of 1902 as being
occupied by an army captain with a double-barrelled name (he
was also a baronet and a Justice of the Peace) while at
Shotover Cottage there was a Ph.D. At Strete there were the
Miss Maddens, who did 'quite a lot for the youth of the place'
according to one respectful account: 'They got cricket clubs
going and things like that and . . . a youth club' (HQT, Kimber,
fol. 3.). A less confident new resident was Dr Drew, a medical
practitioner from Oxford, who had a big house built for him on
Shotover. In 1910 he applied for police protection after a large
group of Quarry youths had started bonfires around him ('near
midnight') on 15 January, election night – 'there was a lawless
spirit in that neighbourhood and he suggested that there should
be telephonic communication between the district police and the
head office' (*Oxford Times*, 29 January 1910, p. 3. col. 5; HQT,
Wright, fols 8–9 from a memory of building his residence).
147 PRO, RG 9/1890/516.
148 PRO, RG 10/1434/20.
149 HQT, J. Kerry, fol. b. 12.
150 HQT, Smith, fols 1–2; conversation with Jim Phillips, November
1969.
151 HQT, J. Kerry, fol. a. 4.
152 HQT, Tolley, fol. b. 3.
153 HQT, J. A. Coppock, fol. a. 5.
154 HQT, Cooper, fol. c. 3.
155 One sign of Quarry's plebeian character was the use of nicknames,
'a sure sign of a low civilization', according to Lancelot Smith,
the well-born hero of Kingsley's novel *Yeast*. A favourite
(though questionable) explanation is that they made up
for the shortage of surnames in the village ('it was no good saying
"Jack Coppock" when there was about six, seven Jack Coppocks');
however this may be, there is no doubt that one of their effects
in Quarry, as in the Andalusian *pueblo* studied by Julian
Pitt-Rivers (*The People of the Sierras*), was to blur class divisions
and assert the village's claim on the individuals within it. (I
am very grateful to Valentine Cunningham of Corpus Christi
College, Oxford, for the excellent Kingsley reference.)
156 HQT, Cooper, fol. a. 1.
157 Samuel, 'The gypsies in Headington Quarry' (unpublished).
158 *St Andrew's Parish Magazine* April 1881 for its foundation and
subsequent years for progress reports. There is a handbill about
it in the Bodleian Library (G. A. Oxon. 317/21).
159 *St Andrew's Parish Magazine*, March 1883.
160 In the 1860s the vicar of Holy Trinity had attempted to found

an evening school in Quarry but it seems to have petered out. Bodleian Library, MS. Oxf. Dioc. papers, c. 33, fol. 222v, visitation returns, 1869. For an earlier failure, MS. Oxf. Dioc. papers, d. 180, fol. 556r, visitation returns, 1860. In the 1870s some Quarry boys started to go to night school in Old Headington, though 'not many' (MS. Oxf. Dioc. papers, c. 341, fol. 219^r, visitation returns, 1875). Cf. also *St Andrew's Parish Magazine*, April 1872, p. 206, which gives the names of three Quarry boys who won prizes. In March 1888 all Quarry boys were excluded from the Old Headington school, for reasons that can only be surmised (*St Andrew's Parish Magazine*, 18 March 1888).

161 *St Andrew's Parish Magazine*, April 1872, p. 206.

162 *Alden's Oxford Almanack*, Oxford, 1899, p. 37.

163 There were two friendly societies in Quarry in the 1900s, a local club based on the 'Chequers', and a branch of the Foresters.

164 According to the memory of William 'Merry' Kimber, recorded by T. W. Chaundy in 'William Kimber', *Journal of the English Folk Song and Dance Society*, n.s. 1956, p. 204.

165 Clare College, Cambridge, Cecil Sharp MSS., Folk Dance Notes.

166 HQT, conversation at the 'Mason's Arms', 21 December 1969.

167 HQT, B. Trafford, fol. 9; J. Kerry, Ed. a. 8.

2 *Work*

1 Oxfordshire Record Office, Symonds MSS., vol. V, p. 90.

2 W. J. Arkell, *Oxford Stone*, London, 1947, p. 46.

3 Vallis papers, MS. account of Quarry; *Post Office Directory*, 1854, pp. 553–4; ibid., 1864, p. 796.

4 HQT, B. Gurl, fol. 13.

5 For a fatal accident there, *Jackson's Oxford Journal*, 15 February 1896, p. 4; and for an account of Mucky Gurl's period of employment there, HQT, B. Gurl, fols 1–4.

6 Felix Coppock, MS. notes on Headington Quarry.

7 'Excursion to Headington, Shotover, and Wheatley', *Proceedings of the Geological Association*, 17, 1901–2, pp. 384–5; Herbert Hurst, *Rambles and Rides around Oxford*, Oxford, n.d., 2nd ed., pp. v–vi.

8 It is referred to as 'Titups', the home of the brickmakers, in a newspaper paragraph of 1877 (*Oxford Times*, 11 August 1877, p. 8, col. 6).

9 HQT, Webb, fol. d. 3.

10 Ruth Fasnacht, *Summertown*, Oxford, 1969, for a good account of its early growth.

11 Hurst, *Rambles and Rides around Oxford*, p. 102.

12 H. Graves and A. B. Evans, *The Roads round Oxford*, Oxford, 1896, p. 116.

13 HQT, Wright, fols 1–2. For complaints about the sanitary

condition of New Headington, and representations about the 'urgent need' for effective draining and made-up roads, Oxford Town Hall muniments, A 7/2, Headington Rural Sanitary Authority minute book, 1882–91, p. 135, 12 February 1885; and *St Andrew's Parish Magazine*, September 1889. For a recollection of Lime Walk, New Headington, in its unmade-up state, HQT, Tolley, fol. a. 1; for complaints about the sanitary condition of New Marston, Headington Union Rural Sanitary Authority M.B., 1882—91, p. 7.

14 *Oxford Times*, 29 September 1877, p. 8, cols 1–3.

15 For Wolvercote Paper Mill, HQT, G. Kerry, fol. 4; for Radley College, HQT, Wright, fol. 8; for the building of Oxford Town Hall and Lady Margaret Hall, two other big jobs of the early 1900s, see HQT, Wright, fol. 8, and J. A. Coppock, fol. b. 1.

16 Mrs Parker, *Oxfordshire Words*, 1881.

17 HQT, Cooper, fol. b. 1. 'Beetles and wedges' were incorporated into the local wooding chant for Guy Fawkes Day. See Bodleian Library, MS. Top, Oxon., d. 191. fols 48, 61.

18 HQT, Cooper, fols b. 2, 4.

19 HQT, Tolley, fol. a. 1.

20 HQT, Morris, fol. 1.

21 HQT, P. Phillips, fol. 4.

22 HQT, Webb, fol. b. 3.

23 HQT, P. Phillips, fol. 6.

24 HQT, Buckland, fol. 5; cf. also Horwood, fol. 1.

25 HQT, W. Kerry, fol. b. 1.

26 HQT, J. Kerry, fol. a. 3.

27 HQT, P. Phillips. fol. 6.

28 HQT, B. Gurl, fol. 4.

29 HQT, East, fols, 5, 6.

30 Ibid.

31 HQT, Cooper, fol. b. 9. for an example.

32 HQT, B. Gurl, fol. 5.

33 Ibid., fol. 17.

34 HQT, Webb, fols d. 3, 14.

35 HQT, J. A. Coppock, fol, a. 3.; Morris, fol. 2.

36 HQT, Morris, fol. 3.

37 HQT, Cooper, fol. c. 10; Morris, fol. 3.

38 HQT, B. Coppock, fol. 4.

39 HQT, Cooper, fol. c. 1.

40 HQT, Cooper, fol. b. 12.

41 HQT, G. Kerry, fol. 2.

42 HQT, Cooper, fol. b. 7a; fols c. 5–6, 7–8, 9.

43 *Oxford Times*, 21 September 1867, p. 5, col. 4.

44 HQT, Wharton, fol. 1.; *Headington Quarry and Shotover, a History*, compiled by G. A. Coppock and B. M. Hill, Oxford, 1933, p. 51.

45 Letter to the writer from Mrs Gladys Coppock, 16 November 1969, recalling her father's work.

46 HQT, P. Phillips, fol. 3.

47 HQT, W. Kerry, fol. b. 5.
48 HQT, Webb, fol. b. 3.
49 *Jackson's Oxford Journal*, 8 April 1893, p. 5, col. 5.
50 HQT, P. Phillips, fol. 3.
51 HQT, Cooper, fols b. 3–4.
52 HQT, B. Gurl, fol. 13.
53 Conversation at the 'Mason's Arms', 28 July 1969.
54 *Forest Hill with Shotover, 1933, The Village Book*, compiled by Elsie Miller, Oxford, 1933, p. 40.
55 HQT, B. Gurl, fols 2–3.
56 J. E. T. Thorold Rogers, *A History of Agriculture and Prices in England*, Oxford, 1882, vol. III, pp. 732–7, reproduces the accounts; Knoop and Jones, 'The English medieval quarry', *Economic History Review*, IX/I, 1938, discusses them.
57 HQT, B. Gurl, fol. 7.
58 HQT, Mrs East, fol. 6.
59 HQT, B. Gurl, fol. 4.
60 HQT, Wright, fol. 2.
61 Ibid., fol. 3.
62 Ibid., fol. 5.
63 Ibid., fol. 2.
64 Conversation at the 'Mason's Arms', January 1970.
65 HQT, Wright, fol. 5.
66 HQT, G. Kerry, fol. 3.
67 HQT, B. Gurl, fols 19–20.
68 HQT, Webb, fol. d. 3.
69 HQT, Webb, fol. d. 3.
70 HQT, B. Gurl, fols 8–9.
71 HQT, B. Gurl, fols 4–6.
72 HQT, Morris, fol. 3.
73 HQT, Cooper, fol. c. 9.
74 HQT, Cooper, fol. c. 3; Kimber, fol. 5.
75 HQT, Morris, fol. 3.
76 Ibid.
77 HQT, B. Gurl, fol. 16.
78 Ibid., fol. 15.
79 HQT, Cooper, fol. b. 3.
80 HQT, J. A. Coppock, fol. b. 3; J. Kerry, fols b. 3–4.
81 *Kelly's Directory*, 1906, p. 454.
82 HQT, Ward, fols b. 6–7, 19–20.
83 HQT, Wright, fols 11, 12.
84 HQT, Ward, fol. b. 3.
85 HQT, East, fol. 1.
86 HQT, Auger, fol. 7.
87 HQT, Ward, fol. a. 7., Webb, fol. d. 9.
88 It was said that their horses were so used to stopping at the 'Rising Sun', a pub at the bottom of Headington Hill, that they would come to a halt there even if the driver forgot to say 'Whoa!'
89 HQT, B. Coppock, fol. 4.

90 HQT, Longford, fol. 8.
91 HQT, B. Coppock, fol. 5.
92 HQT, B. Coppock, fol. 6.
93 HQT, B. Coppock, fols 6–7.
94 Ibid., fol. 7.
95 HQT, Tolley, fol. b. 3.
96 Conversation at the 'Mason's Arms', January 1970.
97 HQT, Webb, fol. d. 12.
98 Conversation with Will Webb, 5 September 1969.
99 HQT, Webb, fol. a. 3.
100 Conversation with Will and Bert Webb, August 1969, and
     HQT, Webb, fol. c. 9.
101 HQT, Webb, fol. a. 3.
102 HQT, B. Trafford, fol. 11.
103 Ibid., fols 10–11.
104 HQT, Kimber, fol. 1.
105 HQT, J. Kerry, fol. a. 5.
106 HQT, Mrs Gurl, fol. 1.
107 HQT, Mrs Kerry, fol. 1.
108 HQT, J. Kerry, fol. a. 5.
109 HQT, Longford, fols 4, 7–8.
110 HQT, Webb, fol. b. 3.
111 HQT, Tolley, fol. b. 2.
112 Conversation with A. G. Vallis, September 1969.
113 HQT, Webb, fol. d. 2.
114 *Oxford Times*, 28 March 1915, p. 1, col. 7.
115 HQT, J. A. Coppock, fol. a. 8.
116 HQT, Kimber, fol. 5.
117 HQT, Miss Horwood, fol. 2.
118 HQT, Ward, fol. b. 1.
119 HQT, Ward, fols b. 2, 7–8.

3   Secondary incomes

1 HQT, Wharton, fol. 1.
2 HQT, J. Phillips, fol. 1.
3 *Jackson's Oxford Journal*, 23 September 1882, p. 8, col. 4;
   30 September 1882, p. 8, col. 3.
4 HQT, Webb, fol. a. 2.
5 HQT, Cooper, fol. b. 8.
6 HQT, B. Gurl, fol. 3.
7 *Jackson's Oxford Journal*, 30 September 1882, p. 8, col. 3 (at
   least two men from Quarry were in this company).
8 HQT, J. A. Coppock, fol. b. 3.
9 Thomas F. Plowman, *Fifty Years of a Showman's Life*, London,
   1919, pp. 73–4. 'Many of us remember seeing the Morris danced
   down the High St. Oxford at Whitsuntide', runs an article in the
   Oxford Times in 1909, adding that the melodies were then played
   upon the pipe and tabor, 'the "whittle and dub" of rustic

parlance' (*Oxford Times*, 17 June 1909, p. 12, col. 3).

10 Clare College, Sharp MSS., Folk Dance Notes, I, fol. 252.

11 HQT, Webb, fol. c. 5.

12 HQT, W. Kerry, fols b. 7–8. These 'Monday beanfeasts' seem to have come to an end in 1911 after a fatal accident when Sticky Parsons drowned in a disused claypit (for this incident see Vallis papers, diary, 24 July 1911).

13 HQT, Kimber, fol. 3; conversation with Fred Tolley, May 1969.

14 Holy Trinity archives, Headington Quarry Mixed School log book, 23 January 1914.

15 Cecil Sharp House, Cecil Sharp MSS., misc. documents, GRQ 35/86, Kimber to Sharp, 22 January 1908.

16 Cecil Sharp House, Sharp Correspondence, Box 2, Kimber to Sharp, 15 December 1905; cf. also Kimber to Sharp, 10 December 1922.

17 Merry Kimber, the concertina-player of the side, was a brick-layer by trade, and so was George Coppock, one of the dancers (in later, more prosperous years, he became a small master builder). Sip Washington, who played the fool in the procession, with a pig's bladder on a stick, was a well-digger; so was old Mac Massey, another of the dancers; young Mac Massey, his son, also a member of the side, was a builder's labourer (for Kimber see T. W. Chaundy, 'William Kimber', *Journal of the English Folk Dance and Song Society*, 1956).

18 Maud Karpeles, *Cecil Sharp*, London, 1967, p. 25.

19 W. Kerry, interview with Jack Holland and Alun Howkins, Nov. 1968.

20 HQT, Wharton, fol. 1.

21 HQT, Ward, fol. 6. 28.

22 HQT, Mrs G. Kerry, fol. 1.

23 HQT, Cooper, fol. c. 8.

24 Ibid., fol. b. 5.

25 HQT, J. A. Coppock, fol. b. 4.

26 HQT, Wright, fol. 15.

27 HQT, Kimber, fol. 5; Smith, fol. 4.

28 HQT, Cooper, fol. a. 5.

29 *Jackson's Oxford Journal*, 19 August 1896, p. 7, col. 4; Bodleian Library, Headington parish council minute book, 14 August, 19 October 1896.

30 HQT, Will Smith, fol. 5.

31 HQT, Wharton, fol. 4.

32 HQT, J. Kerry, fols. a. 1–2; W. Kerry, fol. b. 7, for family tradition about him. *Jackson's Oxford Journal*, 8 January 1898, p. 6, col. 4, for his designation as a 'cricketer'; Kelly's *Directory*, 1887, p. 636, for him as 'poulterer'; and 1871 MS. census returns for him as 'dealer'. For various incidents in a stormy career, *Jackson's Oxford Journal*, 28 April 1888, p. 6, col. 6; *Oxford Times*, 22 April 1905, p. 12. His father, the first Kerry to settle in Quarry, hailed from Wychwood Forest.

33 HQT, W. Kerry, fol. b. 7.
34 HQT, Ward, fol. b. 11.
35 Ibid., fol. 12.
36 HQT, J. A. Coppock, fol. b. 10.
37 HQT, Webb, fol. d. 9.
38 HQT, Webb, fol. c. 9.
39 HQT, Tolley, fol. c. 1.
40 HQT, Mrs Dyer, fols 1–3; for the mowing, HQT, B. Gurl, fol. 18.
41 Oxford Town Hall muniments, y.z.2, printed notice on
    Headington charities, with MS. additions, undated but *circa* 1865.
42 Bodleian Library, G. A. Oxon, c. 317/2.
43 Charity Commission archives, files nos 16067, 15857, various
    papers on Headington charities dated 1887–8.
44 *Oxford Times*, 25 July 1908, p. 5, col. 8; 15 August 1908, p. 12,
    col. 4; 24 October 1908, p. 3, cols 7–8.
45 HQT, Mrs G. Kerry, fols 1–2; Smith, fol. 1; Vallis, fol. c. 2.
46 HQT, Cooper, fol. b. 9.
47 HQT, Ward fols a. 13–14.
48 HQT, Webb, fol. c. 9.
49 HQT, Mrs Gurl, fol. 4.
50 HQT, Auger, fol. 4.
51 HQT, Vallis, fol. a. 2.
52 Vallis papers, diary of Charles Snow.
53 HQT, Tolley, fol. a. 1.
54 HQT, Tolley, fol. b. 1.
55 HQT, Mrs Gurl, fol. 5.
56 HQT, Ward, *passim*.
57 Conversation with Will and Bert Webb, Sept. 1969.
58 PRO, RG 9/890/5161 and *Shrimpton's Oxford Directory*, 1875, p. 84.
59 PRO, RG 9/890/5161; *Post Office Directory*, 1864, p. 796; *Post
    Office Directory*, 1869, p. 872; Kelly's *Directory*, 1877, p. 1006.
60 HQT, Wright, fol. 14.
61 HQT, East fol. 1; for the pickled salmon and potted meats,
    see the report of a theft in *Oxford Times*, 11 December 1909,
    p. 10, col. 8.
62 HQT, Hay, fol. 15.
63 HQT, J. A. Coppock, fols b. 3–4.
64 Vallis papers, diary of Charles Snow.
65 HQT, Vallis, fols c. 1–2.
66 HQT, J. A. Coppock, fol. b. 2.
67 HQT, F. Coppock, fol. b. 2.
68 HQT, Longford, fol. 6.
69 HQT, G. Kerry, fol. 1.
70 HQT, J. Kerry, fol. b. 6; B. Gurl, fol. 17.
71 HQT, Ward, fol. b. 29.
72 HQT, W. Trafford, fol. 1.
73 HQT, B. Trafford, fol. 6.
74 R. E. Moreau, *The Departed Village*, Oxford, 1968, p. 122.
75 HQT, J. A. Coppock, fol. b. 6.

76 HQT, Baker, fols 2–3.
77 HQT, Smith, fol. 2.
78 HQT, Ward, fol. b. 27.
79 HQT, Ward, fol. b. 5.
80 *Oxford Times*, 17 January 1914, p. 7, col. 2; 31 January 1914; in May of the same year, however, an arrears order was served against him for not paying 2*s.* a week maintenance money (*Oxford Times*, 9 May 1914, p. 6, col. 6).
81 HQT, J. A. Coppock, fol. b. 7.
82 HQT, Mrs Montgomery and Miss Coppock, fol. 5.
83 HQT, Ward, fol. b. 14.
84 Vallis papers, diary of Charles Snow.
85 HQT, Tolley, fol. b. 1.
86 HQT, J. A. Coppock, fol. b. 7. The price seems to have been about the same in 1884 when Charles Snow paid D. Bushnell £2 'for 2 Piggs' (Vallis papers, diary of Charles Snow, 27 January – 2 February 1884).
87 HQT, J. A. Coppock, fol. b. 4.
88 Ibid.
89 Cecil Sharp House, Sharp Correspondence, Box 2, Kimber to Sharp, 10 June, 1910.
90 Ibid., Kimber to Sharp, 15 October 1913.
91 HQT, J. A. Coppock, fol. b. 4.
92 HQT, Morris, fol. 6.
93 HQT, B. Gurl, fol. 5.
94 HQT, J. Phillips, fol. 1.
95 For the Pig Club, *Headington Quarry and Shotover, a History*, compiled by G. A. Coppock and B. M. Hill, Oxford, 1933, p. 67; *Oxford Times*, 18 February 1905; 21 March 1908, p. 9, col. 7.
96 HQT, Mrs Kerry, fol. 1.; cf. also J. A. Coppock, fol. b. 9.
97 HQT, Smith, fol. 5.
98 *Jackson's Oxford Journal*, 19 August 1896, p. 7, col. 4.
99 Conversation with Mrs Gladys Coppock, May 1970.
100 Conversation with Jim Phillips, July 1969.
101 HQT, J. A. Coppock, fols b. 6–7.
102 HQT, Wright and Jones, fol. 3.
103 Ibid.
104 HQT, Cooper, fol. a 5.
105 HQT, Kimber, fol. 5.
106 HQT, Wright, fol. 18, Wright and Jones, fol. 2.
107 HQT, W. Kerry, fol. b. 3.
108 HQT, Wright and Jones, fol. 4.
109 Ibid., fol. 3.
110 HQT, Bache, fol. 2.
111 HQT, Wright and Jones, fols 3–4, 7, 8.
112 HQT, Stowe, fol. 2.
113 Three women are remembered as selling home-made sweets in in the early 1900s: Emma Webb, Mrs Huggins and Darkie Coppock.

114 HQT, Kimber, fol. 5; and J. A. Coppock fol. b. 7.
115 HQT, Auger, fol. 2.
116 HQT, Miss Coppock and Mrs Montgomery, fol. 1.
117 HQT, Jack Kerry, fol. a. 9.
118 HQT, J. A. Coppock, fol. b. 8.
119 HQT, Webb, fol. c. 10.
120 HQT, Ward, fols b. 9–10.
121 HQT, Mrs East, fol. 12.
122 HQT, W. Kerry, fols 6–7.
123 HQT, Mrs East, fol. 7.
124 HQT, Wharton, fol. 4. In August 1879 Charles Kerry, aged six, son of Annie Trafford, was killed by a brick-cart when returning from taking his stepfather's breakfast to Mrs Phillips's brickyard. *Oxford Times*, 16 August 1879, p. 8, col. 2.
125 HQT, W. Kerry, fol. b. 5.
126 HQT, Webb, fol. d. 13.
127 HQT, Ward, fol. b. 26.
128 HQT, Ward, fol. b. 27.
129 HQT, Baker, fol. 3.
130 HQT, Ward, fol. b. 8–9.
131 Ibid., fol. a. 12.
132 HQT, Kimber, fol. 3.
133 HQT, Miss Coppock and Mrs Montgomery, fol. 2.
134 HQT, Wright, fols 13–14.
135 Conversations with Jim Phillips, July 1969.
136 HQT, Cooper, fol. a. 3.
137 Conversation with Will and Bert Webb.
138 HQT, B. Trafford, fol. d. 7.

4 Totting and poaching, woodland and waste

1 HQT, B. Trafford, fol. 5; Webb, fol. d. 2.
2 HQT, Webb, fol. d. 2; Auger, fol. 1; Baker, fol. 7; Vallis, fol. a. 5.
3 HQT, L. Coppock, fol. 8; Cooper fol. a. 4.
4 HQT, Ward, fol. b. 10.
5 HQT, Ward, fols b. 27–9.
6 Christopher Hussey, 'Shotover Park, Oxon', *Country Life*, 13 February 1926.
7 Holy Trinity archives, Headington Quarry Mixed School log book, 9 June 1913.
8 For details see Jack Holland, Alun Howkins, Raphael Samuel, *Headington Quarry and the Fight for the Open Magdalens*, History Workshop pamphlet (forthcoming).
9 HQT, Tolley, fol. 1. a.
10 HQT, Wright, fol. 13.
11 Conversation with Fred Tolley, June 1969.
12 HQT, Ward, fol. b. 20. For the ochre pits, see *The Stranger's Guide to Oxford*, Oxford, n.d., p. 265.
13 HQT, B. Gurl, fol. 10.

14 For a prosecution for hollying on Shotover, see *Jackson's Oxford Journal*, 19 November 1881, p. 6, col. 2. According to Waggle Ward, who often went out 'Christmassing', Shotover was not the best place for hollying; and there was no mistletoe there at all: HQT, Ward, fol. b. 24; according to Spot Wright there was one place on Shotover which was good for berried holly. HQT, Wright, fol. 14.

15 HQT, B. Gurl, fol. 11.

16 HQT, W. Kerry, fol. b. 6.

17 HQT, Ward, fol. a. 5.

18 HQT, W. Kerry, fol. a. 2.

19 HQT, Mrs East, fol. 7.

20 HQT, Mrs Gurl, fol. 1.

21 *Jackson's Oxford Journal*, 12 January 1861, p. 5, col. 2.

22 PRO, RG 9/580.

23 Bodleian Library, MS. Top. Oxon., d. 193, 'Village Life', fol. 46ʳ.

24 HQT, conversation with Bert Webb, July 1969.

25 HQT, J. Kerry, fol. b. 6.

26 I have given a fuller account of the Bucklands in a paper on 'The gypsies in Headington Quarry' which I hope to publish shortly.

27 Oxfordshire Record Office, Misc. Mor. IV/I.

28 HQT, B. Trafford, fol 4; B. Gurl, fol. 10; Oxfordshire Record Office, Misc. Mor. IV/I.

29 Herbert Hurst, *Rambles and Rides around Oxford*, Oxford, n.d. (1890?), p. 165.

30 Holland, Howkins and Samuel, op. cit.

31 *Jackson's Oxford Journal*, 14 July 1883, p. 6, col. 2.

32 Holland, Howkins and Samuel, op. cit.

33 HQT, Vallis, fol. a. 1.

34 Conversation at the Mason's Arms, 25 July 1969.

35 HQT, Kimber, fol. 4; Wright and Jones, fol. 6; conversation with Will and Bert Webb, July 1969.

36 HQT, Kimber, fol. 4.

37 *Jackson's Oxford Journal*, 16 March 1895, p. 7, col. 2.

38 Interview with Fred Tolley, June 1969.

39 Ibid.

40 HQT, L. Coppock, fols 7–8.

41 Interview with Fred Tolley, June 1969; and HQT, Tolley, fol. c. 1.

42 HQT, Wright and Jones, fol. 6.

43 HQT, Ward, fol. b. 17.

44 HQT, Wright, fol. 18; for other descriptions see HQT, Wright and Jones, fol. 2; Webbs, fol. a. 5; J. A. Coppock, fol. b. 7.

45 Conversation with Fred Tolley, May 1969.

46 HQT, Buckland, fol. b. 4.

47 HQT, Mrs Montgomery and Miss Coppock, fol. 5.

48 HQT, Auger, fol. 8.

49 HQT, W. Kerry, fol. b. 7.

50 HQT, Baker, fol. 7.

51 For a case involving Bobby Baker and Stunt Kerry, see *Oxford Times*, 6 September 1913, p. 8, col. 5.

52 HQT, Baker, fols 4–6. Another place where horses were put to graze (notwithstanding numerous complaints) was on Quarry Rec. Cf. *Oxford Times*, 24 July 1909, p. 9, col. 7; 23 October 1909, p. 3, col. 8; 23 July 1910, p. 12, col. 2; Headington parish council minute book, 18 October 1897, p. 104; 20 October 1913, pp. 410–2.

53 Oxfordshire Record Office, Misc. Mor. IV/I; and *Jackson's Oxford Journal*, 2 September 1871, p. 6, cols 4–5.

54 *Jackson's Oxford Journal*, 14 May 1892, p. 6, col. 7, and 4 June 1892, p. 7, col. 3, for the Cowley 'right of way' dispute, and for the subject generally, Holland, Howkins and Samuel, op. cit.

55 *Headington Quarry and Shotover, a History*, compiled by G. A. Coppock and B. M. Hill, Oxford, 1933, p. 77.

56 HQT, Tolley, fol. b. 1; for the use of the roadside wastes by another local cow-keeper, see *Jackson's Oxford Journal*, 19 January 1878, p. 6, col. 4; 25 May 1878 p. 8, col. 3.

57 HQT, Lee, fol. 5.

58 HQT, Buckland, fol. b. 2.

59 HQT, Kimber, fol. 4.

60 HQT, Ward, fol. b. 24.

61 HQT, Ward, fol. b. 21.

62 HQT, Ward, fol. b. 24. The faking up of holly was to deceive the customers ('they Londoners knowed no different') not the dealers. For an account of it, HQT, Ward, fols b. 23–4.

63 HQT, East, fol. 7.

64 HQT, Ward fol. b. 21.

65 *Jackson's Oxford Journal*, 12 May 1877, p. 6, col. 5; 21 December 1878, p. 6, col. 4; 18 January 1879, p. 7, col. 3; *Oxford Times*, 26 April 1879, p. 3, col. 5.

66 HQT, Ward, fol. b. 16.

67 Conversation at the 'Mason's Arms', 4 May 1969.

68 HQT, W. Kerry, fol. b. 7.

69 HQT, W. Kerry, fol. a. 7.

70 HQT, Wright fols 12–13. For some uses of the alibi, *Jackson's Oxford Journal*, 12 September 1908, p. 4, col. 1; 20 December 1913, p. 12, col. 4; 10 January 1914, p. 13, cols 3–4.

71 HQT, Ward, fols b. 20–1, 25.

72 HQT, Wright fol. 12; Wright and Jones, fol. 6.

73 HQT, Wright, fol. 15.

74 HQT, Phillips and Gurl, fol. 2.

75 HQT, Cooper, fol. a. 6.

76 Conversation with Mr and Mrs East, August 1969.

77 HQT, Ward, fol. b. 18.

78 HQT, Wright, fol. 15.

79 Ibid., fol. 13.

80 HQT, Ward, fols b. 18, 19.

81 HQT, Ward, fols b. 20, 21.

82 HQT, Wright, fols 14–15.

83 HQT, Ward, fols b. 26–7.

84 HQT, Ward, fols b. 21–2.

85 HQT, Will Smith, fol. 6, and conversation with Fred Tolley, June 1969.

86 HQT, W. Kerry, fol. b. 3. Spot Wright, however, a regular old poacher in his time, recalls weeks when he might get hold of no more than three or four rabbits; HQT, Wright, fol. 18.

87 HQT, Ward, fols b. 14–16.

88 HQT, Ward, fol. b. 10.

89 HQT, Wright, fol. 16.

90 HQT, Ward, fols a. 4–5.

91 For an example, *Jackson's Oxford Journal*, 30 September 1882, p. 8, col. 3.

92 HQT, Buckland, fol. a. 4.

93 HQT, Ward, fol. b. 27.

94 HQT, Tolley, fol. b. 2.

95 HQT, Ward, fol. b. 10.

96 HQT, East, fol. 6.

97 HQT, J. A. Coppock, fol. b. 8; W. Trafford, fol. 6.

98 HQT, Morris, fol. 1.

99 HQT, Horwood, *passim*.

100 HQT, Montgomery and Coppock, fol. 6; Smith, fol. 1.

101 HQT, Webb, fol. a. 5.

102 HQT, Horwood, fol. 3.

103 HQT, Webb, fol. c. 6; Smith, fol. 1; Tolley, fol. b. 3.

104 *Jackson's Oxford Journal*, 18 November 1876, p. 6, col. 5.

105 *Jackson's Oxford Journal*, 27 November 1886, p. 7, col. 5, for the 1886 convictions, and 24 January 1885, p. 6, col. 5; 4 April 1885, p. 6, col. 6, and 18 July 1885 for the 1885 convictions.

106 HQT, Kimber, fol. 1.

107 HQT, Wright, fol. 15.

108 HQT, Wright, fol. 15; B. Horwood, fol. 2; Ward, fol. b. 25; for some convictions against him for briaring, see *Jackson's Oxford Journal*, 23 October 1897, p. 6, col. 3; 30 October 1897, p. 6, col. 3: 10 August 1898, p. 9, col. 2.

109 *Jackson's Oxford Journal*, 25 January 1896, p. 7, col. 7.

110 *Jackson's Oxford Journal*, 30 April 1887, p. 6.

111 Ibid., 7 January 1899, p. 3, col. 4.

112 *Oxford Times*, 12 September 1908, p. 4, col. 1.

113 HQT, Ward, fols b. 25–6.

114 HQT, Auger, fol. 2; cf. also *Headington Quarry and Shotover, a History*, p. 73.

115 *Jackson's Oxford Journal*, 16 March 1895, p. 7, col. 2.

116 HQT, Ward, fol. a. 13.

117 HQT, Webb, fol. a. 1.

118 HQT, Ward, fol. b. 29.

119 HQT, Mrs Hay, fol. 8; Ward, fol. b. 19.

120 HQT, Buckland, fol. 2.

121 HQT, Buckland, fol. 2.; Horwood, fols 2–3.
122 HQT, Smith, fol. 2.
123 HQT, Wright, fol. 17.
124 HQT, B. Gurl, fol. 6.
125 Holy Trinity archives, parochial accounts 1870–91, undated note.

5 Wage labour and capital

1 HQT, Cooper, fols c. 2, 7.
2 PRO, RG 9/890/561.
3 HQT, Longford, fol. 3.
4 *Oxford Times*, 23 January 1901, p. 4, col. 1; 30 January 1909, p. 8, col. 2.
5 HQT, Smith, fol. 4.
6 HQT, Longford, fol. 2; Baker, fol. 6.
7 HQT, Vallis, fol. c. 4.
8 HQT, Webb, fol. d. 9.
9 HQT, Vallis, fol, c. 5.
10 HQT, J. Kerry, fol. a. 4.
11 HQT, Auger, fol. 1.
12 HQT, Webb, fol. c. 13.
13 HQT, Ward, fol. b. 4.
14 HQT, B. Trafford, fol. 3.
15 Bodleian Library, G. A. Oxon. 6. 4 (35).
16 HQT, J. A. Coppock, fol. a. 2.
17 Oxfordshire County Record Office, Misc. Suf. 1/1–4, 6.
18 HQT, Longford, fol. 4.
19 For various occasions on which they came up against the law, see *Oxford Times*, 25 March 1901, p. 4, col. 1; 29 July 1905, p. 9, col. 7; 30 January 1909, p. 8, cols 1–2; 5 July 1913, p. 6, col. 5.
20 HQT, Longford, fol. 4.
21 HQT, P. Phillips, fol. 1.
22 HQT, Edney, fol. b. 2.
23 'A little . . . shop . . . only a little . . . ordinary house, with a window like this . . .' is how Will Smith remembers Stephen Goodgame's shop. HQT, Smith, fol. 2.
24 HQT, Longford, fol. 6.
25 HQT, Montgomery and Coppock, fol. 10; Longford, fol. 5.
26 HQT, Coppock, fol. 1; Auger, fol. 2. There were two prosecutions against him in 1878 for allowing his cows to stray on the highway (*Jackson's Oxford Journal*, 19 January 1878, p. 6, col. 4; 25 May 1878, p. 8, col. 3); he died in July 1906, aged seventy-two.
27 PRO, RG 10/1434/20.
28 Kelly's *Directory*, 1890–1; Kelly's *Directory*, 1896–7, p. 377; *Shrimpton's Oxford Directory*, 1875, p. 84.
29 HQT, B. Gurl, fol. 15; Smith, fol. 2; Longford, fol. 5.
30 HQT, Smith, fol. 2.
31 PRO, RG 10/1434/20.

32 Vallis papers, MS. account of Quarry, fol. 6r.

33 HQT, B. Trafford, fol. 8; Kelly's *Directory*, 1902, p. 422.

34 See J. Holland, A. Howkins and R. Samuel, *Headington Quarry and the Fight for the Open Magdalens*, History Workshop pamphlet (forthcoming).

35 *Post Office Directory*, 1864, p. 796; Kelly's *Directory*, 1883, p. 578; PRO, RG 10/1434/20.

36 Kelly's *Directory*, 1910–11, p. 492.

37 HQT, Longford, fol. 4.

38 Conversation with Miss Goodgame, August 1969.

39 HQT, Smith, fol. 3. The pond where he fed them was the big pond later taken over by Todd Kerry.

40 HQT, J. A. Coppock, fol. b. 7.

41 *Jackson's Oxford Journal*, 9 June 1883, p. 7, col. 2; Phipps seems to have been a difficult man; in 1877 he was accused by some neighbours of beating and ill-treating a horse (*Oxford Times*, 21 July 1877); in 1878 he was forced to send a written apology to the vicar of Holy Trinity for breaking open the churchyard gates (*St Andrew's Parish Magazine*, November 1879, p. 587); in 1879 he was involved in a dispute with another neighbour over the ownership of some stones (*Oxford Times*, 29 November 1879, p. 7, col. 6).

42 Kelly's *Directory*, 1877, p. 1006.

43 *Oxford Times*, 25 July 1908, p. 5, col. 8.

44 PRO, RG 9/890/516.

45 Vallis papers, MS. account of Quarry, fol. 16r for the emigration to Canada.

46 Kelly's *Directory*, 1883, p. 578; Kelly's *Directory*, 1890–1, p. 316; Kelly's *Directory*, 1896–7, p. 377.

47 The fate of the ten listed shopkeepers, publicans, etc., of the 1871 census awaits the release of the MS. returns for the 1881 census in 1981; few of those styled 'shopkeepers' in the census were rated worthy of a mention in the directories of the time, which tends to confirm the impression of their more or less domestic and extempore character.

48 HQT, F. Coppock, fol. b. 2; Vallis, fols cl, 6.

49 *Oxford Times*, 19 March 1913, p. 5, col. 5.

50 R. Samuel, 'The gypsies in Headington Quarry' (unpublished typescript).

51 'Groome's letters to Smart and Crofton,' *Journal of the Gypsy Lore Society*, 3rd ser., no. 2, 1928, p. 58. I am grateful to Thomas Acton who first suggested this source to me.

52 For Razzle Smith see HQT, Webb, fol. c. 16.

53 HQT, Hay, fol. 13.

54 Conversation with Fred Tolley, May 1969.

55 HQT, Cooper, fol. c. 9.

56 HQT, B. Coppock, fol. 4.

57 Cecil Sharp House, Cecil Sharp correspondence, box 2, William Kimber to Cecil Sharp, 1 February 1915.

58 HQT, Morris, fol. 2.
59 HQT, J. A. Coppock, fol. b. 1.
60 HQT, B. Coppock, fol. 3.
61 HQT, Webb, fol. d. 3.
62 Conversation with Will and Bert Webb, June 1969.
63 HQT, J. A. Coppock, fol. a. 12–13.
64 HQT, B. Coppock, fol. 4; cf. also the account in Violet Butler,
    Social Conditions in Oxford, London, 1908.
65 HQT, Auger, fol. 6; J. Phillips, fol. 1.
66 HQT, J. Phillips, fol. 2.
67 'The masons' strike', *Oxford Times*, 12 July 1879, p. 5, col. 5.
68 Vallis papers, diary of Charles Snow.
69 HQT, J. A. Coppock, fol. a. 12.
70 HQT, Bert Coppock, fols 2–3.
71 HQT, J. A. Coppock, fol. a. 15.
72 HQT, Morris, fol. 1.
73 HQT, Bert Coppock, fol. 1.
74 HQT, J. A. Coppock, fol. b. 1.
75 HQT, B. Gurl, fol. 12.
76 HQT, J. A. Coppock, fol. b. 2.
77 HQT, Auger, fol. 5.
78 HQT, G. Kerry, fol. 1.
79 HQT, B. Gurl, fol. 3.
80 HQT, Webb, fol. d. 4; Wright, fol. 11.
81 HQT, B. Gurl, fol. 15.
82 HQT, Webb, fol. a. 3.
83 HQT, Wright, fol. 11.
84 Ibid.
85 *Oxford Times*, 30 January 1909, p. 8, cols 1–2. Another of the
    Wright brothers was at Ilkeston in 1913, when he was arrested
    for a potato theft at Littlemore. *Oxford Times*, 21 February 1914,
    p. 6, col. 7.
86 HQT, Cooper, fol. c. 9.
87 HQT, B. Gurl, fol. 4.
88 HQT, J. Kerry, fol. b. 12.
89 HQT, P. Phillips, fol. 8.
90 HQT, Hay, fol. 15.
91 Her first appearance in a directory is in Kelly's *Directory* for
    1916–17.
92 HQT, Ward, fol. a. 15.
93 HQT, Lee, fol. 6; Webb, fol. d. 5.
94 HQT, Mrs Gurl, fol. 3.
95 HQT, Webb, fol. d. 7.

Subject index

Index of places